THE ORIGINS OF DRACULA

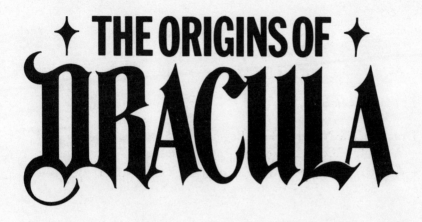

THE ORIGINS OF DRACULA

The Background to Bram Stoker's Gothic Masterpiece

CLIVE LEATHERDALE

WILLIAM KIMBER · LONDON

First published in 1987 by
WILLIAM KIMBER & CO LIMITED
100 Jermyn Street, London, SW1Y 6EE

editorial material and selection
© Clive Leatherdale, 1987

ISBN 0-7183-0657-0

Typeset by Ann Buchan (Typesetters), Middlesex
and printed and bound in Great Britain by
Billing and Sons Limited, Worcester

Contents

List of Illustrations

Preface

No Victorian fictional character has come to assume greater prominence in the popular culture of the late twentieth century than Bram Stoker's Dracula. The evil Count has become a box-office phenomenon around the world.

For many years little thought was given to the origins of *Dracula*, first published in 1897. Bram Stoker was a shadowy individual, leaving behind little information on his famous creation. Or so it was thought. Then, in the 1970s, Stoker's research notes for *Dracula* were discovered in the United States. These notes transform our understanding of the novel. Among them are mentioned some two dozen books which Stoker used as sources, books which, when traced, help to shed light on virtually every aspect of *Dracula*.

Tracing these sources was not always a straightforward matter. Stoker was often content to abbreviate titles, and dispense with the forenames of their authors. To make matters worse, his sources included three Jones's, two Lee's, and a Lea.

It is the aim of the present anthology to present as wide a selection of texts, covering as many thematic issues, as possible – within the limitations of the texts themselves. Some had to be excluded because they are written in French. Others are so wordy and repetitious as to defy editorial surgery. Still others, while intriguing in themselves, seem to have little obvious bearing on *Dracula*.

Given these limitations, *The Origins of Dracula* is a survey of Stoker's sources, reproducing texts on such diverse subjects as: burial customs, vampire epidemics, the history of Transylvania and of Vlad the Impaler, werewolves, the behaviour of bats, naval superstitions, hypnosis, exorcism, and fifteenth century campaigns against diabolism.

Clive Leatherdale

Acknowledgements

Bram Stoker's working notes for his novel *Dracula* are housed in the Rosenbach Museum and Library, Philadelphia, whose kindly staff permitted me to consult them in the delightful setting of their reading room in the summer of 1984.

I am indebted to Robert Leake and the Dracula Society for the use of many of the illustrations in this book. Enquiries to the Dracula Society can be made to:

> The Membership Secretary,
> The Dracula Society,
> 36 Ellison House,
> 100 Wellington Street,
> LONDON SE18 6QF

I should also like to thank the following people for their assistance at various stages in the preparation of this book – Dr Robert Lawson-Peebles, Julia Kruk, Alison Stewart and Isabelle Boutriau.

Clive Leatherdale

Introduction

Count Dracula exerts an immense hold over the modern imagination. Along with his nineteenth-century contemporaries – Frankenstein, Sherlock Holmes, Dr Jekyll – he seems to have assumed a life of his own through innumerable appearances and adaptations on stage and screen. The authors who originally created these immortal characters seem almost to have been detached from them, their names are not always easy to recall, and are often found appended to a film adaptation's list of credits almost as an afterthought. In everyday conversation it is surprising how often the author of one horror novel will be confused with another. Mary Shelley, creator of *Frankenstein*, is frequently accredited with writing *Dracula*, while its actual author – Bram Stoker – well, who has ever heard of him?

Stoker's magic formula was to write a thriller about vampires which still strikes a chilling chord ninety years after its publication. A world best-seller whose sales run into the millions, *Dracula* has also spawned one of the most money-spinning genres in the history of the cinema.

Immortality seems to be at the heart of *Dracula*'s appeal. But immortality is not confined to vampires. Belief in life after death is part and parcel of every world religion. Fear of blood is another universal human trait. It is the one human fluid without which we die. Tears, saliva, urine, semen and other secretions all have their purposes, but blood is what keeps us alive. And if loss of blood causes death, surely imbibing it promotes life. Since earliest times blood has taken on mystical, medical and ceremonial functions: sacrificial offerings to the gods; the letting of bad blood from the sick; transfusions to the anaemic; cosmetic application for renewed youth; mutual exchange to bind friendship, as with blood brothers.

Through blood's association with life and death it became inextricably linked with the soul, the essence of spirituality and individuality. Warriors in many cultures have taken to drinking the blood of the enemy in the belief that the strength and valour of the slain will be transferred with the blood.

It is the unique combination of belief in an afterlife and in the rejuvenating powers of blood that gives rise to the vampire. If blood is essential to life it follows logically that it is essential to those who have departed from this earth but who are now 'living' somewhere else. The dead can obtain their life-giving blood through either of two ways: they can either have it provided for them by means of sacrifice – or they can come and take it themselves, and gorge themselves from the veins of unwilling donors. This, in essence, is vampirism.

Each culture added its own local idiosyncrasies to this simple recipe to produce the range and diversity of blood-sucking species to be found in the annals of folklore. Stoker knew of a peculiar spectre common to parts of Malaysia, described by Isabella Bird: 'A vile fiend called the penangalan takes possession of the forms of women, turns them into witches, and compels them to quit the greater part of their bodies, and fly away by night to gratify a vampire craving for human blood.' (*Golden Chersonese* p. 354)

The penangalan might be a vampire, but it does not sound much like Count Dracula. His folkloric roots are distinctly European and Christian. The resurrection of Christ provides an in-built receptivity among Christian peoples to the idea of bodies rising from their graves. The biblical message 'the blood is the life' adds the second ingredient. St John's exhortation to drink the blood of Christ as a means of becoming closer to God, and the practice of the Eucharist whereby wine is mysteriously transubstantiated into Christ's blood, come precariously close to asking the faithful to commit acts of vampirism for the purpose of attaining everlasting life.

Christian communities, in other words, are predisposed by the very nature of their faith to entertain beliefs of a vampiric nature. Should the Church unwittingly fuel these superstitions it might find itself unable to contain the consequences. Take, for example, the turbulence in southern and eastern Europe between the fifteenth and eighteenth centuries. The bitter schism between Catholicism and Orthodoxy, and the occupation of much of Europe by the forces of Ottoman Islam, virtually manufactured the conditions necessary for popular belief in vampires. In the 1490s the Roman Church was so embattled by enemies, both within its ranks and without, that it gave birth to one of the most notorious publications ever to receive the papal seal. For two centuries it represented Rome's ultimate anti-satanic authority, sanctioning the excesses of the Inquisition. In the name of thwarting the devil the *Malleus Maleficarum* laid down the gruesome procedures recommended in the war against witchcraft and other devilish manifestations, such as incubi and succubi. These unlikely sounding creatures were symptomatic of the mounting spiritual war against the pleasures of the flesh and are the direct antecedents of the vampire. Incubi and succubi constitute, respectively, the male and female form of serpentine spectres whose purpose was to seduce their victims in their sleep and drain them of their vitality.

The Roman and Greek Churches, desperate to resist theological incursion by the other, preyed on the credulity of the masses, warning them of the fateful consequences of false belief. The punishment would not come in this life, but the next. Excommunications were carried out on the slightest pretext, and with the removal of proper burial rites went the removal of God's protection beyond death. Resurrection would not be in Christ's footsteps, but in the devil's.

The Greek Church, in particular, found itself aiding and abetting the conditions for an outbreak of superstitious mania. Whereas Rome had always held that non-dissolution of a body was an indication of sanctity, Orthodoxy put forward an alternative explanation. The devil would use his powers over the excommunicated to arrest decomposition. The corpses of the damned were left intact, waiting to walk again, and it was not long before rumours were sweeping from village to village. Sightings of the walking dead proliferated until an actual epidemic – of hysteria, if nothing else – was raging through the Balkans.

The actual causes of this epidemic have never been satisfactorily explained. It spread, however, on the back of an increasing and ever-widening paranoia. Symptoms such as those of lassitude, weight loss, pallor and apparent anaemia do not point to a single identifiable source: but they were believed to be caused by vampires and they resulted in death – or, it was later surmised, apparent death due to hysterical catalepsy. Without adequate medical provision the slightest indication of death precipitated instant disposal in graves that were makeshift, shallow, and easily exposed. Premature burial therefore became an added source of death and panic, for some of the victims would have awakened, struggled to the surface, wandered back to their homes clad in mud-smeared and blood-stained burial shrouds, and triggered a fresh wave of hysteria, real or apparent symptoms, and real or apparent deaths. It was a vicious circle in which the human imagination was more than adequately equipped to embellish tales of the undead returning from their graves to haunt their grieving loved ones.

This inexplicable epidemic spanned the late 1720s and early 30s. In time it attracted the curiosity of centres of learning in Germany and the West. Within the Christian preconceptions of the time, it was natural that the resulting theses and dissertations sought explanations in theological rather than medical or psychological terms. The most famous of these works was written by the French Benedictine abbot, Dom Augustine Calmet, whose tortuous metaphysical reasonings about whether vampires are alive or dead appear in Chapter 4 of this book.

It will be noticed that there is still some distance between the grimy, blood-spattered spectres of Balkan superstition and the haughty nobility of Dracula in his Gothic castles. Calmet does not suggest that vampires exist for the sole purpose of sucking blood. Consequently they are not described as having the necessary tools of the trade, namely elongated canine teeth. He has nothing to say about safeguards such as garlic, and does not consider it essential that vampires operate only at night. These and other features were added independently: some by folklore, some by literature, some by the cinema.

Folklore is responsible for allying the vampire with the werewolf. The person who transforms into a werewolf in life transforms into a vampire upon death. This accounts for the animalistic features of the vampire – pointed ears, hairy palms, extended canine teeth – and its passion for feasting off its victims. Folklore also suggests a range of homoeopathic safeguards against the powers of evil. These are usually distinguished by their pungent smell (garlic, onions), their symbolic association with purity (salt, running water, the wild rose and silver bullet), or their connection with Christianity and the crucifixion (thorns, crucifix, and Host).

If western academia examined the Balkan vampire outbreak in search of divine explanation, western poets and writers were attracted by its artistic potential. There is a qualitative leap in the imagination from the vampire of peasant superstition to the vampire of literature. Among the obvious characteristics of Count Dracula are his aristocratic background and mien, his erotic charm, and his almost irresistible psychological and physical power. His fictional antecedents are to be found less in the legends of eastern Europe than in the creative imaginations of the Romantics.

Accounts of the vampire epidemic in Hungary and Slavic regions, painstakingly charted and investigated by Calmet and a host of clerics in Germany and elsewhere, found an eager audience in the changing artistic and cultural climate of western Europe. The austere Age of Reason was experiencing a greater freedom of expression filtering through in the last decades of the eighteenth century. Gothicism and Romanticism were not shy of adapting these hair-raising accounts of the undead to serve the purposes of art. Clearly the vampire needed cosmetic treatment if it was to effectively become an object of romance. But cloak the vampire in ermine instead of rags and you had a creature perfectly fitted for a new role.

The Gothic and Romantic era was naturally drawn to the mysteries of life and death, satanic influences, and the perverse capacity of lovers to draw the life-force one from the other. Before the end of the eighteenth century a number of poets – Bürger, Goethe, Coleridge – had explored vampiric themes, such as the dead returning to drink their lover's blood, but without using the term 'vampire'. This omission was rectified in 1797 with Robert Southey's 'Thalaba the Destroyer', and over the course of the next twenty years vampirism enjoyed an artistic vogue that enrolled the most illustrious of the Romantics, including Keats, Shelley and Byron.

It was Lord Byron who, most of all, helped launch the vampire in a fresh direction, one that would culminate with the figure of Dracula. His poem 'The Giaour' includes the lines:

> But first on earth, as Vampyre sent,
> Thy corpse shall from its tomb be rent;
> Then ghastly haunt thy native place,
> And suck the blood of all thy race.

and ends with the message that the vampire is the most accursed of spectres. But Byron's real importance is as a source of inspiration to another. His flight from Britain to Switzerland, in the company of his physician and travelling companion John Polidori, led to the renowned 'ghost writing contest' with fellow poet Percy Shelley and his young wife-to-be, Mary. For once, the illustrious duo had to stand aside. Out of that meeting Mary produced *Frankenstein*, while Polidori capitalised on a fragment of a tale penned by Byron to write the first recognisable vampire story in English prose.

Polidori's *The Vampyre* (1819) is a milestone in English literature. The character of Lord Byron is unmistakably present in the character of Lord Ruthven. Ruthven – the vampire – is not just an aristocrat. He is misanthropic, moody, world weary, coldly evil, aloof, cunning, and fatal to innocent women. In other words, with this tale, not only is the transition of the vampire from the peasantry to the aristocracy successfully accomplished, but in so doing he becomes a shameless womaniser. The vampire genre can be seen to merge with the cult of the Byronic hero to produce a character that owes as much to the libertine as to the undead. *The Vampyre* enjoyed unexpected success, both in Britain and on the Continent. It was translated and performed on the Paris stage and encouraged further literary exploitation of the undead.

Polidori's vampire, Lord Ruthven, possesses none of the menace of Count Dracula. There is very little preoccupation with blood and no mention of protruding canines. But then this is a short story of some two-dozen pages. James Malcolm Rymer's *Varney the Vampire: Or, the Feast of Blood* (1847) was not so constrained. In the course of 868 double-columned pages Sir Francis Varney's gory exploits are set down without a trace of restraint. There is blood a-plenty, plus fangs with which to procure it. Here is the true literary precursor of Dracula, as the following extract might illustrate:

> Her beautifully rounded limbs quivered with the agony of her soul. The glassy, horrible eyes of the figure ran over that angelic form with a hideous satisfaction – horrible profanation. He drags her head to the bed's edge. He forces it back by the long hair still entwined in his grasp. With a plunge he seizes her neck in his fang-like teeth – a gush of blood and a hideous sucking noise follows. The girl has swooned, and the vampire is at his hideous repast!
>
> (*Varney the Vampire* Vol. 1., p.4)

Varney, like Dracula, originates from central Europe, dresses himself in a black cloak, climbs down castle walls, and arrives in Britain aboard a shipwrecked vessel. Likewise his innocent female victims are part entranced, part terrified. While Varney is too vulgar and tasteless to be erotic, the next major development of the vampire is sensuous in the extreme. Sheridan Le Fanu's *Carmilla* (1872) conforms to most of the Gothic conventions – aristocratic cast headed by a Countess Karnstein, central European setting, black stagecoaches, full moons and misty landscapes – but adds an unmistakable eroticism:

> Sometimes after an hour of apathy, my strange and beautiful companion would take my hand and hold it with a fond pressure, renewed again and again; blushing softly, gazing in my face with languid and burning eyes, and breathing so fast that her dress rose and fell with the tumultuous respiration. It was like the ardour of a lover; it embarrassed me; it was hateful and yet overpowering; and with gloating eyes she drew me to her, and her hot lips travelled along my cheek in kisses; and she would whisper, almost in sobs, 'You are mine, you *shall* be mine, and you and I are one for ever'.
>
> (*Carmilla* Chapter 4)

Carmilla's eroticism is enhanced by the fact of vampire and victim being female. In other words it is a tale of lesbian attraction, and the double feminine perspective permits Le Fanu to emphasise the sensuousness of the vampire act to an extent unsurpassed before or since. This female eroticism owes something to the femme fatale of the Romantics, and highlights yet another diversion for the literary vampire. Moreover, in *Carmilla* the character of the vampire is no longer a one-dimensional supernatural fiend but a rational, complex, calculating personality. Not many vampire tales stray from the strict heterosexual orthodoxy of the genre, but *Carmilla*'s lesbianism and the renowned activities of the real-life blood-drinker Elizabeth Bathory (see Chapter 9) would provide a profitable diversion for film makers.

By the time *Dracula* was published the metamorphosis of the vampire from the squalid apparition of peasant superstition to the sinister, calculating aristocrat was complete. These changes need summarising. The vampire of eastern European superstition was something which people accepted almost as an act of faith. These creatures reflected the backgrounds of those most susceptible to belief in them. In other words they were concentrated in rural areas. Vampires plagued only their own localities and generally restricted their attacks to their families and loved ones. They usually began their undead existence within a short time of their burial, and would be customarily described, as we might put it, as zombie-like, blank-eyed and gormless. Their bodies might be reanimated, but apparently not their brains.

The vampire of literature is an altogether more up-market creature, habitually from the higher end of the social spectrum. This gives him (or her) access to travel far beyond his native environment where his anonymity provides his shelter. Not having close relatives, except perhaps the devil, his victims are likely to be randomly selected, though usually from the opposite sex. He may have been dead for centuries, but his intelligence and cunning will have increased in proportion to his age. He is much more 'human' than his folkloric counterpart, and therefore more likely to arouse complex emotions in his victims, even those of pity for his plight.

Ruthven, Varney and Carmilla are just three of innumerable vampire characters to be found in the pages of nineteenth-century fiction. Many other writers preferred to exploit the vampire theme in a psychic, non intra-venous, sense. Heathcliff in Emily Brontë's *Wuthering Heights* possesses the requisite psychic power, facial pallor and sharp, white teeth. The short stories of Edgar Allan Poe are noted for the communication between lovers after their separation by death, and in particular for malevolent females returning to haunt their lovers from beyond the grave.

Clearly it is all a question of how we define the vampire. The looser, broader definition would encompass any process whereby one entity, human or otherwise, derives nourishment and strength in direct proportion to the loss of another's. There is no specific need for blood, sex, death, the devil, garlic or wolf teeth. By this reckoning the vampire motif would embrace such tales as Oscar Wilde's *Picture of Dorian Gray* in which the sinful effects of an artist's debauchery are mysteriously transferred to a portrait of himself; not to mention the works of Brontë, Poe, and countless others.

On the other hand, a stricter definition of vampirism does not necessarily assist matters. If we insist that, to be worthy of the label 'vampire', the creature should possess sharp teeth and be vulnerable to garlic and crucifixes then we must exclude Lord Ruthven from contention. The requirements that it be related to the werewolf and be sponsored by the devil rules out Carmilla. And if it is held that the vampire's sole preoccupation is to drink blood for the explicit purpose of regaining youth and vitality, this would seem to reduce the category to just one – Drácula. It is notable that Stoker's creation has become the yardstick by which we measure all other so-called vampires. Count Dracula, as will be explained, is a unique amalgam of folklore, historical record, and assorted prototypes of the literary vampire. This uniqueness at once sets Dracula apart from earlier, less sophisticated models of the undead, while also undermining all attempts to produce a worthwhile definition of his kind which does not exclude all but himself.

But what of Bram Stoker, architect of this supreme vampire? He was born in 1847 in Clontarf, in the northern suburbs of Dublin, the third of seven children in a Protestant household. We know that he was invalided in his infancy, so that he was bedridden until the age of seven, and that his recovery was so total that he became an athletics champion at Trinity College, where he took honours in mathematics and science. The next ten years were spent following his father's footsteps as a civil servant in Dublin Castle.

The turning point in his life came with an invitation from the distinguished actor, Henry Irving, to manage the business affairs of his newly-acquired theatre company – the London Lyceum. Stoker fulfilled these duties for 27 years until the actor's death in 1905. Stoker's passion for the theatre, which had first brought him to Irving's notice, therefore found a satisfactory outlet, but it meant that his other passion, for writing, was to be only partially fulfilled. Even in his spare hours Stoker achieved an output of nineteen books and so many short stories that they are still being unearthed today. Given his workload this was remarkable enough, but almost everything he wrote would have benefited from the extra care and attention that only a full-time author could have brought to them.

Stoker died in 1912. Although his family had a crypt in the vaults of a Dublin church, sufficiently famous for its preserving effects on human remains that it sustains a minor tourist trade, Stoker preferred to be cremated in London. He left one son – Noel – from his marriage to Florence Balcombe, and a lifetime's writings that can be classified under several headings. A textbook on clerical duties in Irish lawcourts would have had the narrowest market. His other attempts at non-fiction, including a two-volume biography of Henry Irving and a breeze through the great impostors of history, are worth little except as insights into Stoker's mind.

By far the greater part of his fiction was reserved for romances of no special quality, but which are uniformly characterised by a slushy sentimentality which finds little sympathy – and fewer readers – in the sceptical late twentieth century. The consistent message of his romances (reinforced by autobiographical material in his work on Irving) is that women are weak and feeble, given to fainting, possess limited brain power, and want only one thing in life – to meekly submit themselves to the arms of strong, gallant gentlemen, who will guard and protect them from strong un-gallant rogues. Questions of honour must always prevail, even when at preposterous personal expense. And on the occasions in his later fiction when Stoker does ostensibly create more resourceful women he is careful to restrict their talents to intuition rather than ratiocination – which is pointedly made the preserve of men.

It is with his fairy tales and his supernatural epics that Stoker moves into a higher gear. The fairy tales in the anthology *Under the Sunset* were critically well-received, and rightly so. They show wit and imagination, over and above the requisite moralising. Unfortunately they are so nightmarish as to be hardly appropriate for younger readers, and are more properly considered as falling within the scope of his horror fiction.

Stoker was nothing if not a writer of extremes. His gushing romances should not prejudice our reception to his tales of the supernatural – even if they, too, are not infrequently tarnished with the trappings of over-sentimentality. Whether in the form of the short story or the full novel, Stoker was capable of combining the most vivid, if ghastly, imagination with the most meticulous plot. His eery tale of rats and the lonely student in 'The Judge's House', for example, justly earns a place in several reputable anthologies of the finest ghost stories. And the effect Stoker could achieve in 17 pages he could sustain in 450 – the length of *Dracula*.

Examination of the origins of *Dracula* is of importance for several reasons. Stoker is an elusive character, leaving behind few personal papers or effects. In the main, we must make do with his publications and what we can glean from his biography of Henry Irving. Stoker's poor literary reputation, in part caused by works other than *Dracula*, in part by the trivialising effects of the cinema on his principal creation, has not encouraged earnest investigation into the background to the famous Count.

Yet by any reckoning *Dracula* stands apart from Stoker's other novels. It is a one-off. It has a whiff of menace about it, of dark understanding of malign forces, which is easy to sense but difficult to explain. It is a truly chilling book. Mary Shelley's *Frankenstein* is equally visionary, but hers was the innocence of a teenage dream.

Stoker was into his middle years when he wrote *Dracula*, years crammed with reading and discoursing on otherworldly topics. Compared with *Frankenstein*'s naïveté, *Dracula* reads like a compendium of the occult. The reader is never tempted to believe that Frankenstein's monster actually exists, whereas it is part of Stoker's talent to be able to suspend all disbelief. Dracula is real, terrifyingly real. Stoker might never have written on vampires previously, but he leaves the impression that he drew on all his considerable knowledge of the supernatural and compressed it within the covers of a single book.

Impressions, however, were all we had until, in the mid-1970s, Stoker's research papers for *Dracula* were unearthed in the Rosenbach Foundation in Philadelphia. These papers comprise three packages, made up of eighty pages of notes, summaries, data and photographs that transform our understanding of the novel. At a stroke it was confirmed that *Dracula* was not a haphazard venture, conceived and written at a single sitting. According to his papers Stoker began making notes in 1890, when he was 42. It would take another seven years before *Dracula* was finished and published.

His notes show that the novel is set in 1893 and that Whitby played an important part from its inception. They show that initially Stoker had never heard of the historical Dracula and was planning to site the novel not in Transylvania but in Styria. They show notes and recorded conversations on tombstone inscriptions, shipwrecks, meteorological data, train timetables, the behaviour of certain animals at London Zoo, a theory of dreams, treatment of specific head injuries, a newspaper cutting dealing with an apparent vampire attack in New York, typed extracts from several books – and a list of source books and material most of which is quite unexpected and takes us far beyond the basic issue of vampirism. These sources provide the justification for the present book. They explain sub-themes of the novel relating to fear of death, burial customs, the link with werewolves, superstitions of the sea, trance and mesmerism, the diabolic control of the vampire, and the link with the Inquisition – not to mention background information on Dracula and Transylvania.

With the aid of Stoker's sources it is possible to grasp the complexity of Count Dracula. He is less a figment of Stoker's imagination than a multi-layered compound of diverse ingredients. He is partly constructed round the vampire of Balkan superstition, in that he is a close cousin to the werewolf. His 'animalism' is reflected in his wolf-like ears, hairy palms, pointed teeth and feral stench, and distinguishes him from the likes of Ruthven, Varney and Carmilla. Dracula's control over wolves provides a curious twist to the folkloric relationship between the werewolf and the vampire, for the former is more normally considered the parent of the latter: vampires are the offspring of werewolves, not their masters. To reinforce Dracula's animalism Stoker elsewhere describes him as 'lion-like', 'lizard-like' and 'panther-like'. As with most animals, Dracula can see in the dark and operates better at night.

Stoker also adopts the folkloric insistence on vampires casting no shadow, being able to transform themselves into whatever shape they please, having power over the elements, and being at their most virulent on the eve of saints' days. Folklore never specified that vampire operations were restricted to the hours of darkness, and in *Dracula*, too, the Count moves around quite freely in daylight, without any harm befalling him. He simply loses his vampiric powers until the moment of sunset. Responsibility for vampires sizzling and melting under the direct rays of the sun lies with the film makers. It makes good use of their special effects.

Stoker's Dracula, we assume, is physically dead. But if he is, as it were, living in death, simultaneously inhabiting both worlds, then it might be asked whether he is more dead than alive, or more alive than dead. If vampires are really dead, then why do they never speak of life beyond the grave, or communicate its wonders or its terrors to the living? The only time Dracula reflects on his past is when recalling his martial exploits during his pre-vampire existence: he has nothing to say about the four hundred years since he signed up with the devil. On closer inspection it would appear that the only aspect of the vampire that is dead is its body, for its mind has never travelled beyond the experiences of this earth.

With regard to the literary tradition, Stoker borrowed from all the great Romantic myths involving those who would cheat death – the Flying Dutchman, The Wandering Jew, Faust, the Demon Lover. Stoker is known to have taken a special interest in these myths: an early draft of *Dracula* was to have featured a theatre production of the Flying Dutchman; while Stoker later wrote an account on the Wandering Jew in his *Famous Impostors*.

More specifically, Dracula belongs with the aristocratic, woman-chasing vampire tradition established by Lord Ruthven and Sir

Bram Stoker, author of *Dracula,* as a young man.

(Left) *Images of Dracula - 1*
Bust of Vlad the Impaler, on display in the house in which he was born, Sighisoara, Transylvania.

(Below) *Images of Dracula - 2*
'Vlad Tepes' Feast': Painting by T. Aman.

Francis Varney. But even here Stoker keeps his distance. It is wise to remember that at the outset Dracula is a tall, white-haired old man, labouring under a droopy moustache. Even with his energising transfusions of blood the only effect is to make him younger and stronger, not more attractive. He never loses his mask of cruelty or his foul odour. In fact he has no amorous qualities at all, save those artificially induced by his special powers of hypnosis. The sexual exploits in the novel are mostly performed by women, by a batch of femmes fatales that connects Stoker's *Dracula* with Coleridge's 'Christabel' and with other fatally attractive women in nineteenth-century fiction.

Having considered *Dracula*'s folkloric and literary precursors it remains to examine the real-life models Stoker drew upon. The most important of his associates was Sir Henry Irving, who seems to have been to Stoker's vampire what Lord Byron was to Polidori's. Dracula even looks rather like Irving. *Dracula* was dramatised and performed at the Lyceum to accompany its publication. Perhaps Stoker would have liked Irving in the leading role, for the actor, with his hissing, metallic voice and saturnine air, normally relished supernatural roles – such as that of Mephistopheles.

If Irving was a contemporary source, then a more distant one was Countess Elizabeth Bathory – the Blood Countess – whose passion for retaining her youth led to the unspeakable deeds for which she is immortalised in the *Guinness Book of Records*. (More of her in Chapter 9)

However, it is the association with Vlad Dracula – Vlad the Impaler – which has naturally attracted most attention. Stoker's facial description of his Count bears a strong resemblance to that of the Impaler, although both are in effect no more than standard physiognomic depictions of nature's tyrants. How Stoker came upon the historical Dracula has never been fully established and is the subject of Chapter 5.

Finally, Dracula is unique among vampires because of his specifically diabolical origins. It is unusual in vampire fiction for authors to divulge the process of recruitment to the undead. Stoker is not so reticent. Not only does he detail the circumstances of Dracula's rebirth (see Chapter 7), but in so doing he makes clear that it is the devil who is pulling the strings. Stoker adds little touches like the vampire being unable to gain access to the victim's abode at the first instance, unless invited in, thereby conforming to the belief that the devil can only conduct business with willing clients. Having the devil as the adversary also lends *Dracula* a stark religious aspect which permits the book's heroes to think of themselves as Crusaders or Inquisitors. (see Chapter 17)

Dracula is the focus of the novel, but he shares the stage with seven other prominent characters. These include two women – Mina and Lucy – the one marrying Jonathan Harker, the other intending to wed the Hon Arthur Holmwood after spurning the advances of both Dr Seward, who runs a lunatic asylum, and a Texan, Quincey Morris, who does nothing very much – until his death on the final page. The remaining two characters are both linked with Dr Seward: his mad patient, Renfield, who finds himself mixed up with the Count; and his old tutor and master, professor Abraham Van Helsing.

Stoker evidently had considerable difficulty assembling this cast, for in his notes are scribbled numerous names and occupations, few of which found themselves included in the finished work. Stripped of its sub-plots, the story concerns a hapless young solicitor, Jonathan Harker, forced to stand in for his employer and undertake the hazardous journey to Castle Dracula, located on the mountainous frontier between Transylvania, Bukovina and Moldavia. His purpose is to settle the sale of a crumbling estate in Purfleet, east of London, which Dracula wishes to purchase, presumably as a base from which to build a vampire empire in Britain. Details finalised, Harker is left behind, intended bounty for Dracula's three vampire women, while the Count, accompanied by crates of native earth in which to sleep, makes his stealthy way to England as a stowaway aboard the Russian ship *Demeter*, bound for Whitby, Yorkshire.

Upon landing, in a shipwreck, he makes the acquaintance of beautiful Lucy Westenra, whose only problem in life is to select a husband from three simultaneous offers. Being a childhood somnambulist, she is easily snared by Dracula's blazing eyes. Had he chosen someone less well-connected Dracula might have gone undetected, but now unfurls the chain of developments that eventually proves his undoing. As Lucy weakens, her betrothed calls upon the services of his friend, Dr Seward, by chance one of her rejected suitors. His conventional medical training easily baffled, he in turn summons his guru, the ageing Dutch polymath Van Helsing.

From this point the novel is almost Sherlock Holmesian as the master medic-magician-sleuth pits his wits against the master demon. The first round goes to Dracula: Lucy dies, notwithstanding Van Helsing's attentions. She duly stalks the London nights until the Professor exposes her for what she is. Her would-be husband extinguishes her nocturnal habits by means of a stake through her heart, whereupon the hunt is launched for Dracula before he can strike again.

Requesting access to Lucy's correspondence Van Helsing learns of her closest friend, Mina, visits her and is thereby introduced to her husband, Jonathan, miraculously returned from Transylvania. All the information about the Count is pooled, the men set off in pursuit of his boxes of earth, and conveniently leave Mina exposed and unprotected for Dracula's counter-attack, made with Renfield's assistance. The quest is now a race against time: Dracula must be destroyed before Mina's transformation into a vampire is complete. As the net closes he flees back to Transylvania as he came – on board a Russian ship. He is caught at the foot of his castle, the sun already dipping below the horizon, when Harker slices Dracula's throat with his Bowie knife. To avoid too happy a dénouement, Quincey Morris is mortally wounded in the struggle.

For *Dracula* to occupy such a prominent place in contemporary popular culture, clearly its impact must derive from more than its story-line. There seems to be no limit to the number of ways in which the novel can be interpreted. The cinema has gleefully exploited its sexual potential. The extent to which Stoker was aware of *Dracula*'s sexuality is a matter of fierce debate. At the conscious level he would have denied any suggestion of prurience or pornography. Stoker was the most upright of Victorian gentlemen. In his more irascible moments he was given to preaching against the smutty pulp literature streaming from the presses at the turn of the century. His proposed solution was to introduce censorship.

Stoker's unconscious mind is another matter. It is not necessary to delve into his private life – his wife's unsubstantiated frigidity, his resulting illicit unsubstantiated liaisons, and his unsubstantiated contraction of syphilis – in order to detect a troubled and unhealthy view of women. His fiction is full of it, particularly in his later years. In *Dracula* he writes of vampire bites as 'kisses'. It is only necessary to substitute 'sexual intercourse' for 'kisses', and 'semen' for 'blood', to be left with a novel as sexually explicit as any of the time. Impaling, of course, needs no interpretation.

When Jonathan Harker is 'assaulted' by Dracula's she-vampires,

Stoker uses the language of a three-on-one seduction, with Harker reclining in expectation, all coy and passive, worried only that his beloved Mina might find out. Later, the sexual imagery takes a sadistic turn when the undead Lucy is impaled by Arthur, the night after they were to have been married. Their relationship is consummated by his hammering a huge stake through her, accompanied by her orgasmic screech and his post-coital exhaustion. Next it is the turn of oral sex. When Dracula forces Mina's head down upon him Stoker describes her ordeal as like having to swallow milk. This unusual twist to orthodox vampire-victim proceedings, through having the victim suck from the vampire, is lost in the violent sexual symbolism of the episode.

Several critics have maintained that *Dracula*'s sexuality has a Freudian base. This is demonstrated, for example, in the Count's oral preoccupation and his excremental stench. When we add Van Helsing's observation of Dracula's child-like intellectual development, we are presented with a persona which is in Freudian terms pre-phallic: oral, anal, and infantile. The Freudian view is backed up by the numerous familial metaphors – parent-child, sisters-brothers – and Stoker's strange need to kill off as many parental figures as he can. These include Lucy's mother, Arthur's father, Jonathan's mentor and second father, old Mr Swales at Whitby, the mother of a stolen child against whom Dracula directs the wolves, and even Dracula himself when we think of his vampire wife and daughters.

These Oedipal configurations can be linked with the psychoanalytical theory of castration complex, which is centred around the symbolic power of teeth – a feature shared with *Dracula*'s obsession with gleaming, sharp dentures. The cutting of the young male's teeth provides him with his first ability to inflict pain (on his mother's breast), and the subconscious realisation, or dread, of what her teeth might do to him. Maybe, in other words, Stoker is using *Dracula* to work through his own juvenile castration complex. Maybe not. But teeth, along with virtually any other elongated objects, tend to assume phallic connotations. They allow Stoker to portray sexual intercourse by means of a lengthened tooth penetrating the soft white skin of the neck. Freud also proposed, in the case of sexual nightmares involving castration fears, that not only the teeth but the head, too, could act as a penis substitute. What a symbolic sexual punishment, then, that Harker's knife goes not for Dracula's heart but for his throat. Dracula thereby suffers the ultimate sexual revenge.

If Dracula acts as a sexual tyrant he does so in the service of the devil. Stoker emphasises the biblical confrontation underpinning the novel in ways which are sometimes explicit, sometimes subtle. He includes thinly-veiled references to St George and the Dragon. On other occasions Stoker has Mina and Renfield give loosely adapted quotations from both Old and New Testaments. Renfield uses capitalised pronouns when speaking of Dracula, to emphasise His divine status, and elsewhere Stoker uses imagery which comes close to identifying the Count with the Antichrist. More subtly biblical is the very structure of the novel. Stoker may have chosen the format of letters and diaries in which to tell his tale as a means of enhancing authenticity: if *all* the characters come to believe in vampires they cannot *all* be mad. But its effect is to provide a scriptural text in itself, with Gospels according to Jonathan Harker, Mina Harker, and Dr Seward, each recording the events leading up to Dracula's 'crucifixion' from their own perspectives and in their own words.

Gnostic themes can also be read into *Dracula*. At times Stoker seems to borrow from the symbolism of the Tarot, with the unwitting Fool (Harker) venturing out on a voyage of personal discovery and having to surmount the various hazards and hurdles placed in his path, till he arrives at the goal of redemption with Dracula's destruction. The whole novel, however, is also cyclical and wedded to the calendar of the seasons. The book opens in spring, but it is autumn when Dracula meets his doom, so that his ashes are like those of a malign plant, lost among the dying vegetation around him. The action is set first in Transylvania, transfers to England, and returns to Transylvania – exactly retracing Harker's earlier path to the Castle – for the climax. Then, in a postscript written seven years after Dracula's demise – that is, in 1900 – the Harkers introduce their little son. He is linked by all the names of Mina's protectors; and also by their blood. Arthur's, Dr Seward's, Van Helsing's and Quincey Morris's had been transfused into Lucy; Dracula had drunk hers; and Mina his. Which means that young Master Harker has Dracula's blood flowing through his veins. The ashes of one totemic fiend have probably given rise to another.

When all is said, it is Dracula's awesome power which most appeals, or appals. He does not know fear. The weather, the animal world, the minds of men – all are under his control. A brawling mob cannot restrain him for he has the strength of twenty men. He can summon a sexual power over Lucy and Mina which their menfolk cannot match. He provides a harkback to the days when personal autocratic rule was the norm; no wonder that in his heyday Dracula was a shrewd, ruthless political leader, almost a model of the Machiavellian ethos. There is something of Nietzsche's aristocratic, Will-to-Power Superman in him; of Darwin's survival of the fittest taken to its ultimate degree.

Nowadays, Dracula has spread his cloak to symbolise economic domination. Marxists see in him the worst excesses of capitalism; total control over his vampire victims for eternity. His strategic designs to colonise London, moreover, are not to be accomplished by force of arms, but by means of capital – the pile of gold he brought with him. Nor is he at war with everybody. He has his cronies, his conscience-less accomplices in exploitation. Estate agents, solicitors, and his gypsy bodyguard earn his cash, not his teeth. However, for legends to be enduring they must be adaptable. Transylvania's position behind the Iron Curtain has conveniently rubbed off on its most famous inhabitant. American Cold War propaganda seized on the diabolical Count as representing everything evil in the communist world, a godless, merciless tyrant. Dracula the capitalist or Dracula the Red: we can take our pick.

Above all, Dracula has no fear of death. Strictly speaking he died once, but instead of bringing him decay and oblivion he was rewarded by the devil with power beyond his dreams and an ever-expanding harem. At least, this would be his reward but for Van Helsing's intervention. Stoker makes sure the last laugh lies with God. For Dracula is, after all, afraid of one thing. He cannot succeed in a standup fight with God. For all its temptations Stoker's novel allows only one winner. Faith.*

*

With an author as shadowy and unknown as Stoker, it is perhaps to be expected that he should be slighted at every turn. He is an exposed target for innuendo and malign gossip that is not easily rebutted. These attacks take several forms. There are those directed against his personal reputation. One of his biographers declared, specula-

* This analysis is developed fully in my earlier book – *Dracula: The Novel and the Legend – A Study of Bram Stoker's Gothic Masterpiece.*

tively, that Stoker had died of tertiary syphilis.

But if this is a damaging accusation – true or otherwise – there is another which is even more wounding. In the same way that Shakespeare's little-known life prompts disingenuous hints that he might not be responsible for the works that bear his name, so there exist rumours that Stoker should not take credit for *Dracula*. The basis for this view is simplicity itself: Stoker could not write. He was, so it is suggested, a tenth-rate story-teller who needed professional assistance to have *Dracula* knocked into publishable shape.

Such a view could only be held by people unfamiliar with the range of Stoker's works. If he could not write, then every one of his novels and short stories would have needed external polishing. And if so, how do we account for the critical acclaim directed at much of his fiction, especially his earlier works, or his occasional inclusion amongst compilations of some of the foremost writers of his time? For good or ill, Bram Stoker's literary style is unmistakable, not only in a linguistic sense, but also his recurring themes, which surface from one novel to another.

These themes include idealised representations of women, orphaned heroines, racism and class prejudice, the prominence of rescue scenes, treasures and ancient legends, strikingly vivid monsters offset against a cardboard human cast, and conclusions in which the hero ends up with everything: his fairy princess, great wealth or treasure, and the discovery of his manhood. Conspicuous by its absence is any kind of reflection on social injustice or demand for political change. Over-riding all these motifs is Stoker's life-long preoccupation with blurred boundaries. Here is the hallmark of his fiction: the elusive dividing line between life and death, the natural and the supernatural, man and beast, good and evil, scepticism and faith, desire and loathing, dream and reality, lust and purity. Although his imagination was probably his greatest literary asset, it could not be called a flexible imagination, and the aforementioned imprints of his mind are readily detectable in many of his novels, as clear as fingerprints.

A further criticism of *Dracula*'s author is that, as one critic put it: 'it would seem likely that he did some – but very little – research for his fantasy'. These words actually appeared in the introduction to a recent edition of *Dracula*, long after the first published references to Stoker's research notes.

By providing the first book inspired and shaped by Stoker's list of sources, the present author runs obvious risks. Principally they are those of arguing from the sources to the text. Stoker was a widely read man. Each scene in *Dracula* has its origins somewhere or other in the sum experience of his life, of which the knowledge gained through his source-list comprises but a fragment. But his sources we know: his background knowledge we do not. To argue from his sources is inevitably to limit the input which went into *Dracula* to those sources, and in consequence this can lead to some hitherto unvoiced assertions.

For example, take the case of Stoker's adaptation of Vlad Dracula for his own ends. It has always been assumed that Stoker knew of the foul practices of the Impaler. That is surely why he chose Vlad as the model for his Count. But when we read the novel carefully, we search in vain for any reference to the historical Dracula other than to generalised, and muddled, accounts of the Hungarian campaigns against the Turks in the fifteenth century. These are all recorded in the pages of Stoker's listed books. A conclusion drawn strictly from his sources would suggest that Stoker seized on the name Dracula for no other reason than that it means 'Devil'. (Chapter 5) In other words it is Dracula's Satanic aspect which is important for Stoker, not his wretched practice of impaling people. Stoker may have learned of this practice, and more besides, from authorities like Arminius Vambéry and others (Chapters 5 and 8), but this extra information is not necessary for Stoker to have created Dracula exactly as he appears in the novel.

Another problem concerns the presumed accuracy of Stoker's sources. Many of them are outdated, have been overtaken by modern scholarship, and are little more than museum pieces, valuable only for the insights they provide into the nineteenth century world. It is not the intention here to comment on these sources and highlight errors of fact or opinions no longer fashionable. These sources are intended purely to show the kind of world Stoker lived in, and which played their part in the birth of the most enduring of modern myths. Of the extracts which follow, all but one are taken directly from texts listed in Stoker's research notes. The intruder is Chapter 4, dealing with the folkloric vampire, which is included to shed further light on the vampiric origins of *Dracula*.

CHAPTER ONE

The Meaning of Mourning

Sabine Baring-Gould

Fear of death – or, rather, that which lies beyond it – is common to all cultures. Death is life's only certainty. For that reason the human mind has spawned innumerable beliefs and practices designed to counter its ill-effects, whether through faith in the grandest religion or the most trifling superstition. Equally universal to all but the modern atheist is the acceptance that death is not the end, but another beginning. It is not the antithesis of birth, but is akin to it – a form of rebirth.

Acceptance that the dead are, in fact, alive leads to the obvious question. Where? To some it is a place called heaven, or, alternatively, hell. To others, nirvana or some distant kingdom in the sky. In many cultures the dead are thought to inhabit the earth as naturally as do the living. The dead therefore become objects of competition for scarce resources, posing an economic as well as a spiritual threat to those left behind. Fear of the dead in these circumstances is understandable. After all, they vastly outnumber the living.

The Reverend Sabine Baring-Gould was a prolific writer and folklorist, thirteen years Bram Stoker's senior. Perhaps best known for his sixteen-volume *The Lives of the Saints* and the hymn 'Onward Christian Soldiers', Baring-Gould wrote over a hundred books. These covered a wide range, including travel guides, biographies, over fifty novels, and a collection of works on myth, folklore and fairy tales. He even composed an opera.

In 'The Meaning of Mourning' from an anthology of *Curiosities of Olden Times*, Baring-Gould surveys the psychological relationship between the living and the dead. His brittle distinction between the savage and the civilised mind, and the disdain heaped upon the former, we should accept as commonplace within the Victorian world in which he lived. Bram Stoker's writings are likewise prone to cultural elitism.

Baring-Gould reveals how the attribution of human sentiments to the deceased leads to an image of the dead as condemned to a wretched, miserable existence in an all-embracing darkness. They are thought to be cold, wet, hungry and lonely, yearning for nourishment, warmth and companionship. The temptation for them to seek physical and material satisfaction is both natural and unavoidable. It is entirely reasonable that, as the dead are assumed to be alive, they will seek communion with the living. How could they do otherwise?

This unshakable desire to return is matched by a collective stupidity. The dead are held to be bereft of even basic intelligence, and easily outwitted. There are various means of keeping them at bay. The dead can be coaxed into remaining in their resting places by the liberal provision of food and other comforts at the time of burial. Alternatively, it is necessary to resort to deception. Mourners are advised to take tortuous routes home from the graveyard so that any pursuing ghost will lose its way. Perhaps the practice of closing the eyes of the deceased originated in the desire to deprive it of sight, and the wherewithal to return home. The wearing of unfamiliar clothes and facial make-up during the burial ceremony further assists in protecting the mourners by disguising them to the dead.

Should bribery and deception fail in their common objective, then sterner measures are called for. Given the complex relationship between body and soul, and the widely-held assumption that the human spirit cannot function outside the body, physical restraints against resurrection assume a utilitarian character. These restraints include immobilising the corpse with ropes, impaling it by means of nails or a stake, or even snapping the deceased's legs. Nobody can walk with broken legs. Not even the dead. Severing the head was also to be recommended. As insurance, large stones piled upon the grave would hopefully resist all the incumbent's efforts to budge them.

In 'The Meaning of Mourning' Baring-Gould employs the collective term 'ghosts' to apply to the range of apparitions from beyond the grave. Vampirism is not specifically mentioned by name. Baring-Gould is concerned here neither with diabolic agencies instrumental in physical reanimation, nor with the search for blood as the ostensible purpose of it. But by outlining the psychological tensions in operation between the living and the dead, he demonstrates the ease with which the imagination can concoct its own horrors.

*

The Meaning of Mourning

A strip of black cloth an inch and a half in width stitched round the sleeve – that is the final, or perhaps penultimate expression (for it may dwindle further to a black thread) of the usage of wearing mourning on the decease of a relative.

The usage is one that commends itself to us as an outward and visible sign of the inward sentiment of bereavement, and not one in ten thousand who adopt mourning has any idea that it ever possessed a signification of another sort. And yet the correlations of general custom – of mourning fashions, lead us to the inexorable conclusion that in its inception the practice had quite a different signification from that now attributed to it, nay more, that it is solely because its primitive meaning has been absolutely forgotten, and an entirely novel significance given to it, that mourning is still employed after a death.

Look back through the telescope of anthropology at our primitive ancestors in their naked savagery, and we see them daub themselves with soot mingled with tallow. When the savage assumed clothes and became a civilised man, he replaced the fat and lampblack with black cloth, and this black cloth has descended to us in the nineteenth century as the customary and intelligible trappings of woe.

The Chinaman when in a condition of bereavement assumes white garments, and we may be pretty certain that his barbarous ancestor, like the Andaman Islander of the present day, pipeclayed his naked body after the decease and funeral of a relative. In Egypt yellow was the symbol of sorrow for a death, and that points back to the ancestral nude Egyptian having smeared himself with yellow ochre.

Black was not the universal hue of mourning in Europe. In Castile white obtained on the death of its princes. Herrera states that the last time white was thus employed was in 1498, on the death of Prince John. This use of white in Castile indicates chalk or pipeclay as the daub affected by the ancestors of the house of Castile in primeval time as a badge of bereavement.

Various explanations have been offered to account for the

variance of colour. White has been supposed to denote purity; and to this day white gloves and hat-bands and scarves are employed at the funeral of a young girl, as in the old ballad of 'The Bride's Burial':

> A garland fresh and fair
> Of lilies there was made,
> In signs of her virginity,
> And on her coffin laid.
> Six pretty maidens, *all in white*,
> Did bear her to the ground,
> The bells did ring in solemn swing
> And made a doleful sound.

Yellow has been supposed to symbolise that death is the end of human hopes, because falling leaves are sere; black is taken as the privation of light; and purple or violet also affected as a blending of joy with sorrow. Christian moralists have declaimed against black as heathen, as denoting an aspect of death devoid of hope, and gradually purple is taking its place in the trappings of the hearse, if not of the mourners, and the pall is now very generally violet.

But these explanations are afterthoughts, and an attempt to give reason for the divergence of usage which might satisfy, but these are really no explanations at all. The usage goes back to a period when there were no such refinements of thought. If violet or purple has been traditional, it is so merely because the ancestral Briton stained himself with woad on the death of a relative.

The pipeclay, lampblack, yellow ochre, and woad of the primeval mourners must be brought into range with a whole series of other mourning usages, and then the result is something of an 'eye-opener.' It reveals a condition of mind and an aspect of death that causes not a little surprise and amusement. It is one of the most astonishing, and, perhaps, shocking traits of barbarous life, that death revolutionises completely the feelings of the survivors towards their deceased husbands, wives, parents, and other relatives.

A married couple may have been sincerely attached to each other so long as the vital spark was twinkling, but the moment it is extinguished the dead partner becomes, not a sadly sweet reminiscence, but an object of the liveliest terror to the survivor. He or she does everything that ingenuity can suggest to get him or herself out of all association in body and spirit with the late lamented. Death is held to be thoroughly demoralising to the deceased. However exemplary a person he or she may have been in life, after death the ghost is little less than a plaguing, spiteful spirit.

There is in the savage no tender clinging to the remembrance of the loved one, he is translated into a terrible bugbear, who must be evaded and avoided by every contrivance conceivable. This is due, doubtless, mainly to the inability of the uncultivated mind to discriminate between what is seen waking from what presents itself in phantasy to the dreaming head. After a funeral, it is natural enough for the mourners to dream of the dead, and they at once conclude that they have been visited by his *revenant*. After a funeral feast, a great gorging of pork or beef, it is very natural that the sense of oppression and pain felt should be associated with the dear departed, and should translate itself into the idea that he has come from his grave to sit on the chests of those who have bewailed him.

Moreover, the savage associates the idea of desolation, death, discomfort, with the condition of the soul after death, and believes that the ghosts do all they can to return to their former haunts and associates for the sake of the warmth and food, the shelter of the huts, and the entertainment of the society of their fellows. But the living men and women are not at all eager to receive the ghosts into the family circle, and they accordingly adopt all kinds of 'dodges', expedients to prevent the departed from making these irksome and undesired visits.

The Venerable Bede tells us that Laurence, Archbishop of Canterbury, resolved on flying from England because he was hopeless of effecting any good under the successor of Ethelbert, king of Kent. The night before he fled he slept on the floor of the church, and dreamed that St Peter cudgelled him soundly for resolving to abandon his sacred charge. In the morning he awoke stiff and full of aches and pains. Turned into modern language, we should say that Archbishop Laurence was attacked with rheumatism on account of his having slept on the cold stones of the church. His mind had been troubled before he went to sleep with doubts whether he were doing right in abandoning his duty, and very naturally this trouble of conscience coloured his dream, and gave to his rheumatic twinges the complexion it assumed.

Now Archbishop Laurence regarded the Prince of the Apostles in precisely the light in which a savage views his deceased relatives and ancestors. He associates his maladies, his pains, with theirs, if he should happen to dream of them. If, however, when in pain, he dreams of a living person, then he holds that this living person has cast a magical spell over him.

Among nature's men, before they have gone through the mill of civilisation, plenty to eat and to drink, and some one to talk to, are the essentials of happiness. They see that the dead have none of these requisites, they consider that they are miserable without them. The writer remembers how, when he was a boy, and attended a funeral of a relative in November, he could not sleep all night – a bitter, frosty night – with the thought how cold it must be to the dead in the vault, without blankets, hot bottle, or fire. It was in vain for him to reason against the feeling; the feeling was so strong on him that he was conscious of an uncomfortable expectation of the dead coming to claim a share of the banket, fire, or hot bottle. Now the savage never reasons against such a feeling, and he assumes that the dead will return, as a matter of course, for what he cannot have in the grave.

The ghost is very anxious to assert its former rights. A widow has to get rid of the ghost of her first husband before she can marry again. In Parma a widow about to be remarried is pelted with sticks and stones, not in the least because the Parmans object to remarriage, but in order to scare away the ghost of No 1, who is hanging about his wife, and who will resent his displacement in her affections by No 2.

To the present day, in some of the villages of the ancient Duchy of Teck, in Würtemberg, it is customary when a corpse is being conveyed to the cemetery, for relatives and friends to surround the dead, and in turn talk to it – assure it what a blessed rest it is going to, how anxious the kinsfolk are that it may be comfortable, how handsome will be the cross set over the grave, how much all desire that it may sleep soundly and not by any means leave the grave and come haunting old scenes and friends, how unreasonable such conduct as the latter hinted at would be, how it would alter the regard entertained for the deceased, how disrespectful to the Almighty who gives rest to the good, and how it would be regarded as an admission of an uneasy conscience. Lively comparisons are drawn between the joys of Paradise and the vale of tears that has been quitted, so as to take away from the deceased all desire to return.

This is a survival of primitive usage and mode of thought, and has its analogies in many places and among diverse races.

The Dacotah Indians address the ghost of the dead in the same 'soft solder', to induce it to take the road to the world of spirits and not to come sauntering back to its wigwam. In Siam and in China it is much the same; persuasion, flattery, threats are employed.

Unhappily all ghosts are not open to persuasion, and see through the designs of the mourners, and with them severer measures have to be resorted to. Among the Sclavs of the Danube and the Czechs, the bereaved, after the funeral, on going home turn themselves about after every few steps and throw sticks, stones, mud, even hot coals in the direction of the churchyard, so as to frighten the spirit back to the grave so considerately provided for it. A Finnish tribe has not even the decency to wait till the corpse is covered with soil; they fire pistols and guns after it as it goes to its grave, and lies in it.

In *Hamlet*, at the funeral of Ophelia, the priest says–

> For charitable prayers,
> Shards, flints, and pebbles should be thrown on her.

Unquestionably it must have been customary in England thus to pelt a ghost that was suspected of the intention to wander. The stake driven through the suicide's body was a summary and complete way of ensuring that the ghost would not be troublesome.

Those Finns who fired guns after a dead man had another expedient for holding him fast, and that was to nail him down in his coffin. The Arabs tie his legs together. The Wallacks drive a long nail through the skull; and this usage explains the many skulls that have been exhumed in Germany thus perforated. The Icelanders, when a ghost proved troublesome, opened the grave, cut off the dead man's head, and made the body sit on it. That, they concluded, would effectually puzzle it how to get about. The Californian Indians were wont to break the spine of the corpse so as to paralyse his lower limbs, and make 'walking' impossible. Spirit and body to the unreasoning mind are intimately associated. A hurt done to the body wounds the soul. Mrs Crowe, in her *Night Side of Nature*, tells a story reversing this. A gentleman in Germany was dying – he expressed great desire to see his son, who was a ne'er-do-well, and was squandering his money in Paris. At that same time the young man was sitting on a bench in the Bois de Boulogne, with a switch in his hand. Suddenly he saw his old father before him. Convinced that he saw a phantom, he raised his switch, and cut the apparition once, twice, and thrice across the face; and it vanished. At that moment the dying father uttered a scream, and held his hands to his face – 'My boy! my boy! He is striking me again – again!' and he died. The Algonquin Indians beat the walls of the death-chamber to drive out the ghost; in Sumatra, a priest is employed with a broom to sweep the ghost out. In Scotland, and in North Germany, the chairs on which a coffin has rested are reversed, lest the dead man should take the fancy to sit on them instead of going to his grave. In ancient Mexico, certain professional ghost ejectors were employed, who, after a funeral, were invited to visit and thoroughly explore the house whence the dead had been removed, and if they found the ghost lurking about, in corners, in cupboards, under beds – anywhere, to kick it out. In Siberia, after forty days' 'law' given to the ghost, if it be still found loafing about, the Schaman is sent for, who drums it out. He extorts brandy, which he professes to require, as he has to conduct the deceased personally to the land of spirits, where he will make it and the other guests so fuddled that they will forget the way back to earth.

In North Germany a troublesome ghost is bagged, and the bag emptied in some lone spot, or in the garden of a neighbour against whom a grudge is entertained.

Another mode of getting rid of the spirit of the dear departed is to confuse it as to its way home. This is done in various ways. Sometimes the road by which it has been carried to its resting-place is swept to efface the footprints, and a false track is made into a wood or on to a moor, so that the ghost may take the wrong road. Sometimes ashes are strewn on the road to hide the footprints. Sometimes the dead is carried rapidly three or four times round the house so as to make him giddy, and not know in which direction he is carried. The universal practice of closing the eyes of the dead may be thought to have originated in the desire that he might be prevented from seeing his way.

In many places it was, and is, customary for the dead body to be taken out of the house, not through the door, but by a hole knocked in the wall for the purpose, and backwards. In Iceland in the historic period this custom was reserved for such as died in their seats and not in their beds. One or two instances occur in the Sagas. In Corea, blinders made of black silk are put on the dead man's eyes, to prevent him from finding his way home.

Many savage nations entirely abandon a hut or a camp in which a death has occurred for precisely the same reason – of throwing out the dead man's spirit.

It was a common practice in England till quite recently for the room in which a death had occurred to be closed for some time, and this is merely a survival of the custom of abandoning the place where a spirit has left the body. The Esquimaux take out their dying relatives to huts constructed of blocks of ice or snow, and leave them there to expire, for ghosts are as stupid as they are troublesome, they have no more wits than a peacock, they can only find their way to the place where they died.

Other usages are to divert a stream and bring the corpse in the river-bed, or lay it beyond running water, which according to ghost-lore it cannot pass. Or again, fires are lighted across its path, and it shrinks from passing through flames. As for water, ghosts loathe it. Among the Matamba negroes a widow is flung into the water and dipped repeatedly so as to wash off the ghost of the dead husband, which is supposed to be clinging to her. In New Zealand, among the Maoris, all who have followed the corpse dive into water so as to throw off the ghost which is sneaking home after them. In Tahiti, all who have assisted at a burial run as hard as they can to the sea and take headers into it for the same object. It is the same in New Guinea. We see the same idea reduced to a mere form in ancient Rome, where in place of the dive through water, a vessel of water was carried twice round those who had followed the corpse, and they were sprinkled. The custom of washing and purification after a funeral practised by the Jews is a reminiscence of the usage, with a novel explanation given to it.

In the South Pacific, in the Hervey Islands, after a death men turn out to pummel and fight the returning spirit, and give it a good drubbing in the air.

Now, perhaps, the reader may have been brought to understand what the sundry mourning costumes originally meant. They were disguises whereby to deceive the ghosts, so that they might not recognise and pester with their undesired attentions the relatives who live. Indians who are wont to paint themselves habitually, go after a funeral totally unbedecked with colour. On the other hand, other savages daub themselves fantastically with various colours, making themselves as unlike what they were previously as is possible. The Coreans when in mourning assume hats with low rims that conceal their features.

The Papuans conceal themselves under extinguishers made of banana leaves. Elsewhere in New Guinea they envelop themselves in a wickerwork frame in which they can hardly walk. Among the Mpongues of Western Africa, those who on ordinary occasions wear garments walk in complete nudity when suffering bereavement.

Valerius Maximus tells us that among the Lycians it was customary in mourning for the men to disguise themselves in women's garments.

The custom of cutting the hair short, and of scratching and disfiguring the face, and of rending the garments, all originated from the same thought – to make the survivors irrecognisable by the ghost of the deceased. Plutarch asserts that the Sacæ, after a death, went down into pits and hid themselves for days from the light of the sun. Australian widows near the north-west bend of the Murray shave their heads and plaster them with pipeclay, which, when dry, forms a close-fitting skull-cap. The spirit of the late lamented on returning to his better half either does not recognise his spouse, or is so disgusted with her appearance that he leaves her for ever.

There is almost no end to the expedients adopted for getting rid of the dead. Piles of stones are heaped over them, they are buried deep in the earth, they are walled up in natural caves, they are enclosed in megalithic structures, they are burned, they are sunk in the sea. They are threatened, they are cajoled, they are hoodwinked. Every sort of trickery is had recourse to, to throw them off the scent of home and of their living relations.

The wives, horses, dogs slain and buried with them, the copious supplies of food and drink laid on their graves, are bribes to induce them to be content with their situation. Nay, further – in very many places no food may be eaten in the house of mourning for many days after an interment. The object of course is to disappoint the returning spirit, which comes seeking a meal, finds none, comes again next day, finds none again, and after a while desists from returning out of sheer disgust.

A vast amount of misdirected ingenuity is expended in bamboozling and bullying the unhappy ghosts; but the feature most striking in these proceedings is the unanimous agreement in considering these ghosts as such imbeciles. When they put off their outward husk, they divest themselves of all that cunning which is the form that intelligence takes in the savage. Not only so, but although they remember and crave after home comforts, they absolutely forget the tricks they had themselves played on the souls of the dead in their own lifetime; they walk and blunder into the traps which they had themselves laid for other ghosts in the days of their flesh.

Perhaps the lowest abyss of dunder-headedness they have been supposed to reach is when made to mistake their own identity.

Recently near Mentone a series of prehistoric interments in caves have been exposed. They reveal the dead men as having had their heads daubed over with red oxide of iron. Still extant races of savages paint, plaster, and disfigure their dead. The prehistoric Greeks masked them. The Aztecs masked their deceased kings, and the Siamese do so still. We cannot say with absolute certainty what the object is – but we are probably not far out when we conjecture the purpose to be to make the dead forget who they are when they look at their reflection in the water. There was a favourite song sung some sixty years ago relative to a little old woman who got 'muzzy'. Whilst in this condition some naughty boys cut her skirts at her knees. When she woke up and saw her condition, 'Lawk!' said the little old woman, 'this never is me!' And certain ancient peoples treated their dead in something the same way; they disguised and disfigured them so that each ghost waking up might exclaim, 'Lawk! this never is me!' And so having lost its identity, did not consider it had a right to revisit its old home and molest its old acquaintances.

From Curiosities of Olden Times *(1895) pages 1–16.*

CHAPTER TWO

Fetishistic Superstitions and Burial Customs

Rushton M. Dorman

We know from his own writings that Bram Stoker was greatly enamoured with the United States of America. Between 1883 and 1904 he toured frequently with Henry Irving's theatre company. So impressed was he with virtually every aspect of American life that he delivered a lecture on the subject of Britain's ex-colony to the London Institution in 1885. 'A Glimpse of America', as the lecture was called, was published the following year.

Stoker had little to say about the American Indian. But shortly before Irving's company embarked on its first trans-Atlantic voyage a Chicago anthropologist, Rushton M. Dorman, published a volume on *The Origin of Primitive Superstitions*. The title conveyed little. It was left to the sub-title to divulge the exact nature of the contents – *And their Development into the Worship of Spirits and the Doctrine of Spiritual Agency among the Aboriginees of America.*

Dorman's task had been to explore the pagan mythologies of the indigenous populations of North and South America, from Alaska to Patagonia. Although confining his attentions to the New World, his objective was to demonstrate that the psychological basis of primitive religious superstition springs from common perceptions of a hostile environment, shared by all mankind. Local conditions impose only minor variations in the expression of worship and ritual.

According to Dorman, all superstitions are traceable to a common origin, founded on error and ignorance. His modest aim is to illuminate the nature of these errors for the sake of nineteenth century enlightenment. Implicit in his book is the Darwinian assumption that evolution in a spiritual sense is as logical as that found in the physical, natural, world. The idea that societies advance along a line from barbarity to civilisation is something that Dorman does not seek to question. His tone is unwittingly condescending to the peoples of whom he writes. And lest he causes too many ripples among his readers with his tacit Darwinism, he reassures them that Christianity has nothing to fear from religious evolution – provided its 'purity' be maintained.

Dorman appears to have been something of an armchair anthropologist compared, for example, with the Indian investigations of Benjamin Smith Barton a century earlier. Nevertheless, his book provides detailed examples of Indian religious practices, even if his explanations for those practices are less convincing. His chapters range over demonology, transmigration of spirits, ancestor worship, amulets, the worship of animals, trees, mountains and heavenly bodies, the animistic theories of meteorology, and the miraculous powers of witch-doctors. Below are reproduced some of his accounts on the fetishistic nature of cannibalism and the reasoning behind various Indian burial rites.

Vampirism is linked to cannibalism and to the Eucharist. Dorman notes the widely-held belief that consumption of flesh and blood effectively transfers the qualities of the deceased to the living. To eat from the body of a brave man, and particularly from his heart, is to partake of his valour. Nor is this conviction confined to pagan climes. Jesus Christ, according to St John's Gospel, declared: 'Who so eateth my flesh and drinketh my blood hath eternal life; and I will raise him up at the last day. For my flesh is meat indeed, and my blood is drink indeed. He that eateth my flesh and drinketh my blood dwelleth in me and I in him.'

On the question of burial customs, Baring-Gould has already related how fear of the returning dead could best be countered by dismembering the corpse upon internment. Here Dorman offers corroboration, for in cultures where personal resurrection at some future date is taken for granted it becomes imperative that the body of the deceased should remain intact. Otherwise the physical perfection of the reanimated entity is likely to be irrevocably impaired. This explains why, in east European folklore, decapitation is strongly recommended as a precaution against possible future vampires. Cremation provides similar safeguards by pre-empting the possibility of resurrection. Paradoxically, according to Dorman, consummation by fire is held by the American Indian to preserve, not destroy, the essential oneness necessary to reanimation.

*

Fetishistic Superstitions and Burial Customs
All primitive religious belief is polytheistic. All savage tribes are full

of the terror of invisible spirits which have been liberated by death. These spirits fill all nature, animate and inanimate. They are in the air, the wind, the storm, in the rock, the hill, the vale, in the river, the waterfall. They transmigrate into human beings, animals, plants, and even into inanimate stones, idols, and heavenly bodies, which are supposed to be animate thereafter. Hence originates the worship of ancestors, and also of animals, plants, stones, idols, and the heavenly bodies. Death, the liberator, and burial, have their religious ceremonies, and the tomb becomes the temple. These spirits liberated by death, or by sleep or a comatose condition, which are its equivalents in savage life, are abroad on the earth for a time, and can avenge themselves for past or present wrongs, in disease, which is a form of transmigration. They can appear in dreams, which is a form of prophecy.

Among primitive peoples the cure of diseases was given over to sorcerers, who were supposed to have some control over the evil-disposed spirits. This sorcery developed into the priestcraft of higher cultures, where exorcism of evil spirits still survives as one of the offices of the priests. In our own day those peculiar diseases which have defied medical skill, such as insanity, hysteria, and epilepsy, are relegated in many countries for cure to the priesthood. Even the primitive fetishism survives in the use of charms and amulets, and in the heraldic devices on many national flags and the armorial bearings of many families . . .

Among the Ojibways early cannibalism appears to have passed into their traditional history embodied in a myth. They had an imaginary being whose deeds were horrible in the extreme. The ghostly man-eater, a species of vampire, had his residence on an island (imaginary) in the centre of Lake Superior. He had the appearance of the human form, yet intangible, with long nails with which he dug up dead bodies and devoured them, or robbed the burial-scaffold of its burden. He travelled with lightning speed from one place to another, and whenever the Indian heard strange songs above his wigwam, it was the ghostly man-eater hurrying upon the wings of the wind from a recent banquet to his mysterious island home. This spiritual monstrosity appears to have been doomed to this life as a punishment for an act of cannibalism, when he killed and fed upon the body of a youth who was the last remnant of a once powerful tribe. Having thus extinguished the last hope of an Indian race for perpetuation by this bloody act, the Ojibways have handed down his infamy in their folk-lore.

Another mythological character which belongs to our subject was a giant, who came from the north and sought the hospitality of an Indian village bordering on the Lake of the Woods. He was entertained at their expense, and when the feast was ready the giant, disdaining the wild rice and game, destroyed with one exception the inhabitants who had gathered at his feast, and devoured their dead bodies. The youth who escaped carried revenge in his heart, and when he became a great hunter he invited the cannibal giant to a feast, and into his bowl of soup he placed a bitter root, which soon deprived him of his strength. He prepared to sleep, and under him was spread his robe of weasel-skins, and over him was thrown his net woven by a mammoth spider. When deep sleep had fallen upon him, the guests despatched him with their clubs, and his flesh became alive very soon with little animals and birds, who fed upon it. Truly he was a fit companion for the giant Ymer of the Norse folk-lore.

The Indians of Brazil and Paraguay formerly delighted in human flesh. They confessed, after the introduction of Christianity, that the flesh of animals tasted insipid to them in comparison with that of men. The Botecudos sucked the blood from living victims, thinking they would imbibe spiritual force.

The Brazilians had human flesh salted and smoked and hung up in their houses. One man boasted that he had partaken of the bodies of three hundred enemies. But it was a stronger passion than hunger that gave these accursed banquets their highest relish. Children were raised by their captives from tribal women for the express purpose of being eaten. In their great cannibal feasts the women were the most ravenous cannibals, and even the children had the brains and tongue allotted to them. Every part of the body was devoured. One of the children raised from captives, whom the Portuguese offered to redeem and save from a feast to which she was dedicated, preferred, she said, to be buried in the bellies of her lords and masters whom she loved.

Among the Brazilians, the first food given a child when weaning it from its mother's milk was the flesh of an enemy. The bones of those eaten were laid up in piles before their houses, and the rank and estimation of a family were in proportion to the size of its heap.

Prisoners dedicated to a cannibal feast were treated well, had attendants appointed for them and women given them. They were fattened, and paraded up and down with great ceremony. Every guest invited to the feast came and touched the prisoner, who was treated like a god. Mr Southey thinks the motive for their cannibalism was some savage notion of superstition.

The priests of Guatemala ate the bodies of those who were sacrificed. It was considered sacred meat.

Cieza, speaking of the Peruvians, says, 'All the Indians of this country eat human flesh.' Cieza saw them eat in one day more than a hundred men and women they had taken in war. Drawing blood from the nose of a child in Peru was a relic of cannibalism. The more uncivilized Peruvians always ate the flesh of those whom they sacrificed to their gods; and the bodies of the victims were cut up and exposed for sale, and sold in the public markets. Peruvian mythology had its giants who were cannibals, who were exterminated by a resplendent young man who came riding upon the clouds, shining like the sun, and hurling flames of fire.

Cannibalism prevailed among the Mexicans. The bodies of those slain on the field of battle were devoured by those voracious cannibals who followed the armies to feed on the dead bodies. The towns had wooden cages where they kept and fattened, for the purpose of eating, the captives in war. Human flesh, exquisitely prepared, was found upon the table of Montezuma, and was eaten by the Mexicans, not for the purpose of allaying appetite, but from religious motives. All the Nahua nations practised this religious cannibalism. That cannibalism as a source of food, unconnected with religious rites, was ever practised, there is little evidence. Sahagun and Las Casas regard the cannibalism of the Nahuas as an abhorrent feature of their religion, and not as an unnatural appetite. They ate the flesh of their sacrificed foes only.

The Mayas also ate the flesh of human victims sacrificed to the gods. In Nicaragua, the high-priest received the heart, the king the feet and hands, the captors took the thighs, and the tripe was given to the trumpeters. The natives of Honduras said the Spaniards were too tough and bitter to be eaten. 'The Mosquito men never gave quarter to any but women; but as many men and children as they take they tie and throw upon a barbecue, as they call it, which is a rack of stakes doing the office of a gridiron, and make a good fire underneath, which, with the help of the sun overhead at noon, soon

(Right) *Images of Dracula - 3*
Painting by Bruce Wightman of
Dracula as he is described by
Bram Stoker in the novel. The
Count is an old man, with
white hair and a long
moustache, 'without a single
speck of colour about him
anywhere'.

(Below) *Images of Dracula - 4*
William Huntly starring as
Dracula, in the Hamilton
Deane stage adaptation of the
novel in the 1920's. The opera
cloak and evening dress
present an image which is still
with us through the Hammer
films.

Northern Transylvania c. 1865. The inset shows the extent of railway development at that time.
By the 1890s the railway extended eastwards to Klausenburg and Bistritz. The Borgo Pass,
north-east of Bistritz, is the area Bram Stoker chose to site Castle Dracula.

Wall plaque commemorating a house in Sighisoara lived in by Dracula's father, Vlad Dracul. Dracula was probably born here.

dresses their bodies fit for their teeth, which food they esteem best of any. But before this cookery, whilst the prisoner lives, they draw out his finger and toe nails, and knock out his teeth with stones, which teeth and nails they wear about their necks like a necklace.'

Many Brazilian tribes manifested their love for the dead by reducing the bones to powder, and mingling it with a bread which they then ate. Love, as well as hatred, leads to cannibalism, and an Artemisia could be found in every Tapuya widow.

Among the Tapuyas, when an infant died it was eaten by the parents. Adults were eaten by the kindred, and their bones were pounded and reserved for marriage-feasts, as being the most precious thing that could be offered. When they became old they offered themselves to their children, who devoured them after putting them to death. They thought their spiritual substance became incorporated.

The Xomanas and Passes burned the bones of the dead, and drank the ashes, and in this way, they thought, they received into their bodies the spirits of their deceased friends.

The Maypuris devoured their sick and infirm.

The Arawaks pounded the bones of their dead lords into powder, and drank them.

The ancient Peruvians ate their deceased parents.

I have dwelt longer upon the painful subject of cannibalism than might seem desirable, in order to show its religious character and prevalence everywhere. Instead of being confined to savage peoples, as is generally supposed, it prevailed to a greater extent and with more horrible rites among the most civilized. Its religious inception was the cause of this.

The origin of a religious rite among the aboriginal Americans similar to the eucharistic among Roman Catholics is undoubtedly based upon the primitive superstition, that by eating a part of any animate body, or body supposed to be animate, the partaker is endowed with the qualities of that body. This superstition was very prevalent among the various tribes who thought they became endowed with the qualities of the animal eaten. It developed itself in cannibalism, which had a strangely protracted life in the semi-civilization of America, and it manifested itself in the eucharistic idol and feast of the Aztecs. This singular rite was called Teoqualo – that is, 'the eating of the god.' A figure of Huitzilopochtli was made in dough, and after certain ceremonies they made a pretence of killing it and dividing it into morsels, which were eaten by the worshippers as a sacred food.

The superstition underlying idolatry explains this apparently meaningless rite. They supposed their idol was animate, and the spiritual substance inhered in the material of the idol and passed into their bodies with it and was assimilated. Thus a transmigration of a portion of the spiritual substance of a god was accomplished. One of these eucharistic ceremonies is thus described by Herrera:

> An idol made of all the varieties of the seeds and grain of the country was made and moistened with the blood of children and virgins; this idol was broken into small bits, and given by way of communion to men and women to eat, who, to prepare for that festival, bathed and dressed their heads and scarce slept all the night. They prayed, and as soon as it was day were all in the temple to receive that communion, with such singular silence and devotion that though there was an infinite multitude there seemed to be nobody. If any of the idol was left, the priests ate it. Montezuma went to this ceremony attended by abundance of quality and richly dressed.

Mendieta mentions the same ceremony, and says, 'Gods were eaten in this way; they made idols of seeds, and ate them as though they were the bodies of their gods.' These seed idols have a special significance, because the mysterious vitality of a seed and its germinating power impressed itself on all the American tribes, and manifested itself in many rites and ceremonies. The tobacco-plant was supposed to be imbued with the spiritual body of the goddess Ciuacoatl, and was eaten in the eucharistic ceremony to her. The Totomacs had a communion in the following way. Every three years they killed three boys and took out their hearts. From their blood, mixed with certain seeds, they made a paste which was considered a eucharist and a most sacred thing, and was partaken of every six months by men above twenty-five and women above sixteen. They called the paste, food of our souls. . .

Burial-customs and ceremonies are closely connected with the subject of the worship of human spirits. In the performance of this 'last act' we can find valuable evidence to aid in our researches on primitive religion. The rites and ceremonies attending the disposition of the dead were religious in their nature, and religious rites are unconscious commentaries on religious beliefs.

The great care of primitive peoples in preserving the bodies of the dead has been instigated by many of their superstitions, prominent among which was their belief in a resurrection. The doctrine of the resurrection was the most deeply-rooted and wide-spread conviction of the Indian mind. It is indissolubly connected with their highest theories of a future life. The Delawares told Loskiel, 'We Indians shall not forever die. Even the grains of corn grow up and become living things.' The Indians thought the soul would return to the bones and be clothed again with flesh.

Their belief that dreams were produced by the soul's departure from and return to the body was akin to their belief in resurrection. The only difference between sleep and death to the primitive mind consisted in the extent of time the soul was absent. In both the soul would return; in both the body would reawake. The custom which we have noticed of burying the dead quickly after death in many tribes, and with no medical skill to know whether life was extinct, resulted often in the return of the supposed dead man to life, and thus afforded practical proof of a resurrection to the savage mind. This doctrine of a resurrection manifested itself in Oriental art in the production of the topes. In Egypt the pyramids are an evidence of it. In Greek literature *Antigone* is an expression of this thought. . .

The object among all the American tribes, in all their various burial-customs, was to preserve the bones of the dead. The belief underlying all these customs was that the soul, or a part of the soul, dwelt in the bones. Language illustrates this theory. The Iroquois word for bone is *esken*; for soul, *atisken* – literally, that which is within the bone. In an Athapascan dialect, bone is *yani*, soul is *i-yani*. Mythology adds more decisive testimony. In one of the Aztec legends, after one of the destructions of the world, Xolotl descended to Mictlan, the realm of the dead, and brought thence a bone of the perished race. This, sprinkled with blood, grew on the fourth day into a youth, the father of the present race. Among the Quiches, the hero-gods Hunahpu and Xblanque succumbed to the darksome powers of death. Their bodies were burned, and their bones ground to powder and thrown into the waters; but these ashes, sinking to the bottom of the stream, were, in the twinkling of an eye, changed into handsome youths, with the same features as before. Among many of the tribes the practice of pulverizing the bones of the dead and mixing them with the food was defended by asserting that the souls of the dead remained in the bones and lived again in the living. Even

the animals were supposed to follow the same law. Hardly any of the
hunting tribes, before their manners were vitiated by foreign
influence, permitted the bones of game to be broken or left carelessly
about the encampment. They were left in heaps or thrown into the
water. The Yuricares of Bolivia carried this superstition to such an
inconvenient extent that they preserved even small fish-bones from
harm, saying the fish would desert the rivers unless this was done.
The traveller on our prairies often notices the buffalo-skulls
arranged in circles and symmetrical piles by the careful hands of the
native hunters. Among the Peruvians, so careful were they lest any of
the body should be lost, they preserved even the parings of the nails
and clippings of the hair. Among the Choctaws the spirits of the dead
will return to the bones in the bone-mounds, and flesh will knit
together their loose joints, and they shall again inhabit their ancient
territory. The Peruvians expected the mummified body to be again
inhabited by its soul.

This belief can be traced among all the primitive peoples of the
world. Among the Tartars the pyramid of horses' heads found by
Pallas is analogous to bone-pyramids of the buffalo and deer in
America. The Hebrew rabbis taught that the coccyx remained at
death the germ of a second life, and would develop into the purified
body as the plant from the seed.

Among the Iroquois the spirit stayed near the body for a time, and,
unless burial was performed, was very unhappy; and among the
Brazilian tribes the spirits of the dead were not at rest when the body
was unburied, and, if they had had a Creon, an Antigone would have
undoubtedly arisen to perform the sacred rites of burial. It will be
noticed, then, that there was no uniform custom prevalent among
the American nations in their mode of burial, but that diversity of
custom prevailed in many instances in the same tribe – that climate
and the nature of the soil, and other natural influences, together with
the pursuits of the various peoples, had their effect on the formation
of burial-customs, and these a reflex action again on their religious
beliefs and superstitions. Yet through it all there are plain
indications of a belief that the preservation of the bones of the dead in
their integrity was necessary to the peace and happiness of the
departed spirit. Hence the security of these was sought in all their
various customs. In the suspension of the bodies in trees or on
scaffolds or otherwise, their preservation, after the dissolution of the
flesh, was attended to. In cremation, the residuum of calcined bones

was preserved by interment or a deposit in urns or images of the deceased, or by heaping a mound over them. Interment in the earth had the same object in view, as also in caves and other secret and protected places. Thus security is sought in secrecy or by inaccessibility, or both. Among the Chibchas, sepulchres were concealed by trees planted for that purpose. The greatest danger to the remains of the dead arose from the depredations of animals, yet enemies outside or inside the tribe or clan or family were much feared, the possession of any part of a living or dead person by one seeking revenge being looked upon with exceeding great superstitious fear. The origin and progress of sorcery are traceable to this superstition. Among all primitive peoples, where a belief in the renewal of life or the resurrection exists, the peace and happiness of the spirit, which remains in or about the body, depend upon success in preventing the body or any part of it from being devoured or destroyed in any manner. Of course, among peoples to whom the art of preserving the bodies of the dead by embalming or other means was unknown, the destructibility of all but the skeleton or bones was recognized as unavoidable, and their superstition must be modified to that extent. It maintained itself and increased in strength as to the indestructible parts, even including the nails and hair, through all the stages of savagery and barbarism and into our modern civilization. The caciques of Bogota were protected from desecration by diverting the course of a river and making the grave in its bed, and then letting the stream return to its natural course. Alaric, the leader of the Goths, was secretly buried in the same manner. The imposing pyramids of Mexico, Peru, and the sepulchral mounds of both Americas were intended for, and became, obstacles to the desecration of the remains of distinguished dead, as well as memorials of their greatness; but the temples of the more civilized nations mark the highest stage of the progress of this idea in America, as elsewhere. In these temples the interment of heroes took place, and a priestly hierarchy arose to guard and attend at the sacred precincts of their shrines, and offer sacrifice to their idol likenesses stuffed with their ashes and bones. In addition to their religious care in the preservation of the dead, their comfort was also regarded. Hence protections against pressing earth or stones were provided for; also a way for the spirit to have access to the body was considered of vital importance by most of the aborigines. Embalming and the other customs have the same purpose in view, namely, the arrest of decay. It is quite curious to find embalmment and its antithesis, cremation, practised in the same tribe; yet, since the principal idea underlying both practices is the same – namely, the preservation of all the parts of the dead – there is no inconsistency here. In both, the destructible parts of the body are preserved to a great extent, for what fire destroys is supposed to be dematerialized and ushered quickly into the world of spirits. Hence it became a very common instrument in sending to the dead the sacrifices offered by their living friends, and the Algonkin would throw his choicest bit of venison into the fire and send it to his hungry spirit-relative, before a morsel had been touched by the living, with as much religious fervor as would the Greek offer a bullock on the sacrificial altar or the Chinaman of our day burn paper houses and money for use in the spirit-world. It must be borne in mind that this spirit-world was in earlier times in and among the living world, and not banished, as in our modern civilization, to some unknown far-off country 'from whose bourn no traveller returns.' Thus, whether cremation or embalmment took place, the spirit was ready and waiting for a rehabitation of its fleshly tenement-house, none the less real because the flames had wafted it into the shadowland. With the belief that reanimation will be prevented if the other self finds a mutilated corpse, or none at all, there goes the belief that to insure reanimation putrefaction must be stopped. Naturally there arises the inference that if destruction of the body by animals or otherwise prevents revival, decomposition of it may prevent revival. That this idea is not found among men in very low states is undoubtedly due to the fact that no methods of arresting decomposition have been discovered by them. Hence cremation is found among lower tribes, and survives when this more approved method is discovered; and even among those who are acquainted with the process much greater care is taken to preserve the bodies of kings and distinguished men than the mass of the people. Hence the latter are often carelessly looked after. Distinctions of caste, which are apt to arise in the higher stages of human progress under certain conditions of development, tend to destroy the belief in the immortality of the lower class. Such glaring examples of this are found in some of the more advanced American nations that immortality has been denied to all but a few of the upper class. Hence, while great care is taken in the preservation of their bodies by the erection over them of pyramids and temples, the common people die with 'none so poor as to do them reverence.'

The belief in the resurrection of the body was universal among primitive peoples, and owed its origin often to cases of resuscitation. Among the tribes of the West there was a superstition against touching dead bodies, or those supposed to be dead; and hence there have been many cases where the natives have been buried alive. Two cases of this kind are mentioned by Lee and Frost among the natives of Oregon. Among these tribes there are a few resurrection-traditions, growing undoubtedly out of this careless habit. The Virginians had fictions concerning the resurrection of certain persons from the dead. Hariot gives two instances of this. He says:

> They told me that a wicked man having been dead and buried, the next day the earth of the grave was seen to move, whereupon, being taken up again, he told where his soul had been, and that he was very near entering into Popogusso, had not one of the gods saved him and given him leave to return again and teach his friends what they should do to avoid that terrible place of torment. Another revival from the dead occurred the same year, and it was told me for strange news that one being dead, buried, and taken up again as the first, showed that although his body had laid dead in the grave, yet his soul was alive, and had travelled far in the long, broad way, on both sides whereof grew most delicate and pleasant trees, bearing more rare and excellent fruits than ever he had seen before. He at length came to most fair houses, near which he met his father that had been dead before, who gave him great charge to go back again and show his friends what good they were to do to enjoy the pleasures of that place.

In cases of the falling sickness, catalepsy, or any diseases where the person is in a lethargic state, the savage believes that the soul has left the body and returns to it again when revival takes place. This has perhaps suggested in many cases their belief in a resurrection. The Ojibways say of such cases that the soul could not get into the spirit-land and had to come back. They conceive the person to be dead, and the revival is a resurrection. The savage believes that the insensibility of death is, like all the other insensibilities, only temporary.

Among the Eskimos, if a man wished to become of the highest order of priests, it was requisite that he should be drowned and eaten by sea-monsters; then, when his bones were washed ashore, his spirit, which had spent all this time gathering information about the secrets of the invisible world, would return to them, and he would rejoin his tribe.

There are curious traditions of resurrections among them. An Eskimo female carried home a bird, and, having cut it up, found in its crop the bones of her lost brother. She singled these all out and kept them together, when, behold, they moved. The brother quickly revived, and seemed entirely unhurt. An Eskimo man and wife who were old and unable to provide for themselves, in their extremity decided to go to the tomb of their dead foster-son. The grave was opened and the body appealed to, when, lo, it began to move. The son arose from the dead, went home with them, got a kayak, and thereafter provided for his aged parents. Many stories are told of such resurrections among the Eskimos. In one case a son revived three times, after as many burials.

The natives of Canada had a universally received tradition that their dead bodies were to rise again.

The Peruvians thought the bodies of the dead arose from their graves. Some of them asserted that they had seen them walking about after burial. Atahuallpa requested the Spaniards that he might be hanged instead of burned. He said then his body would rise again. The Chibchas also believed that the dead would be raised. The natives of Quimbaya thought that the bodies of the dead would come to life again. Those of Guazacualco thought the dead would rise again, and therefore hung their bones to the bough of a tree, that they might be easily found. Among many of the tribes of South America it was within the power of the sorcerers, they thought, to bring the dead to life.

The Bois Brulé tribe carried their belief in the resurrection so far that if a leg or a foot should be separated from the rest of the body the stray member would be hunted for till found. All of the aborigines preserved with almost as much care the bones of animals. They said these bones contained the spirits of the slain animals, and that some time in the future they would rise, reclothe themselves with flesh, and stock the earth anew.

From Rushton M. Dorman, The Origin of Primitive Superstitions *(1881) pages 14–15, 148–153, 163–164, 193–199.*

CHAPTER THREE

Vampyrism

Herbert Mayo

Stoker could have picked up his background information on the vampire mania that swept eastern Europe in the 1720s–30s from any of several sources. He read the following account by Herbert Mayo, possibly among others.

Mayo did not set out to shed new light on the subject. He had grander ambitions. As a professor of anatomy in London, he wrote his book *On the Truths Contained in Popular Superstitions – with an Account of Mesmerism* with the aim of expounding a new approach to our understanding of the magnetic state. All but the first four of the fourteen chapters are given to a discussion on trance, mesmerism and hypnotism. These are of considerable interest regarding *Dracula* and will be given proper attention in due course. Mayo, as befits a medical man, also hoped to undermine belief in supernatural phenomena, such as vampirism, insisting that they are capable of rational, natural explanation. This does not stop him apologising, in his prefatory remarks, for failing to adopt a more serious tone in some of his earlier chapters, including the one here reproduced. Interestingly, his book is compiled, like *Dracula*, in the form of letters. They comprise Mayo's half of an imaginary correspondence with a presumably equally imaginary friend, Archy.

Notwithstanding his occasional levity, it is worthwhile noting Mayo's precise definition of the vampire – essentially a corpse that sucks blood for the purpose of resisting decomposition. This contrasts with the more fashionable, somewhat metaphorical interpretation which prefers to extend vampirism to include the process of psychic energy transfer between two people, or even between a person and an artifact. Modern disingenuity and scepticism has largely dispensed with the earlier vampire prerequisites of reanimation and blood-sucking. This would not have appealed to Herbert Mayo. Nor to Bram Stoker.

Mayo retells the case of Arnod Paole, a supposed vampire from

Belgrade. Most of the folkloric paraphernalia of vampirism are set out in this episode – how the corpse regenerates fresh skin and nails, how the pestilence spreads to the local community, and the steps to be taken to exterminate the source of the contagion. Mayo also draws attention to the widespread practice of premature burial, not just in eastern Europe, but also in New York, where a crude experiment revealed that at least one person in every 200 could expect to be buried alive. That such mistakes could be made in such numbers Mayo attributes largely to the medical malfunction which he terms the 'death trance'. Interestingly, Mayo's assertion that there is no sure proof of death short of putrefaction was reaffirmed by the British Medical Council as late as 1885, not long before Stoker commenced work on *Dracula*.

Persons of a weak and hysterical disposition – and Mayo emphasises that young ladies are particularly prone to this condition – are especially susceptible to imagining they are in the presence of the supernatural. They are also the most likely to succumb to the affliction of suspended animation, the appearance of death, and the unspeakable fate of premature burial that sometimes ensues. In other words, belief in a supposed vampire attack could produce symptoms sometimes fatal in their effects.

Nor could an actual epidemic of death-trance victims be ruled out, given the contagious effects of hysteria. For in time of plague or vampire paranoia this meant hasty burial in shallow graves. Some victims would have regained consciousness within the grave and succumbed to asphyxia or starvation. Others would have succeeded in breaking out of their confines and tried to return home. Their dishevelled appearance would have triggered a panic: they would have been taken for the living dead, when in fact they had never died.

When the time comes to determine whether or not vampires really exist, Mayo hedges his bets. For all his early insistence on the cause of the epidemic being attributable to death-trance and premature burial, he is clearly not satisfied with his own solution. He is more assured when discussing the causes of the epidemic panic which invariably attended the discovery of a living dead, for this leads him conveniently to his theories on trance. But he is forced to end on a metaphysical note: if vampires do not disturb the soil when returning to their graves then they must, after all, be spectral rather than physical in nature.

*

Vampyrism

In acknowledging my former letter, you express an eager desire to
learn, as you phrase it, 'all about Vampyrs, if there ever were such
things'. I will not delay satisfying your curiosity, although by so
doing I interrupt the logical order of my communications. It is,
perhaps, all the better. The proper place of this subject falls in the
midst of a philosophical disquisition; and it would have been a pity
not to present it to you in its pristine colouring. But how came your
late tutor, Mr H., to leave you in ignorance upon a point on which, in
my time, schoolboys much your juniors entertained decided
opinions?

Were there ever such things as Vampyrs? *Tantamne rem tam
negligenter!** I turn to the learned pages of Horst for a luminous and
precise definition of the destructive and mysterious beings whose
existence you have ventured to consider problematical.

'A Vampyr is a dead body which continues to live in the grave;
which it leaves, however, by night, for the purpose of sucking the
blood of the living, whereby it is nourished and preserved in good
condition, instead of becoming decomposed like other dead bodies.'

Upon my word, you really deserve, since Mr George Coombe has
clearly shown, in his admirable work on the *Constitution of Man*, and
its adaptation to the surrounding world, that ignorance is a
statutable crime before nature, and punished by the laws of
Providence – you deserve, I say, unless you contrive to make Mr H.
your substitute, which I think would be just, yourself to be the
subject of the nocturnal visit of a Vampyr. Your scepticism will abate
pretty considerably when you see him stealthily entering your room,
yet are powerless under the fascination of his fixed and leaden eye –
when you are conscious, as you lie motionless with terror, of his
nearer and nearer approach – when you feel his face, fresh with the
smell of the grave, bent over your throat, while his keen teeth make a
fine incision in your jugular, preparatory to his commencing his
plain but nutritive repast.

You would look a little paler the next morning, but that would be
all for the moment; for Fischer informs us that the bite of a Vampyr
leaves in general no mark upon the person. But he fearfully adds, 'it
(the bite) is nevertheless speedily fatal,' unless the bitten person
protect himself by eating some of the earth from the grave of the

* From Latin 'Such a great subject so negligently treated' – C.L.

Vampyr, and smearing himself with his blood. Unfortunately, indeed, these measures are seldom, if ever, of more than temporary use. Fischer adds, 'if through these precautions the life of the victim be prolonged for a period, sooner or later he ends with becoming a Vampyr himself; that is to say, he dies and is buried, but continues to lead a Vampyr life in the grave, nourishing himself by infecting others, and promiscuously propagating Vampyrism.'

This is no romancer's dream. It is a succinct account of a superstition which to this day survives in the east of Europe, where little more than a century ago it was frightfully prevalent. At that period Vampyrism spread like a pestilence through Servia and Wallachia, causing numerous deaths, and disturbing all the land with fear of the mysterious visitation, against which no one felt himself secure.

Here is something like a good solid practical popular delusion. Do I believe it? To be sure I do. The facts are matter of history: the people died like rotted sheep; and the cause and method of their dying was, in their belief, what has just been stated. You suppose, then, they died frightened out of their lives, as men have died whose pardon has been proclaimed when their necks were already on the block, of the belief that they were going to die? Well, if that were all, the subject would still be worth examining. But there is more in it than that, as the following o'er true tale will convince you, the essential points of which are authenticated by documentary evidence.

In the spring of 1727, there returned from the Levant to the village of Meduegna, near Belgrade, one Arnod Paole, who, in a few years of military service and varied adventure, had amassed enough to purchase a cottage and an acre or two of land in his native place, where he gave out that he meant to pass the remainder of his days. He kept his word. Arnod had yet scarcely reached the prime of manhood; and though he must have encountered the rough as well as the smooth of life, and have mingled with many a wild and reckless companion, yet his naturally good disposition and honest principles had preserved him unscathed in the scenes he had passed through. At all events, such were the thoughts expressed by his neighbours as they discussed his return and settlement among them in the Stube of the village Hof. Nor did the frank and open countenance of Arnod, his obliging habits and steady conduct, argue their judgment incorrect. Nevertheless, there was something occasionally noticeable in his ways – a look and tone that betrayed inward disquiet. Often would he refuse to join his friends, or on some sudden plea abruptly quit their society. And he still more unaccountably, and as it seemed systematically, avoided meeting his pretty neighbour, Nina, whose father occupied the next tenement to his own. At the age of seventeen, Nina was as charming a picture of youth, cheerfulness, innocence, and confidence, as you could have seen in all the world. You could not look into her limpid eyes, which steadily returned your gaze, without seeing to the bottom of the pure and transparent spring of her thoughts. Why, then, did Arnod shrink from meeting her? He was young; had a little property; had health and industry; and he had told his friends he had formed no ties in other lands. Why, then, did he avoid the fascination of the pretty Nina, who seemed a being made to chase from any brow the clouds of gathering care? But he did so; yet less and less resolutely, for he felt the charm of her presence. Who could have done otherwise? And how could he long resist – he didn't – the impulse of his fondness for the innocent girl who often sought to cheer his fits of depression?

And they were to be united – were betrothed; yet still an anxious gloom would fitfully overcast his countenance, even in the sunshine of those hours.

'What is it, dear Arnod, that makes you sad? It cannot be on my account, I know, for you were sad before you ever noticed me; and that, I think,' (and you should have seen the deepening rose upon her cheeks) 'surely first made me notice you.'

'Nina,' he answered, 'I have done, I fear, a great wrong in trying to gain your affections. Nina, I have a fixed impression that I shall not live; yet, knowing this, I have selfishly made my existence necessary to your happiness.'

'How strangely you talk, dear Arnod! Who in the village is stronger and healthier than you? You feared no danger when you were a soldier. What danger do you fear as a villager of Meduegna?'

'It haunts me, Nina.'

'But, Arnod, you were sad before you thought of me. Did you then fear to die?'

'Ah, Nina, it is something worse than death.' And his vigorous frame shook with agony.

'Arnod, I conjure you, tell me.'

'It was in Cossova this fate befell me. Here you have hitherto escaped the terrible scourge. But there they died, and the dead visited the living. I experienced the first frightful visitation, and I fled; but not till I had sought his grave, and exacted the dread expiation from the Vampyr.'

Nina's blood ran cold. She stood horror-stricken. But her young heart soon mastered her first despair. With a touching voice she spoke–

'Fear not, dear Arnod; fear not now. I will be your shield, or I will die with you!'

And she encircled his neck with her gentle arms, and returning hope shone, Iris-like, amid her falling tears. Afterwards they found a reasonable ground for banishing or allaying their apprehension in the length of time which had elapsed since Arnod left Cossova, during which no fearful visitant had again approached him; and they fondly trusted *that* gave them security.

It is a strange world. The ills we fear are commonly not those which overwhelm us. The blows that reach us are for the most part unforeseen. One day, about a week after this conversation, Arnod missed his footing when on the top of a loaded hay-waggon, and fell from it to the ground. He was picked up insensible, and carried home, where, after lingering a short time, he died. His interment, as usual, followed immediately. His fate was sad and premature. But what pencil could paint Nina's grief!

Twenty or thirty days after his decease, says the perfectly authenticated report of these transactions, several of the neighbour-hood complained that they were haunted by the deceased Arnod; and, what was more to the purpose, four of them died. The evil, looked at sceptically, was bad enough, but, aggravated by the suggestions of superstition, it spread a panic through the whole district. To allay the popular terror, and if possible to get at the root of the evil, a determination was come to publicly to disinter the body of Arnod, with the view of ascertaining whether he really was a Vampyr, and, in that event, of treating him conformably. The day fixed for this proceeding was the fortieth after his burial.

It was on a grey morning in early August that the commission visited the quiet cemetery of Meduegna, which, surrounded with a wall of unhewn stone, lies sheltered by the mountain that, rising in undulating green slopes, irregularly planted with fruit-trees, ends in an abrupt craggy ridge, feathered with underwood. The graves were, for the most part, neatly kept, with borders of box, or something like it, and flowers between; and at the head of most a small wooden cross, painted black, bearing the name of the tenant. Here and there a stone had been raised. One of considerable height, a single narrow slab, ornamented with grotesque Gothic carvings, dominated over the rest. Near this lay the grave of Arnod Paole, towards which the party moved. The work of throwing out the earth was begun by the grey crooked old sexton, who lived in the Leichenhaus, beyond the great crucifix. He seemed unconcerned enough; no Vampyr would think of extracting a supper out of him. Nearest the grave stood two military surgeons, or feldscherers, from Belgrade, and a drummer-boy, who held their case of instruments. The boy looked on with keen interest; and when the coffin was exposed and rather roughly drawn out of the grave, his pale face and bright intent eye showed how the scene moved him. The sexton lifted the lid of the coffin; the body had become inclined to one side. Then turning it straight, 'Ha! ha!' said he, pointing to fresh blood upon the lips – 'Ha! ha! What! Your mouth not wiped since last night's work?' The spectators shuddered; the drummer-boy sank forward, fainting, and upset the instrument-case, scattering its contents; the senior surgeon, infected with the horror of the scene, repressed a hasty exclamation, and simply crossed himself. They threw water on the drummer-boy, and he recovered, but would not leave the spot. Then they inspected the body of Arnod. It looked as if it had not been dead a day. On handling it, the scarfskin came off, but below were *new skin and new nails!* How could *they* have come there but from its foul feeding! The case was clear enough; there lay before them the thing they dreaded – the Vampyr. So, without more ado, they simply drove a stake through poor Arnod's chest, whereupon a quantity of blood gushed forth, and the corpse uttered an audible groan. 'Murder! oh, murder!' shrieked the drummer-boy, as he rushed wildly, with convulsed gestures, from the cemetery.

The drummer-boy was not far from the mark. But, quitting the romancing vein, which had led me to try and restore the original colours of the picture, let me confine myself, in describing the rest of the scene and what followed, to the words of my authority.

The body of Arnod was then burnt to ashes, which were returned to the grave. The authorities further staked and burnt the bodies of the four others which were supposed to have been infected by Arnod. No mention is made of the state in which they were found. The adoption of these decisive measures failed, however, entirely to extinguish the evil, which continued still to hang about the village.

About five years afterwards it had again become very rife, and many died through it; whereupon the authorities determined to make another and a complete clearance of the Vampyrs in the cemetery, and with that object they had all the graves, to which present suspicion attached, opened, and their contents officially anatomised, of which procedure the following is the medical report, here and there *abridged* only:

1. A woman of the name of Stana, twenty years of age, who had died three months before of a three-days' illness following her confinement. She had before her death avowed that she had *anointed* herself with the blood of a Vampyr, to liberate herself from his persecution. Nevertheless, she, as well as her infant, whose body through careless interment had been half eaten by the dogs, had died. Her body was entirely free from decomposition. On opening it, the chest was found full of recently effused blood, and the bowels had exactly the appearances of sound health. The skin and nails of her hands and feet were loose and came off, but underneath lay new skin and nails.

2. A woman of the name of Miliza, who had died at the end of a three-months' illness. The body had been buried ninety and odd days. In the chest was liquid blood. The viscera were as in the former instance. The body was declared by a heyduk, who recognised it, to be in better condition, and fatter, than it had been in the woman's legitimate lifetime.

3. The body of a child eight years old, that had likewise been buried ninety days: it was in the Vampyr condition.

4. The son of a heyduk named Milloc, sixteen years old. The body had lain in the grave nine weeks. He had died after three days' indisposition, and was in the condition of a Vampyr.

5. Joachim, likewise son of a heyduk, seventeen years old. He had died after three days' illness; had been buried eight weeks and some days; was found in the Vampyr state.

6. A woman of the name of Rusha, who had died of an illness of ten days' duration, and had been six weeks buried, in whom likewise fresh blood was found in the chest.

(The reader will understand, that to *see* blood in the chest, it is first necessary to *cut* the chest open.)

7. The body of a girl of ten years of age, who had died two months before. It was likewise in the Vampyr state, perfectly undecomposed, with blood in the chest.

8. The body of the wife of one Hadnuck, buried seven weeks before; and that of her infant, eight weeks old, buried only twenty-one days. They were both in a state of decomposition, though buried in the same ground, and closely adjoining the others.

9. A servant, by name Rhade, twenty-three years of age; he had died after an illness of three months' duration, and the body had been buried five weeks. It was in a state of decomposition.

10. The body of the heyduk Stanco, sixty years of age, who had died six weeks previously. There was much blood and other fluid in the chest and abdomen, and the body was in the Vampyr condition.

11. Millac, a heyduk, twenty-five years old. The body had been in the earth six weeks. It was perfectly in the Vampyr condition.

12. Stanjoika, the wife of a heyduk, twenty years old; had died after an illness of three days, and had been buried eighteen. The countenance was florid. There was blood in the chest and in the heart. The viscera were perfectly sound; the skin remarkably fresh.

The document which gives the above particulars is signed by three regimental surgeons, and formally countersigned by a lieutenant-colonel and sub-lieutenant. It bears the date of 'June 7, 1732, Meduegna near Belgrade.' No doubt can be entertained of its authenticity, or of its *general* fidelity; the less that it does not stand alone, but is supported by a mass of evidence to the same effect. It appears to establish beyond question, that where the fear of Vampyrism prevails, and there occur several deaths, in the popular belief connected with it, the bodies, when disinterred weeks after burial, present the appearance of corpses from which life has only recently departed.

What inference shall we draw from this fact? – that Vampyrism is true in the popular sense? – and that these fresh-looking and well-conditioned corpses had some mysterious source of preternatural nourishment? That would be to adopt, not to solve the superstition. Let us content ourselves with a notion not so monstrous, but still startling enough: that the bodies, which were found in the so-called Vampyr state, instead of being in a new or mystical condition, were simply alive in the common way, or had been so for some time subsequent to their interment; that, in short, they were the bodies of persons who had been buried alive, and whose life, where it yet lingered, was finally extinguished through the ignorance and barbarity of those who disinterred them. In the following sketch of a similar scene to that above described, the correctness of this inference comes out with terrific force.

Erasmus Francisci, in his remarks upon the description of the Dukedom of Krain by Valvasor, speaks of a man of the name of Grando, in the district of Kring, who died, was buried, and became a Vampyr, and as such was exhumed for the purpose of having a stake thrust through him.

> When they opened his grave, after he had been long buried, his face was found with a colour, and his features made natural sorts of movements, as if the dead man smiled. He even opened his mouth as if he would inhale fresh air. They held the crucifix before him, and called in a loud voice, 'See, this is Jesus Christ who redeemed your soul from hell, and died for you.' After the sound had acted on his organs of hearing, and he had connected perhaps some ideas with it, tears began to flow from the dead man's eyes. Finally, when after a short prayer for his poor soul, they proceeded to hack off his head, the corpse uttered a screech, and turned and rolled just as if it had been alive – and the grave was full of blood.

We have thus succeeded in interpreting one of the unknown terms in the Vampyr-theorem. The suspicious character, who had some dark way of nourishing himself in the grave, turns out to be an unfortunate gentleman (or lady) whom his friends had buried under a mistake while he was still alive, and who, if they afterwards mercifully let him alone, died sooner or later either naturally or of the premature interment – in either case, it is to be hoped, with no interval of restored consciousness. The state which thus passed for death and led to such fatal consequences, apart from superstition, deserves our serious consideration; for, although of very rare, it is of continual occurrence, and society is not sufficiently on its guard against a contingency so dreadful when overlooked. When the nurse or the doctor has announced that all is over – that the valued friend or relative has breathed his last – no doubt crosses any one's mind of the reality of the sad event. Disease is now so well understood – every step in its march laid down and foreseen – the approach of danger accurately estimated – the liability of the patient, according to his powers of resisting it, to succumb earlier or to hold out longer – all is theoretically so clear, that a wholesome suspicion of error in the verdict of the attendants seldom suggests itself. The evil I am considering ought not, however, to be attributed to redundance of knowledge: it arises from its partial lack – from a too general neglect of one very important section in pathological science. The laity, if not the doctors too, constantly lose sight of the fact, that there exists an alternative to the fatal event of ordinary disease; that a patient is liable at any period of illness to deviate, or, as it were, to slide off, from the customary line of disease into another and a deceptive route – *instead of death, to encounter apparent death.*

The Germans express this condition of the living body by the term *scheintod*, which signifies exactly *apparent death*; and it is perhaps a better term than our English equivalent, 'suspended animation'. But both these expressions are generic terms, and a specific term is still wanted to denote the present class of instances. To meet this exigency, I propose, for reasons which will afterwards appear, to employ the term 'death-trance' to designate the cases we are investigating.

Death-trance is, then, one of the forms of suspended animation: there are several others. After incomplete poisoning, after suffocation in either of its various ways, after exposure to cold in infants newly born, a state is occasionally met with, of which (however each may still differ from the rest) the common feature is an apparent suspension of the vital actions. But all of these so-cited instances agree in another important respect, which second inter-agreement separates them as a class from death-trance. They represent, each and all, a period of conflict between the effects of certain deleterious impressions and the vital principle, the latter struggling against the weight and force of the former. Such is not the case in death-trance.

Death-trance is a positive status – a period of repose – the duration of which is sometimes definite and predetermined, though unknown. Thus the patient, the term of the death-trance having expired, occasionally suddenly wakes, entirely and at once restored. Oftener, however, the machinery which has been stopped seems to require to be jogged – then it goes on again.

The basis of death-trance is suspension of the action of the heart, and of the breathing, and of voluntary motion; generally likewise feeling and intelligence, and the vegetative changes in the body, are suspended. With these phenomena is joined loss of external warmth; so that the usual evidence of life is gone. But there have occurred varieties of this condition, in which occasional slight manifestations of one or other of the vital actions have been observed.

Death-trance may occur as a primary affection, suddenly or gradually. The diseases the course of which it is liable, as it were, to bifurcate, or to graft itself upon, are first and principally all disorders of the nervous system. But in any form of disease, when the body is brought to a certain degree of debility, death-trance may supervene. Age and sex have to do with its occurrence; which is more frequent in the young than in the old, in women than in men – differences evidently connected with greater irritability of the nervous system. Accordingly, women in labour are among the most liable to death-trance, and it is from such a case that I will give a first instance of the affection as portrayed by a medical witness. (*Journal des Savans*, 1749.)

M Rigaudeaux, surgeon to the military hospital, and licensed accoucheur at Douai, was sent for on the 8th of September 1745, to attend the wife of Francis Dumont, residing two leagues from the town. He was late in getting there; it was half-past eight A.M. – too late, it seemed; the patient was declared to have died at six o'clock, after eighteen hours of ineffectual labour-pains. M Rigaudeaux inspected the body; there was no pulse or breath; the mouth was full of froth, the abdomen tumid. He brought away the infant, which he committed to the care of the nurses, who, after trying to reanimate it for three hours, gave up the attempt, and prepared to lay it out, when it opened its mouth. They then gave it wine, and it was speedily recovered. M Rigaudeaux, who returned to the house as this occurred, inspected again the body of the mother. (It had been already nailed down in a coffin.) He examined it with the utmost care; but he came to the conclusion that it was certainly dead. Nevertheless, as the joints of the limbs were still flexible, although seven hours had elapsed since its apparent death, he left the strictest injunctions to watch the body carefully, to apply stimulants to the nostrils from time to time, to slap the palms of the hands, and the like. At half-past three o'clock symptoms of returning animation showed themselves, and the patient recovered.

The period during which every ordinary sign of life may be absent, without the prevention of their return, is unknown, but in well-authenticated cases it has much exceeded the period observed in the above instance. Here is an example borrowed from the *Journal des Savans*, 1741.

There was a Colonel Russell, whose wife, to whom he was affectionately attached, died, or appeared to do so. But he would not allow the body to be buried; and threatened to shoot any one who should interfere to remove it for that purpose. His conduct was guided by reason as well as by affection and instinct. He said he would not part from the body till its decomposition had begun. Eight days had passed, during which the body of his wife gave no sign of life; when, as he sat bedewing her hand with his tears, the church-bell tolled, and, to his unspeakable amazement, his wife sat up, and said – 'That is the last bell; we shall be too late.' She recovered.

There are cases on record of persons who could spontaneously fall into death-trance. Monti, in a letter to Haller, adverts to several; and mentions, in particular, a peasant upon whom, when he assumed this state, the flies would settle; breathing, the pulse, and all ordinary signs of life disappeared. A priest of the name of Caelius Rhodaginus had the same faculty. But the most celebrated instance is that of Colonel Townshend, mentioned in the surgical works of Gooch, by whom and by Dr Cheyne and Dr Baynard, and by Mr Shrine, an apothecary, the performance of Colonel Townshend was seen and attested. They had long attended him, for he was a habitual invalid, and he had often invited them to witness the phenomenon of his dying and coming to life again; but they had hitherto refused, from fear of the consequences to himself: at last they assented. Accordingly, in their presence, Colonel Townshend laid himself down on his back, and Dr Cheyne undertook to observe his pulse; Dr Baynard laid his hand on his heart, and Mr Shrine had a looking-glass to hold to his mouth. After a few seconds, pulse, breathing, and the action of the heart, were no longer to be observed. Each of the witnesses satisfied himself of the entire cessation of these phenomena. When the death-trance had lasted half-an-hour, the doctors began to fear that their patient had pushed the experiment too far, and was dead in earnest; and they were preparing to leave the house, when a slight movement of the body attracted their attention. They renewed their routine observation; when the pulse and sensible motion of the heart gradually returned, and breathing, and consciousness. The tale ends abruptly. Colonel Townshend, on recovering, sent for his attorney, made his will, and died, for good and all, six hours afterwards.

Although many have recovered from death-trance, and there seems to be in each case a definite period to its duration, yet its event is not always so fortunate. The patient sometimes really dies during its continuance, either unavoidably, or in consequence of adequate measures not being taken to stimulate him to waken, or to support life. The following very good instance rests on the authority of Dr

Schmidt, a physician of the hospital of Paderborn, where it occurred, (*Rheinisch-Westphälischer Anzeiger*, 1835, No. 57 and 58.)

A young man of the name of Caspar Kreite, from Berne, died in the hospital of Paderborn, but his body could not be interred for three weeks, for the following reasons. During the first twenty-four hours after drawing its last breath, the corpse opened its eyes, and the pulse could be felt, for a few minutes, beating feebly and irregularly. On the third and fourth day, points of the skin, which had been burned to test the reality of his death, suppurated. On the fifth day the corpse changed the position of one hand: on the ninth day a vesicular eruption appeared on the back. For nine days there was a vertical fold of the skin of the forehead – a sort of frown – and the features had not the character of death. The lips remained red till the eighteenth day; and the joints preserved their flexibility from first to last. He lay in this state in a warm room for nineteen days, without any farther alteration than a sensible wasting in flesh. Till after the nineteenth day no discoloration of the body, or odour of putrefaction, was observed. He had been cured of ague, and laboured under a slight chest affection; but there had been no adequate cause for his death. It is evident that this person was much more alive than many are in the death-trance; and one half suspects that stimulants and nourishment, properly introduced, might have entirely reanimated him.

I might exemplify death-trance by many a well-authenticated romantic story. – A noise heard in a vault; the people, instead of breaking open the door, go for the keys, and for authority to act, and return too late; the unfortunate person is found dead, having previously gnawn her hand and arm in agony. – A lady is buried with a jewel of value on her finger; thieves open the vault to possess themselves of the treasure; the ring cannot be drawn from the finger, and the thieves proceed to cut the finger off; the lady, wakening from her trance, scares the thieves away, and recovers. – A young married lady dies and is buried; a former admirer, to whom her parents had refused her hand, bribes the sexton to let him see once more the form he loved. The body opportunely comes to life at this moment, and flies from Paris with its first lover to England, where they are married. Venturing to return to France, the lady is recognised, and is reclaimed by her previous husband through a suit at law; her counsel demurs, on the ground of the desertion and burial; but the law not admitting this plea, she flies again to England with her preserver, to avoid the judgment of the parliament of Paris, in the acts of which the case stands recorded. There are one or two other cases that I dare not cite, the particulars of which transcend the wildest flights of imagination.

It may be thought that these are all tales of the olden time; and that the very case I have given from the hospital at Paderborn shows that now medical men are sufficiently circumspect, and the public really on its guard to prevent a living person being interred as one dead. And I grant that in England, among all but the poorest class, the danger is practically inconsiderable of being buried alive. But that it still exists for every class, and that for the poor the danger is great and serious, I am afraid there is too much reason for believing. It is stated in Froriep's *Notizen*, 1829, No. 522, that, agreeably to a then recent ordinance in New York, coffins presented for burial were kept above ground eight days; open at the head, and so arranged, that the least movement of the body would ring a bell, through strings attached to the hands and feet. It will hardly be credited, that *out of twelve hundred* whose interment had been thus postponed, *six returned to life* – one in every two hundred! The arrangement thus beneficently adopted at New York is, however, imperfect, as it makes time the criterion for interment. The time is *not* known during which a body in death-trance may remain alive. Nothing but one positive condition of the body, which I will presently mention, authenticates death. It is frightful to think how, in the south of Europe, within twenty-four hours after the last breath bodies are shovelled into pits among heaped corpses; and to imagine what fearful agonies of despair must sometimes be encountered by unhappy beings, who wake amid the unutterable horrors of such a grave. But it is enough to look at home, and to make no delay in providing there for the careful watching of the bodies of the poor, till life has certainly departed. Many do not dream how barbarous and backward the vaunted nineteenth century will appear to posterity!

But there is another danger to which society is obnoxious through not making sufficient account of the contingency of death-trance, that appears to me more urgent and menacing than even the risk of being buried alive.

The danger I advert to is not *this*; but this is something–

The Cardinal Espinosa, prime minister under Philip the Second of Spain, died, as it was supposed, after a short illness. His rank entitled him to be embalmed. Accordingly, the body was opened for that purpose. The lungs and heart had just been brought into view, when the latter was seen to beat. The cardinal awakening at the fatal moment, had still strength enough left to seize with his hand the knife of the anatomist!

But it is *this*–

On the 23d of September 1763, the Abbé Prevost, the French novelist and compiler of travels, was seized with a fit in the forest of Chantilly. The body was found, and conveyed to the residence of the nearest clergyman. It was supposed that death had taken place through apoplexy. But the local authorities, desiring to be satisfied of the fact, ordered the body to be examined. During the process, the poor abbé uttered a cry of agony – It was too late.

It is to be observed that cases of sudden and unexplained death are, on the one hand, the cases most likely to furnish a large percentage of death-trance; and, on the other, are just those in which the anxiety of friends or the over-zealousness of a coroner is liable to lead to premature anatomisation. Nor does it even follow that, because the body happily did not wake while being dissected, the spark of life was therefore extinct. This view, however, is too painful to be followed out in reference to the past. But it imperatively suggests the necessity of forbidding necroscopic examinations, before there is perfect evidence that life has departed – that is, of extending to this practice the rule which ought to be made absolute in reference to interment.

Thus comes out the practical importance of the question, how is it to be known that the body is no longer alive?

The entire absence of the ordinary signs of life is insufficient to prove the absence of life. The body may be externally cold; the pulse not be felt; breathing may have ceased; no bodily motion may occur; the limbs may be stiff (through spasm); the sphincter muscles relaxed; no blood may flow from an opened vein; the eyes may have become glassy; there may be partial *mortification* to offend the sense with the smell of death; and yet the body may be alive.

The only security we *at present* know of, that life has left the body, is the supervention of chemical decomposition, shown in commencing change of colour of the integuments of the abdomen and throat to blue and green, and an attendant cadaverous fœtor.

To return from this important digression to the former subject of the Vampyr superstition. The second element which we have yet to explain is the Vampyr visit and its consequence – the lapse of the

Castle Dracula Looking up to Poenari Fortress from the road, 1,480 steps lead up to the Castle ruins.

Castle Dracula Poenari Fortress was a battlement used by Vlad the Impaler, whose ruins are still standing. The fortress is situated near the Transylvanian-Wallachian frontier, hundreds of miles from Bram Stoker's location for Castle Dracula, in the Borgo Pass.

party visited into death-trance. There are two ways of dealing with this knot; one is to cut it, the other to untie it.

It may be cut, by denying the supposed connection between the Vampyr visit and the supervention of death-trance in the second party. Nor is the explanation thus obtained devoid of plausibility. There is no reason why death-trance should not, in certain seasons and places, be *epidemic*. Then the persons most liable to it would be those of weak and irritable nervous systems. Again, a first effect of the epidemic might be further to shake the nerves of weaker subjects. These are exactly the persons who are likely to be infected with imaginary terrors, and to dream, or even to fancy, they have seen Mr or Mrs such a one, the last victims of the epidemic. The dream or impression upon the senses might again recur, and the sickening patient have already talked of it to his neighbours, before he himself was seized with death-trance. On this supposition, the Vampyr visit would sink into the subordinate rank of a mere premonitory symptom.

To myself, I must confess, this explanation, the best I am yet in a position to offer, appears barren and jejune; and not at all to do justice to the force and frequency, or, as tradition represents the matter, the universality of the Vampyr visit as a precursor of the victim's fate. Imagine how strong must have been the conviction of the reality of the apparition, how common a feature it must have been, to have led to the laying down of the unnatural and repulsive process customarily followed at the Vampyr's grave, as the regular and proper preventive of ulterior consequences.

I am disposed, therefore, rather to try and untie this knot, and with that object to wait, hoping that something may turn up in the progress of these inquiries to assist me in its solution. In the mean time, I would beg leave to consider this second half of the problem a compound phenomenon, the solutions of the two parts of which may not emerge simultaneously. The Vampyr visit is one thing; its presumed contagious effect another.

The Vampyr visit! Well, it is clear the Vampyr could not have left his grave bodily – or, at all events, if he could, he never could have buried himself again. Yet in his grave they always found him. So the body could not have been the visitant. Then, in popular language, it was the ghost of the Vampyr that haunted its future victim. The ghostly nature of the visitant could not have been identified at a luckier moment. The very subject which I next propose to undertake is the analysis of ghosts. I have, therefore, only to throw the Vampyr ghost into the crucible with the rest; and to-morrow I may perhaps be able to report the rational composition of the whole batch.

From On the Truths Contained in Popular Superstitions *(1851) pages 22–43*

CHAPTER FOUR

Are Vampires Really Dead?

Dom Augustine Calmet

Herbert Mayo wrote about vampires from the standpoint of a physician and surgeon. A century earlier Dom Augustine Calmet had written about them as a Benedictine abbot. One might expect there to be no common ground on such a potentially heated clash between church and science, faith and reason. We would be wrong, for that would be to underestimate Calmet.

For seekers after vampire lore Calmet is the eminence grise. Much of the works of later commentators is indebted to his pioneering study *Traité sur les Apparitions des Esprits, et sur les Vampires, ou les Revenans de Hongrie, de Moravie &c*, published in several editions either side of 1750. It was translated into English in 1850 by the Rev Henry Christmas under the title *The Phantom World: or, The Philosophy of Spirits and Apparitions.*

A secluded scholar throughout his life, Calmet has left us a vast library of theological and historical thought. His treatise on apparitions and vampires spans two volumes, though the first reads like a lengthy preamble, as he wanders amongst good and bad angels, magic throughout the world, sorcerers, possession by the devil, and arguments for and against the principles of apparitions.

We can sense Calmet getting into his stride in Volume Two, as he turns his intellect to the problematic existence of revenants and vampires in central and eastern Europe. His was a long life – 1672 to 1757 – and he actually lived through the vampire plague of the early eighteenth century reported by Mayo and which threw up tales of Arnod Paole and others. Calmet was into middle age when the lurid accounts of reanimated bloodsuckers began filtering west from Hungary, Moravia, Poland and Silesia, and it is to address this epidemic that his work is principally dedicated.

His style is long-winded and repetitive. He puts before us an extensive catalogue of apocryphal case studies none of which could possibly be authenticated in any way. As Calmet makes this very

point himself, one sometimes wonders why he went to such trouble to
reproduce them. But Calmet, we might say, leaves no stone
unturned in his quest for truth. He reminds us that vampire
superstition has a long and respectable history, seeking illumination
in the writings of Plato, Homer and St Augustine, as well as
searching for instances from biblical times. He goes beyond
superficial explanations linked with trance or premature burial,
though he ponders (as does Professor Van Helsing in *Dracula*) the
fact that certain creatures can hibernate for months, and even be
discovered alive after years of incarceration.

Calmet is aware of the unfortunate effects of the Orthodox and
Roman schism in the Christian church. The plague from the east
seemed to be restricted to regions under Orthodox domination,
where scepticism on the matter of vampires amounted almost to
heresy. Divergence of view on the causes of bodily dissolution
seemed to contribute to the schism. Rome interpreted incorruptibility as a reward for sanctity, while the Greek Church extended its
application to include the excommunicated. Saints and sinners were
apparently sharing a common afterlife.

Calmet is at his most probing when asking questions of a
metaphysical nature. How can a three-dimensional body pass
through the soil above its grave without disturbing it? Throughout
he is obsessed with one question to which he returns again and again.
Are vampires really dead? If they are dead – as opposed to victims of
premature burial who have managed to free themselves – then their
existence can only be at the will of God. God alone has the power to
resurrect from the grave: even the Devil can only do so with His
permission. But then what could God's purpose be?

In fairness, Calmet's conclusion is measured and unwavering. He
might entertain doubts about God's ulterior motives, but his
intellectual rejection of the idea of vampires is unequivocal – indeed,
surprisingly unequivocal when we remember the age in which he
lived and the shadow of the Holy Inquisition in the background.

It must be owned that Calmet's name does not feature among the
list of sources Bram Stoker compiled for *Dracula* – though a reference
to another of Calmet's works does appear in one source.*

✳

---

* Calmet's *Ecclesiastical and Civil History of Lorraine* in Henry Lea's *Superstition and
Force* p. 207.

Are Vampires Really Dead?

Some advantage of these instances and these arguments may be derived in favour of vampirism, by saying that the ghosts of Hungary, Moravia, and Poland are not really dead; that they continue to live in their graves, although without motion and without respiration; the blood which is found in them being fine and red, the flexibility of their limbs, the cries which they utter when their heart is pierced or their head being cut off, all prove that they still exist.

That is not the principal difficulty which arrests my judgment; it is, to know how they come out of their graves without any appearance of the earth having been removed, and how they have replaced it as it was; how they appear dressed in their clothes, go and come, and eat. If it is so, why do they return to their graves? why do they not remain amongst the living? why do they suck the blood of their relations? why do they haunt and fatigue persons who ought to be dear to them, and who have done nothing to offend them? If all this is only imagination on the part of those who are molested, whence comes it that these vampires are found in their graves in an uncorrupted state, full of blood, supple, and pliable; that their feet are found to be in a muddy condition the day after they have run about and frightened the neighbours, and that nothing similar is remarked in the other corpses interred at the same time and in the same cemetery? Whence does it happen that they neither come back nor infest the place any more when they are burned or impaled? Would it be, again, the imagination of the living and their prejudices which reassure them after these executions? Whence comes it that these scenes recur so frequently in those countries, that the people are not cured of their prejudices, and daily experience, instead of destroying, only augments and strengthens them? . . .

[Many] authors have reasoned a great deal on these events. 1. Some have believed them to be miraculous. 2. Others have looked upon them simply as the effect of a heated imagination, or a sort of prepossession. 3. Others again have believed that there was nothing in them all but what was very simple and very natural, these persons not being dead, but acting naturally upon other bodies. 4. Others have asserted that it was the work of the devil himself; amongst these, some have advanced the opinion that there were certain benign demons, differing from those who are malevolent and hostile to mankind, to which benign demons they have attributed

playful and harmless operations, in contradistinction to those bad
demons who inspire the minds of men with crime and sin, ill use
them, kill them, and occasion them an infinity of evils. But what
greater evils can one have to fear from veritable demons and the most
malignant spirits, than those which the ghouls of Hungary inflict on
the persons whose blood they suck, and thus cause to die? 5. Others
will have it that it is not the dead who eat their own flesh or clothes,
but serpents, rats, moles, ferrets, or other voracious animals, or even
what the peasants call *striges*, which are birds that devour animals
and men, and suck their blood. Some have said that these instances
are principally remarked in women, and, above all, in a time of
pestilence; but there are instances of ghouls of both sexes, and
principally of men; although those who die of plague, poison,
hydrophobia, drunkenness, and any epidemical malady, are more
apt to return, apparently because their blood coagulates with more
difficulty; and sometimes some are buried who are not quite dead, on
account of the danger there is in leaving them long without
sepulture, from fear of the infection they would cause.

It is added, that these vampires are known only to certain
countries, as Hungary, Moravia, and Silesia, where those maladies
are more common, and where the people, being badly fed, are
subject to certain disorders occasioned by the climate and the food,
and augmented by prejudice, fancy, and fright, which are capable of
producing or of increasing the most dangerous maladies, as daily
experience proves too well. As to what some have asserted, that the
dead have been heard to eat and chew like pigs in their graves, it is
manifestly fabulous, and such an idea can have its foundation only in
ridiculous prepossessions of the mind . . .

That bodies which have died of violent maladies, or which have
been executed when full of health, or have simply swooned, should
vegetate underground in their graves; that their beards, hair, and
nails should grow; that they should emit blood, be supple and pliant;
that they should have no bad smell, &c., – all these things do not
embarrass us: the vegetation of the human body may produce all
these effects. That they should even eat and devour what is about
them, the madness with which a man interred alive must be
transported when he awakes from his torpor, or his swoon, must
naturally lead him to these violent excesses. But the grand difficulty
is to explain how the vampires come out of their graves to haunt the
living, and how they return to them again. For all the accounts that

we see suppose the thing as certain, without informing us either of the way or the circumstances, which would, however, be the most interesting part of the narrative.

How a body covered with four or five feet of earth, having no room to move about and disengage itself, wrapped up in linen, covered with pitch, can make its way out, and come back upon the earth, and there occasion such effects as are related of it; and how after that it returns to its former state, and re-enters underground, where it is found sound, whole, and full of blood, and in the same condition as a living body? this is the question. Will it be said that these bodies evaporate through the ground without opening it, like the water and vapours which enter into the earth, or proceed from it, without sensibly deranging its particles? It were to be wished that the accounts which have been given us concerning the return of the vampires had been more minute in their explanations of this subject.

Supposing that their bodies do not stir from their graves, that it is only their phantoms which appear to the living, what cause produces and animates these phantoms? Can it be the spirit of the defunct, which has not yet forsaken them, or some demon, which makes their apparition in a fantastic and borrowed body? And if these bodies are merely phantomic, how can they suck the blood of living people? We always find ourselves in a difficulty to know if these appearances are natural or miraculous.

A sensible priest related to me, a little while ago, that, travelling in Moravia, he was invited by M. Jeanin, a canon of the cathedral at Olmutz, to accompany him to their village, called Liebava, where he had been appointed commissioner by the consistory of the bishopric, to take information concerning the fact of a certain famous vampire, which had caused much confusion in this village of Liebava some years before.

The case proceeded. They heard the witnesses, they observed the usual forms of the law. The witnesses deposed that a certain notable inhabitant of Liebava had often disturbed the living in their beds at night, that he had come out of the cemetery, and had appeared in several houses three or four years ago; that his troublesome visits had ceased because a Hungarian stranger, passing through the village at the time of these reports, had boasted that he could put an end to them, and make the vampire disappear. To perform his promise, he mounted on the church steeple, and observed the moment when the vampire came out of his grave, leaving near it the linen clothes in which he had been enveloped, and then went to disturb the inhabitants of the village.

The Hungarian, having seen him come out of his grave, went down quickly from the steeple, took up the linen envelops of the vampire, and carried them with him up the tower. The vampire having returned from his prowlings, cried loudly against the Hungarian, who made him a sign from the top of the tower that if he wished to have his clothes again he must fetch them; the vampire began to ascend the steeple, but the Hungarian threw him down backwards from the ladder, and cut his head off with a spade. Such was the end of this tragedy.

The person who related this story to me saw nothing, neither did the noble who had been sent as commissioner; they only heard the report of the peasants of the place, people extremely ignorant, superstitious and credulous, and most exceedingly prejudiced on the subject of vampirism.

But supposing that there be any reality in the fact of these apparitions of vampires, shall they be attributed to God, to angels, to the spirits of these ghosts, or to the devil? In this last case, will it be said that the devil can subtilize these bodies, and give them power to penetrate through the ground without disturbing it, to glide through the cracks and joints of a door, to pass through a key-hole, to lengthen or shorten themselves, to reduce themselves to the nature of air, or water, to evaporate through the ground – in short, to put them in the same state in which we believe the bodies of the blessed will be after the resurrection, and in which was that of our Saviour after his resurrection, who showed himself only to whom he thought proper, and who without opening the doors appeared suddenly in the midst of his disciples?

But should it be allowed that the demon could reanimate these bodies, and give them the power of motion for a time, could he also lengthen, diminish, rarify, subtilize the bodies of these ghosts, and give them the faculty of penetrating through the ground, the doors and windows? There is no appearance of his having received this power from God, and we cannot even conceive that an earthly body, material and gross, can be reduced to that state of subtilty and spiritualization without destroying the configuration of its parts and spoiling the economy of its structure; which would be contrary to the intention of the demon, and render this body incapable of appearing, showing itself, acting and speaking, and, in short, of being cut to pieces and burned, as is commonly seen and practised in Moravia, Poland, and Silesia. These difficulties exist in regard to those persons of whom we have made mention, who, being excommunicated, rose from their tombs, and left the church in sight of everybody.

We must then keep silence on this article, since it has not pleased God to reveal to us either the extent of the demon's power, or the way in which these things can be done. There is very much appearance of illusion; and even if some reality were mixed up with it, we may easily console ourselves for our ignorance in that respect, since there are so many natural things which take place within us and around us, of which the cause and manner are unknown to us.

Those who have recourse to the fascination of the senses to explain what is related concerning the apparition of vampires, throw themselves into as great a perplexity as those who acknowledge sincerely the reality of these events; for fascination consists either in the suspension of the senses, which cannot see what is passing before their sight, like that with which the men of Sodom were struck when they could not discover the door of Lot's house, though it was before their eyes; or that of the disciples at Emmaus, of whom it is said 'that their eyes were holden, so that they might not recognise Jesus Christ, who was talking with them on the way, and whom they knew not again until the breaking of the bread revealed him to them;' – or else it consists in an object being represented to the senses in a different form from that it wears in reality, as that of the Maobites, who believed they saw the waters tinged with the blood of the Israelites, although nothing was there but the simple waters, on which the rays of the sun being reflected, gave them a reddish hue; or that of the Syrian soldiers sent to take Elisha, who were led by this prophet into Samaria, without their recognising either the prophet or the city.

This fascination, in what way soever it may be conceived, is certainly above the usual power known unto man, consequently man cannot naturally produce it; but is it above the natural powers of an angel or a demon? That is unknown to us, and obliges us to suspend our judgment on this question.

There is another kind of fascination, which consists in this, that the sight of a person or a thing, the praise bestowed upon them, the envy felt towards them, produce in the object certain bad effects, against which the ancients took great care to guard themselves and their children, by making them wear round their neck preservatives, or amulets, or charms.

A great number of passages on this subject might be cited from the Greek and Latin authors; and I find that at this day, in various parts of Christendom, people are persuaded of the efficacy of these fascinations. But we must own three things; first, that the effect of these pretended fascinations (or spells) is very doubtful; the second, that if it were certain, it is very difficult, not to say impossible, to explain it; and, lastly, that it cannot be rationally applied to the matter of apparitions or of vampires.

If the vampires or ghosts are not really resuscitated nor their bodies spiritualized and subtilized, as we believe we have proved; and if our senses are not deceived by fascination, as we have just seen it; I doubt if there be any other way to act on this question than to absolutely deny the return of these vampires, or to believe that they are only asleep or torpid; for if they truly are resuscitated, and if what is told of their return be true – if they speak, act, reason – if they suck the blood of the living, they must know what passes in the other world, and they ought to inform their relations and friends of it, and that is what they do not. On the contrary, they treat them as enemies; torment them, take away their life, suck their blood, cause them to die with lassitude.

If they are predestinated and blessed, whence happens it that they disturb and torment the living, their nearest relations, their children, and all that for nothing, and simply for the sake of doing harm? If these are persons who have still something to expiate in purgatory, and who require the prayers of the living, why do they not explain their condition? If they are reprobate and condemned, what have they to do on this earth? Can we conceive that God allows them thus to come without reason or necessity and molest their families, and even cause their death?

If these *revenans* are really dead, whatever state they may be in in the other world, they play a very bad part here. . . .

To resume in a few words all that we have related in this dissertation: we have therein shown that a resurrection, properly so called, of a person who has been dead for a considerable time, and whose body was either corrupted, or stinking, or ready to putrefy, like that of Pierre, who had been three years buried, and was resuscitated by St Stanislaus, or that of Lazarus, who had been four days in the tomb, and already possessing a corpse-like smell, – such a resurrection can be the work of the Almighty power of God alone.

That persons who have been drowned, fallen into syncope, into a lethargy or trance, or looked upon as dead, in any manner whatever, can be cured and brought back to life, even to their former state of life, without any miracle, but by the power of medicine alone, or by natural efforts, or by dint of patience; so that nature re-establishes herself in her former state, that the heart resumes its pulsation, and the blood circulates freely again in the arteries, and the vital and animal spirits in the nerves.

That the oupires, or vampires, or *revenans* of Moravia, Hungary, Poland, &c., of which such extraordinary things are related, so detailed, so circumstantial, invested with all the necessary formalities to make them believed, and to prove them even judicially before judges, and at the most exact and severe tribunals; that all which is said of their return to life; of their apparition, and the confusion which they cause in the towns and country places; of their killing people by sucking their blood, or in making a sign to them to follow them; that all those things are mere illusions, and the consequence of a heated and prejudiced imagination. They cannot cite any witness who is sensible, grave and unprejudiced, who can testify that he has seen, touched, interrogated these ghosts, who can affirm the reality of their return, and of the effects which are attributed to them.

I shall not deny that some persons may have died of fright, imagining that their near relatives called them to the tomb; that others have thought they heard some one rap at their doors, worry them, disturb them, in a word, occasion them mortal maladies; and that these persons judicially interrogated, have replied that they had seen and heard what their panic-struck imagination had represented to them. But I require unprejudiced witnesses, free from terror and disinterested, quite calm, who can affirm upon serious reflection, that they have seen, heard, and interrogated these vampires, and who have been the witnesses of their operations; and I am persuaded that no such witness will be found. . . .

I have already proposed the objection formed upon the impossibility of these vampires coming out of their graves, and returning to them again, without its appearing that they have disturbed the earth, either in coming out or going in again. No one has ever replied to this difficulty, and never will. To say that the demon subtilizes and spiritualizes the bodies of vampires, is a thing asserted without proof or likelihood.

The fluidity of the blood, the ruddiness, the suppleness of these vampires, ought not to surprise any one, any more than the growth of the nails and hair, and their bodies remaining undecayed. We see every day, bodies which remain uncorrupted, and retain a ruddy colour after death. This ought not to appear strange in those who die without malady and a sudden death; or of certain maladies, known to our physicians, which do not deprive the blood of its fluidity, or the limbs of their suppleness.

With regard to the growth of the hair and nails in bodies which are not yet decayed, the thing is quite natural. There remains in those bodies a certain slow and imperceptible circulation of the humours, which causes this growth of the nails and hair, in the same way that we every day see common bulbs grow and shoot, although without any nourishment derived from the earth.

The same may be said of flowers, and in general of all that depends on vegetation in animals and plants.

The belief of the common people of Greece in the return to earth of the vroucolacas, is not much better founded than that of vampires and ghosts. It is only the ignorance, the prejudice, the terror of the Greeks, which have given rise to this vain and ridiculous belief, and which they keep up even to this very day. The narrative which we have reported after M. Tournefort, an ocular witness and a good philosopher, may suffice to undeceive those who would maintain the contrary.

The incorruption of the bodies of those who died in a state of excommunication, has still less foundation than the return of the vampires, and the vexations of the living caused by the vroucolacas; antiquity has had no similar belief. The schismatic Greeks, and the heretics separated from the Church of Rome, who certainly died excommunicated, ought, upon this principle, to remain uncorrupted; which is contrary to experience, and repugnant to good sense. And if the Greeks pretend to be the true Church, all the Roman Catholics, who have a separate communion from them, ought then also to remain undecayed. The instances cited by the Greeks either prove nothing, or prove too much. Those bodies which have not decayed, were really excommunicated, or not. If they were canonically and really excommunicated, then the question falls to the ground. If they were not really and canonically excommunicated, then it must be proved that there was no other cause of incorruption, – which can never be proved.

Moreover, any thing so equivocal as incorruption, cannot be

adduced as a proof in so serious a matter as this. It is owned, that often the bodies of saints are preserved from decay; that is looked upon as certain, among the Greeks as among the Latins – therefore, we cannot thence conclude that this same incorruption is a proof that a person is excommunicated.

In short, this proof is universal and general, or only particular. I mean to say, either all excommunicated persons remain undecayed, or only a few of them. We cannot maintain that all those who die in a state of excommunication, are incorruptible. For then all the Greeks towards the Latins, and the Latins towards the Greeks, would be undecayed, which is not the case. That proof then is very frivolous, and nothing can be concluded from it. I mistrust, a great deal, all those stories which are related to prove this pretended incorruptibility of excommunicated persons. If well examined, many of them would doubtless be found to be false.

Whatever respect I may feel for St Gregory the Great, who relates some instances of deceased persons who died in a state of excommunication going out of the church before the eyes of every one present; and whatever consideration may be due to other authors whom I have cited, and who relate other circumstances of a similar nature, and even still more incredible, I cannot believe that we have these legends with all the circumstances belonging to them; and after the reasons for doubt which I have recorded at the end of these stories, I believe I may again say, that God, to inspire the people with still greater fear of excommunication, and a greater regard for the sentences and censures of the Church, has willed on these occasions, for reasons unknown to us, to show forth his power, and work a miracle in the sight of the faithful; for how can we explain all these things without having recourse to the miraculous? All that is said of persons who being dead chew under ground in their graves, is so pitiful, so puerile, that it is not worthy of being seriously refuted.

From Augustine Calmet, The Phantom World *(Vol. II) (1850) pages 175–176, 183–184, 208–215, 240–241, 244–248.*

CHAPTER FIVE

An Account of Wallachia, Moldavia . . . and Dracula

William Wilkinson

Sheridan Le Fanu's short novel *Carmilla* lifted the vampire motif to new heights of literary creativity. Its impact on Le Fanu's Irish compatriot, Bram Stoker, was such that Stoker came near to plagiarism. His research notes show that he intended initially to locate his novel in Styria, home of Carmilla, and also to feature a vampire countess uncomfortably like her. But he soon changed his mind. He shifted the site of his novel eastwards to Transylvania and built its central character around a certain Voyvode (Prince) Dracula, a fifteenth-century warrior renowned for the ferocity of his campaigns against the Turks.

The modern state of Romania comprises three provinces – Transylvania, Wallachia and Moldavia. Transylvania is historically and culturally considered separate from the other two by virtue of its seclusion behind the Carpathian Alps. Although in pre-Roman times all three were part of the kingdom of Dacia, their later history diverged. In Stoker's time Transylvania was administered by Hungary as part of the Austria-Hungary Empire, and only joined Wallachia and Moldavia as a constituent part of Romania at the end of the First World War.

As for Dracula, although he was born in the Transylvanian town of Sighisoara, it was over Wallachia, to the south, that he ruled – briefly in 1448, again between 1456–62, and finally for a few weeks until his death in 1476. Not surprisingly, the castles of Voyvode Dracula are to be found where he ruled, in Wallachia. Bram Stoker, however, realising that Hungary and its provinces were more steeped in vampire lore than was the Romanian territory of Wallachia, chose to relocate Castle Dracula further north, close to the remote Borgo Pass which connects Transylvania with Moldavia.

Stoker was introduced to Mr Dracula in the public library at Whitby, where he researched aspects of his novel in the summer of 1890. There he came across William Wilkinson's *An Account of the*

Principalities of Wallachia and Moldavia, published in 1820. Wilkinson was a former British Consul-Resident at Bucharest. Strictly speaking, Wilkinson slightly confuses matters when speaking of two Draculas, father and son, because it is the son who interests us. His father is more usually known as Dracul – minus the 'a'. Nevertheless, in Wilkinson we read a sentence that must have fired Stoker's imagination: 'Dracula in the Wallachian language means Devil.'

Devil or not, Dracula became known in the West by another name – Vlad the Impaler. This was in recognition of his favourite form of torture and execution. Vlad may have learned of the Turkish practice of impalement from his time spent as a hostage of the Sultan in his younger days. In any case, the methods by which he cemented his rule over Wallachia, by wholesale impalement of those who opposed him, not to mention the fate of thousands of Turkish troops who fell into his hands in battle, quickly made him one of the most notorious figures of the age. Woodcuts of him feasting in the open air among rows of impaled bodies provide some of the most vivid surviving portraits of the life and times of Vlad the Impaler.

Whether Stoker knew of this side to Dracula's character is uncertain. Wilkinson doesn't mention it. However, at the point where he mentions Dracula's son he refers the reader to page 296 of the *Generall Historie of the Turkes* by the Oxford scholar Richard Knolles, first published in 1603 and which records an early account of 'Dracula's' battles with the Turks. Even if Stoker did follow up this reference it would only have misled him, for it actually relates to Dracula's father and brother. But if, out of curiosity, he happened to flip through to page 362, he would have unearthed a harrowing description of Wladus Dracula's tortures and executions – two square miles of gallows, gibbets, wheels and stakes, upon which were suspended some twenty thousand bodies.

But did Stoker read that account, or others in similar vein? None of the other books on his list of Transylvanian sources spares a word for Dracula, never mind his atrocities. In the novel Count Dracula relates his encounters with the Turks, but there is no mention of impalement. This would be either because Stoker wants Count Dracula to present himself in a favourable light, or because Stoker did not know any other light in which to present him. This latter view is reinforced when Van Helsing comes to survey Dracula's human existence. The professor seems equally blind to Dracula's darker side. He makes no mention of the name 'Vlad', nor his sobriquet 'the

Impaler', nor his unspeakable cruelties. Indeed, he prefers to describe Dracula as 'in life a most wonderful man. Soldier, statesman, and alchemist. . .'. Did Van Helsing (or Stoker) really know who Dracula was?

The nearest that Stoker's sources come to locating an authentic biographical sketch of Vlad the Impaler is to be found in a fleeting reference to Major Johnson's *On the Track of the Crescent to* James Samuelson's *Roumania: Past and Present*. If Stoker pursued this reference he would have found elsewhere in Samuelson the following account of the Impaler, tagged on to an appreciation of another anti-Turk campaigner, John Hunniades, who also happened to be nicknamed 'The Devil'.

> As we have said, the Turks were so much afraid of Hunniades that they are said to have given him the name of 'the Devil', but the same designation, as well as that of the Impaler, has also been bestowed upon Vlad, a voivode of Wallachia, who was probably the ally of Hunniades, and who, if one-tenth of what has been related of him be true, has a much better claim to the title. He is represented to have been one of the most atrocious and cruel tyrants who ever disgraced even those dark ages. One day he massacred 500 boyars who were dissatisfied with his rule. The torture of men, women, and children, seems to have been his delight. Certain Turkish envoys, when admitted into his presence, refused to remove their turbans, whereupon he had them nailed to their heads. He burned 400 missionaries and impaled 500 gipsies to secure their property. In order to strike terror into Mohammed II, he crossed over into Bulgaria, defeated the Turks, and brought back with him 25,000 prisoners, men, women, and children, whom he is said to have impaled upon a large plain called Praelatu.
>
> (*James Samuelson* Roumania: Past and Present *(1882) p. 170.*)

It is curious that whereas Van Helsing never explicitly identifies Dracula with the 'Impaler'. Samuelson's account tends to confuse Dracula with his father (p. 180). Which leads to the question: were Dracula and the Impaler in Stoker's mind one and the same person?

What follows is the first section of Wilkinson's *Account*, tracing the history of Wallachia and Moldavia from pre-Roman Dacia up to the brief, but crucial, reference to Dracula. It is worth bearing in mind that but for Stoker's discovery of Wilkinson's book he might have gone ahead and called his monster 'Count Wampyr' – his uninspiring but original choice of name.

*

An Account of Wallachia, Moldavia . . . and Dracula

The principalities of Wallachia and Moldavia, situated between 43°
40′ and 48° 50′ north latitude, 23° and 29° 30′ east longitude,
occupying a space of 350 miles in length, and 160 in breadth, are
separated from the Austrian provinces of Temesvar, Transylvania,
and Boukovina, by the Carpathian mountains; from Russia, by the
river Pruth; and from Bulgaria (the ancient Mœsia), by the Danube.

It is sufficiently ascertained that these two provinces, joined to
those of Transylvania and Temesvar, composed the kingdom of
Dacia, finally conquered by the Romans.

The Dacians were originally a Scythian or Sarmatian tribe,
resembling, in language and manners, the Thracians; the Greeks,
indeed, considered them as a part of the Thracian nation.

They were a sober and vigorous people, capable of enduring any
hardships and privations in war: they did not fear exposing
themselves to the greatest dangers, because they looked upon death
as the beginning of a much happier life; and this doctrine, according
to Strabo, they held from a philosopher named Zamolxis, who was
held in high repute by them.

The progress of the Roman arms, which, under the reign of
Augustus, were carried to the banks of the Danube, brought them
into contact with the Dacians, who were at that time governed by a
warlike prince named Bærebestes, who boldly set the Roman
conquerors at defiance. After his death, they were divided into four
or five different principalities, and their strength was a good deal
broken by the Romans; but their last king Decebalus, one of the
ablest and most enterprising warriors of his time, re-united them
into one body towards the 87th year of the Christian æra.

The first irruption of the Dacians into the territory of the empire,
took place during the latter part of Augustus's reign; and, at times
repulsed, at other times successful, they continued to annoy the
Romans without any decisive advantage taking place on either side.
At last the Emperor Domitian, determined to put a stop to their
depredations, marched in person against them.

The particulars of the war which ensued are sufficiently detailed in
the Roman history. The result of it having been such as to compel
Domitian to sue for peace; he consented to pay to Decebalus an
annual sum in the shape of a pension, but which, in fact, was nothing
less than a tribute. It was regularly paid by the Romans until the
year 102, when the Emperor Trajan declared his resolution to

discontinue it; and the Dacians thereby considering themselves no longer bound to observe the treaty of peace, crossed the Danube, and laid waste the Roman territory. Upon these acts of hostility, Trajan put himself at the head of a numerous army, and marching against them, forced them to retire, passed the Danube in pursuit, engaged and defeated their successive forces, and finally compelled Decebalus to acknowledge himself his vassal. Trajan then returned to Rome, where he received the honour of a triumph, and the title of *Dacicus*.

But not long after, Decebalus, eager to shake off the Roman yoke, invaded and plundered the territory of his neighbours the Iazygæ, who were also tributary to the empire, on their refusal to join him against the Romans. Trajan again took the field at the head of a vast army, determined to chastise and subdue the Dacians. He reached the banks of the Danube in autumn, and he thought it prudent to wait there the return of the fine season, that he might carry on military operations with more facility and success. It was during this interval, that he caused his famous bridge to be built over the Danube, under the direction of the architect Apollodorus of Damascus; and its present remains are sufficiently visible to verify the ancient accounts of this stupendous work. When the water is very low, some of the piles stand two or three feet above it, and render that part of the river difficult of navigation; they are looked upon as rocks by the natives of each side.

At the return of the spring, when the bridge was completed, the Roman army marched over it, and commenced hostilities. The war was long and difficult, but it terminated in the complete subjugation of the Dacians, and in the death of their king, Decebalus, who, finding it impossible to avoid being made prisoner, killed himself that he might not fall alive into the conquerors' hands.

Dacia was thus converted into a Roman province, and Trajan shortly after sent colonies to increase its population. New cities were built, and pavements were constructed on the high roads, for the greater facilities of communication.* It was governed by a Roman pro-prætor until the year 274.

* A great Roman pavement is still visible in Wallachia. It begins at a small town called *Caracalla*, situated near the borders of the Danube, about three miles from the place where the great river Olt falls into it: and it runs up in a straight line with this river, as far as the Carpathians, where its traces are lost. It probably led to the Dacian capital, Zarmiss, which is now a Transylvanian town, and contains many ruins of Roman monuments of an inferior kind. The Latin language is almost the only one spoken by its present inhabitants.

Under the reign of Gallienus, when the empire was already declining, various parts of Dacia were seized by the Goths, and other barbarous nations.

A few Roman legions yet remained in the country, under the reign of the Emperor Aurelian, who, returning from Gaul, came down to Illyria, and finding a great part of Dacia in the hands of the barbarians, foresaw the impossibility of maintaining any possessions in the midst of them, and he withdrew a good number of the Roman inhabitants to the other side of the Danube, and settled them in Mæsia.

During the space of a hundred years from that period, those of the natives who had remained behind, and their descendants, were incessantly exposed to the rapacities of a variety of barbarous tribes, who came into the country for plunder.

Towards the year 361, the Goths, more powerful than the rest, seemed to have been left in exclusive possession of the province, and were inclined to make a permanent stay in it. They embraced the Christian religion, and established it in Dacia; since when, to the present moment, it has never ceased to be predominant amongst its inhabitants.

In 376, the Hunns, having over-run the countries possessed by the Goths, forced Athanaric, King of the Vizigoths, to retire with all his forces to that part of Dacia, situated between the rivers Dniester and Danube, now called Moldavia. He raised a wall between the latter river and the Pruth, by which he thought himself sufficiently protected against the attacks of his enemies. The Hunns, however, were not stopped by it; and their approach spread such consternation among the Goths of the interior, that those who had the means of escaping, to the number of some hundred thousand, fled for refuge into the Roman territory, and were permitted by the Emperor Valens, to settle in Thrace, upon condition that they should live peaceably there, and serve, when required, in the Roman armies.

The Hunns having penetrated into Dacia, were left masters of it until the year 453, when Ardaric, King of the Gepidæ, a people previously conquered by Attila and the Hunns, revolted against them, in consequence of Attila's death. His son and successor, Ellach, marched against them, but being defeated and slain, the Hunns were driven back into Scythia, and the Gepidæ remained masters of all Dacia. They entered into a sort of alliance with the

Romans, who agreed to pay them a pension. In 550, their first quarrels with their neighbours, the Lombards, took place; and being sometimes assisted by the Emperor Justinian, they carried on frequent hostilities against them, for the space of eight years, at the end of which both nations resolved to decide the fate of the war by one great battle. The Lombards, under their King Alboin, had previously formed an alliance with the Avars, a people of Scythian extraction; and, assisted by them, they marched to action. Both sides fought with equal valor; but at last victory declared in favour of the Lombards, who, pursuing the Gepidæ, made a great slaughter among them. The Gepidæ, either destroyed, dispersed, or subdued, never after had a king of their own, and ceased to be a nation.

Alboin's achievements in Dacia attracted the notice of Narses, sent by Justinian to conquer Italy: he made offers to him, and finally engaged him to join the expedition with all his forces. The Lombards thus abandoned their possessions in Dacia and Pannonia to their friends and neighbours the Avars. These, also known by the name of White-Hunns, remained in them until their own destruction by the Franks and Bulgarians. In the seventh century, being joined by other barbarous tribes, they pushed their incursions as far as the gates of Constantinople, where they were so completely defeated by the Emperor Heraclius, that they could not recover the blow: it was the original cause of their rapid decline.

Towards the close of the same century, a nation, known under the names of Slaves and Bulgarians, came from the interior of Russia to that part of Mæsia, which has since been called Bulgaria. Soon after a great number of Slaves, headed by their chief Krumo, crossed the Danube, and settled in Dacia, where they have since been known under the name of Wallachs. Opinion varies with respect to the origin of this name. Some historians pretend that the Slaves distinguished by it the Romans of Mæsia; whilst others maintain that they meant by it a people who led a pastoral life, and had given it to the inhabitants of Mæsia, most of whom were shepherds; and that a great number of these, having joined the Slaves in Dacia, the name by degrees became a general one amongst its inhabitants. The modern Wallachians, however, exclude it altogether from their language, and call themselves 'Rummunn' or Romans, giving to their country the name of Roman-land, 'Tsara-Rumaneska'.

Some former inhabitants of Dacia, joined by a number of Slaves and Bulgarians, separated from the new settlers, and went to the lower part of Dacia lying between the rivers Olt and Danube, where they fixed their habitations. They formed themselves into a nation, and chose for their chief one Bessarabba, to whom they gave the Slavonic title of *Bann* or regent. The country within his jurisdiction was called Bannat; and it retains to this day the name of Bannat of Crayova, the latter being that of its present capital. Several other petty independent states arose at the same time in various parts of Dacia; but they were frequently annexed to the same sceptre, at other periods dismembered, according to the warlike ardour or indolence and incapacity of their various chiefs. Their general system, however, consisted in making war against the Romans of the lower empire, in which they were seconded by the Slaves and Bulgarians of Mæsia, whom they looked upon as their natural allies. This state of things continued to the close of the ninth century, at which period the Slaves having fallen into decline, various hordes, originally Scythians, successively undertook the conquest of Dacia, driving each other out of it, according to the momentary superiority of the one over the other. The most remarkable of these were the Hazars, the Patzinaces, the Moangoures, the Ouzes, the Koumans, and other Tartars.

The natives were treated as slaves by all these hordes of barbarian intruders, and great numbers of them were continually retiring to the other side of the Carpathians; where they settled under their own chiefs, sometimes independent, at others tributary to the kings of Hungary. The most conspicuous and thriving of these colonies were those of Fagarash and Maramosh.

The devastations continued in the plains finally drove out all the natives, and in the eleventh century the Tartars retired, leaving the country a complete desert. It remained in this state until the year 1241, when the inhabitants of Fagarash, conducted by their chief Raddo Negro (Rodolphus the Black), crossed the mountains, and took possession of that tract of country, which is now called upper Wallachia. Nearly at the same time, the inhabitants of Maramosh under their chief Bogdan, came and settled in that part which is by some called Moldavia, from the name of the river Moldau, which crosses it to fall into the Danube, and by the natives and Turks, Bogdania. Raddo Negro and his followers halted at the foot of the mountains, where they laid the foundation of a city, to which they gave the name of Kimpolung. At present it is reduced to an indifferent village; but its original extent is marked by old walls in ruin; and some inscriptions in its cathedral church attest it to have been Raddo's capital. His successors transferred their residence to Tirgovist, more pleasantly situated in the plains.

Some Wallachian, Transylvanian, and Hungarian authors differ in opinion with respect to the exact period of Raddo's and Bogdan's establishment in Wallachia and in Moldavia, and fix it at a different year of the early part of the thirteenth century; but as they give no satisfactory explanation on the subject, I am disposed to differ from them all, in placing that event in the year 1241, on the strength of the following considerations: – 1st. It does not appear probable that the kings of Hungary, who, at the commencement of the thirteenth century were very powerful, and who looked upon Fagarash and Maramosh as dependencies of their crown, would have suffered their inhabitants to desert them, in order to settle in foreign countries: 2dly, It would seem strange that Raddo, Bogdan, and their followers should have quitted their homes in a prosperous country, and come to inhabit a desert, without some extraordinary event had necessitated so remarkable an emigration: and 3dly, the best Hungarian historians place in the year 1240 the invasion of Battou-Han in the northern countries; and add, that having crossed Russia and Poland at the head of 500,000 men, he entered Hungary in the year 1241, where he staid three years, during which he put every thing to fire and sword, and finally retired because nothing more was left to satisfy his thirst of blood. It appears, then, extremely probable that the ravages of Battou-Han, and the terror he spread in the adjacent provinces, were the only causes of this emigration, which no historian has yet otherwise accounted for.

Bogdan and Raddo assumed the Slavonic title of Voïvode, equivalent to that of commanding prince. When tranquillity was restored in Hungary, they acknowledged the supremacy of the Hungarian king; but it does not appear that the formalities of the recognition had been such as to bind their successors; for, at the early part of the principalities, some Voïvodes disputed it with success; and from the commencement of the fourteenth century, their independency was acknowledged by Hungary.

The Bannat of Crayova had been little molested during the great incursions of the barbarians: in the ninth century it had become tributary to the kings of Hungary, who afterwards held it as a sort of refuge for the knights going to, and coming from, the Holy Land; but soon after Raddo's arrival, the Bann submitted to him the supreme sovereignty of the Bannat, and it has since then been annexed to the principality of Wallachia.

During the latter part of his life, Raddo raised another city, distant about thirty miles south-west of Kimpolung, on the borders of the river Argis: he gave it the name of Courté d'Argis, and resided in it occasionally. He also built a church here, which, two hundred years after, one of the Voïvodes beautified in a very conspicuous manner. The whole of the exterior work is entirely of carved marble, something in the style of the steeple of St Stephen's church at Vienna, but far more elegant. The whole produces a very striking effect; and, as it has perfectly preserved its original beauty, it is certainly a monument that the Wallachians may boast of in any part of Europe.

The Voïvodate was not made hereditary; and although it devolved sometimes from father to son, the successor was obliged to go through the formality of being elected by the chiefs of the nation.

Several successors of Raddo strengthened the government, the population increased, and a great number of small towns and villages were built in the country. Frequent hostilities against the Hungarians, arising from the claims of sovereignty of the latter, accustomed the Wallachians to war; and in 1391 the Voïvoide Mirtza collected a numerous force, and attacked the neighbouring possessions of the Turks with the view of rescuing them from their hands. The Sultan Bajazet being at that moment employed in Asia in a troublesome war with the Prince of Castomona, had left his conquests near the Danube without the means of defence. But when the news of their invasion reached him, he suspended his operations in Asia, and returned to Adrianople, from whence he sent a numerous army to Wallachia. The Voïvode marched to meet the Turks; and, after a bloody battle, he was defeated, and compelled to become tributary to the Sultan. The annual amount of the tribute was fixed at three thousand piasters.*

Wallachia continued to pay it until the year 1444; when Ladislas King of Hungary, preparing to make war against the Turks, engaged the Voïvode Dracula to form an alliance with him. The Hungarian troops marched through the principality and were joined by four thousand Wallachians under the command of Dracula's son.†

---

* Knolles's *History of Turkey*. p. 204 and Tounousli's, Ιςορια Ιης βλαχιας, p. 247.
  A piaster and a half is equal to an English shilling.
† Knolles's *History*, p. 296.

The Hungarians being defeated at the celebrated battle of Varna, Hunniades their general, and regent of the kingdom during Ladislas's minority, returned in haste to make new preparations for carrying on the war. But the Voïvode, fearful of the Sultan's vengeance, arrested and kept him prisoner during a year, pretending thereby to show to the Turks that he treated him as an enemy. The moment Hunniades reached Hungary, he assembled an army and placed himself at the head of it, returned to Wallachia, attacked and defeated the Voïvode, and caused him to be beheaded in his presence; after which he raised to the Voïvodate one of the primates of the country, of the name of Dan.

The Wallachians under this Voïvode joined again the Hungarians in 1448, and made war on Turkey; but being totally defeated at the battle of Cossova, in Bulgaria, and finding it no longer possible to make any stand against the Turks, they submitted again to the annual tribute, which they paid until the year 1460, when the Sultan Mahomet II being occupied in completing the conquest of the islands in the Archipelago, afforded them a new opportunity of shaking off the yoke. Their Voïvode, also named Dracula*, did not remain satisfied with mere prudent measures of defence: with an army he crossed the Danube and attacked the few Turkish troops that were stationed in his neighbourhood; but this attempt, like those of his predecessors, was only attended with momentary success. Mahomet having turned his arms against him, drove him back to Wallachia, whither he pursued and defeated him. The Voïvode escaped into Hungary, and the Sultan caused his brother Bladus to be named in his place. He made a treaty with Bladus, by which he bound the Wallachians to perpetual tribute; and laid the foundations of that slavery, from which no efforts have yet had the power of extricating them with any lasting efficacy.

From An Account of the Principalities of Wallachia and Moldavia *(1820) pages 1–19*

---

* Dracula in the Wallachian language means Devil. The Wallachians were, at that time, as they are at present, used to give this as a surname to any person who rendered himself conspicuous either by courage, cruel actions, or cunning.

CHAPTER SIX

On the Track of Transylvania

Major E. C. Johnson

Transylvania was, and is, a hotch-potch of races and nationalities, a consequence of interminable wars and migrations. In Stoker's day the population numbered around two million, comprising 1,200,000 Romanians (or Wallachs), 530,000 Hungarians (combining Magyars with the original Széklers), 200,000 Saxons, plus sizable Jewish, Armenian and Slav minorities.

Stoker never went to Transylvania. All the information on that country that appears in *Dracula* can be traced to the notes he made from the handful of books on his source-list. These books, in the main, were written by British official servants – soldiers, administrators, or their wives. The portraits they present share many features: implicit belief in British superiority; irritation at minor inconveniences; a patronising desire to effect change; and a degree of racism – particularly anti-semitism – that might take the modern reader by surprise. All these features can be observed in Harker's travels in *Dracula*, and Stoker's own anti-semitism is detectable in his creation of his own Jewish stereotype. As for Count Dracula, in the novel Stoker allows him to speak of himself, his dynasty, and his people.

'We Szekelys have a right to be proud, for in our veins flows the blood of many brave races who fought as the lion fights, for lordship. Here, in the whirlpool of European races, the Ugric tribe bore down from Iceland the fighting spirit which Thor and Wodin gave them, which their Berserkers displayed to such fell intent on the seaboards of Europe, ay, and of Asia and Africa too, till the peoples thought that the were wolves themselves had come. Here, too, when they came, they found the Huns, whose warlike fury had swept the earth like a living flame, till the dying peoples held that in their veins ran the blood of those old witches, who, expelled from Scythia had mated with the devils in the desert. Fools, fools! What devil or what witch was ever so great as Attila, whose blood is in these veins?' He held up his arms. 'Is it a wonder that we were a conquering

race; that we were proud; that when the Magyar, the Lombard, the
Avar, the Bulgar, or the Turk poured his thousands on our frontiers, we
drove them back? Is it strange that when Arpad and his legions swept
through the Hungarian fatherland he found us here when he reached the
frontier; that the Honfoglalas was completed here? And when the
Hungarian flood swept eastwards, the Szekelys were claimed as kindred
by the victorious Magyars, and to us for centuries was trusted the
guarding of the frontier of Turkey-land; ay, and more than that, endless
duty of the frontier guard, for, as the Turks say, "water sleeps, and
enemy is sleepless". Who more gladly than we throughout the Four
Nations received the "bloody sword", or at its warlike call flocked
quicker to the standard of the King? When was redeemed that great
shame of my nation, the shame of Cassova, when the flags of the Wallach
and the Magyar went down beneath the Crescent? Who was it but one of
my own race who as Voivode crossed the Danube and beat the Turk on
his own ground? This was a Dracula indeed! Woe was it that his own
unworthy brother, when he had fallen, sold his people to the Turk and
brought the shame of slavery on them! Was it not this Dracula, indeed,
who inspired that other of his race who in a later age again and again
brought his forces over the great river into Turkey-land; who, when he
was beaten back, came again, and again, and again, though he had to
come alone from the bloody field where his troops were being
slaughtered, since he knew that he alone could ultimately triumph! They
said that he thought only of himself. Bah! what good are peasants
without a leader? Where ends the war without a brain and heart to
conduct it? Again, when, after the battle of Mohacs, we threw off the
Hungarian yoke, we of the Dracula blood were amongst their leaders, for
our spirit would not brook that we were not free. Ah, young sir, the
Szekelys – and the Dracula as their heart's blood, their brains, and their
swords – can boast a record that mushroom growths like the Hapsburgs
and the Romanoffs can never reach. The warlike days are over. Blood is
too precious a thing in these days of dishonourable peace; and the glories
of the great races are as a tale that is told.'

(*Dracula* Chapter 3)

The extracts that follow are taken from Major E.C. Johnson's *On the
Track of the Crescent – Erratic Notes from the Piræus to Pesth*. They reveal
the combination of popular history and popular prejudice common
to all Stoker's sources, and which likewise colour *Dracula*'s pages. It
can be seen that Stoker relied heavily on Johnson, as, for example,
with Johnson's assertion that the Székelys (Stoker adopts his
Hungarian spelling) are descended from Attila and were the
guardians of the frontier with Turkey. We also find the nobility of
Transylvania referred to as 'counts', which title is unknown in

Romania. Readers can judge for themselves Johnson's likening of Széklers and Wallachs to the Irish and Scots.

✻

On the Track of Transylvania

At last I reached the market-place, an immense *piacz* in front of one of the cathedrals. Here hundreds of little wooden booths had been set up, and here funny little female figures in sheepskin jackets, voluminous short petticoats, large boots, and with coloured handkerchiefs on their heads, waddled about in the mire, and sold wool, toys, clothing, groceries, and all kinds of miscellaneous goods. I noticed that all the Wallachs wore the coloured apron in front and behind, which I had observed in Roumania and at Mehadia. The men – any one of whom would have made the fortune of a transpontine theatrical manager as 'heavy villain,' wore immense hats, large white loose-sleeved shirts, with the tails outside, sheepskin, and hussar jackets, embroidered in worsted and coloured thread, large white trousers, and the usual enormous boots (I much wished that I had been similarly accoutred). The men were lounging about in groups, eagerly discussing (I suppose) the all-absorbing topic of the election. Members of the fallen nation who are waiting for the Messiah were also present, and occupying the period of suspense by their usual and congenial employment – fleecing the Christian.

One thing which must strike every traveller in Hungary is the immense number of Jews, and no one who has been in that country can be still puzzled as to the whereabouts of the lost tribes; for at least one third of the Jews on the whole earth – some 3,000,000 – are in Hungary and Poland. Who can mistake them? The oval face; the 'parrotty' beak, out of all proportion to the other features; the stooping gait and long, flowing beard; the furtive glances from under the shaggy eyebrow, now cringing, now vindictive; the black skullcap, from under which two oily 'kiss-me-quick' curls protrude, brushed well forward over the ears on each side of the low, thoughtful brow; the protruding lower lip; the receding chin; the bony hands, accustomed to roll together, either in supplication, or satisfaction at having 'done a Christian in the eye;' the tight-fitting cassock-like garment of seedy, shining cloth, or threadbare silk, generally with tight sleeves, sometimes varied by a black or red sash round the waist, and always long skirts, lined with fur in winter, reaching to the top of his high boots; – all these show unmistakably the Hungarian branch of that race 'against whom is every man's hand,' and who returns the compliment with compound interest.

Here they have no Greeks with whom to compete, as at Constantinople, and consequently enjoy a monopoly of all the drink-shops, and pull the strings of all commercial enterprise, as they are the *vis* in the midst of the national *inertia*. In this way they are patient and industrious. There they stand at their shop-doors, stiff-necked as their theology, and as motionless as the Highland gentleman who displays his 'understandings' in a kilt at the door of tobacconists' in this country, whose thumb is always conveying something to his nasal dust-bin, which never reaches it. Those who know how pitiless the Jews are when they have the too-confiding peasantry in their clutches can understand the dreadful outbursts of anti-Semitic fury now, alas! so common in Russia, Poland, and Hungary, and the sanguinary vengeance taken on them and theirs by their improvident and exasperated victims, who have got deeper and deeper into their meshes, till the terrible day of reckoning.

Many German anthropologists are of opinion that the Jews of Germany, Poland, and Hungary, are not of the Semitic race, but the descendants of a Turanian tribe called 'Chazars,' who inhabited the Crimea in the third century, and were converted to be chosen people by an immigration of Jews from the south. This tribe then spread over central Europe, and by the persecutions of the twelfth and thirteenth centuries were driven back into Poland and Hungary. The type of those I saw, however, seemed decidedly Semitic, and even of an aggravated form.

This strange people have a great talent. It is shrewdness in driving bargains, and a marvellous aptitude for conducting financial operations, in consequence of which they have accumulated most of the wealth of the world, and control an immense proportion of the business transactions on the civilised globe. They have, however, never added one grain to the food supply of men, or done any physical work or handicraft labour. As a nation, they have never excelled in, or shown a taste for, architecture, sculpture, or painting; nor do they seem to have scientific minds. The grand exceptions to this rule, who tower over the rest of their race as giants of genius, appear to have been the descendants of mixed marriages – Jewish men with Saxon women, or Saxon men with half-Jewish women; for a pure Jewess, like a pure gipsy, will seldom or never link herself with a Saxon male. Thus the type is retained, and will remain all over the world as long as this rule is observed. In England it has lately been somewhat relaxed, with the invariable and gratifying result of the gradual disappearance of the type. Even the most beautiful Jewesses I have ever seen (those of Morocco) will not bear long inspection, as the disproportion of the nose to the rest of the face *grows upon you as you look*, and, when they smile, the mouth enlarges too much, and the magnificent eyes contract.

In the market-place, vehicles of all sorts were massed and arranged like parks of artillery; strange, primitive-looking waggons, for three horses, made of planks nailed together; and one-horse carts, called *szekér*, all entirely innocent of springs, and looking as if they had been employed to convey Noah and his suite out of the Ark. When the glorious monarch of the day was descending in a great ball of fire behind the domes and steeples of the pretty town, and when church-bells of all sizes and tones had announced sunset, and the termination of the fair, the booths disappeared as if by magic. Oxen, with heavy yokes on their necks, were harnessed to the pre-historic waggons, into which numbers of people were packed like herrings, and moved off, amid laughter and merriment, through the stodgy sea of mud to their far-off homes.

Now began the din. As I leaned over the bridge which crosses the Körös, and watched the rays of the moon as they were reflected in the calm water, from coffee-shops and 'publics' the wild wail of Czigán music arose, and the sounds as of many feet showed that the popular goddess Csárdás was being worshipped with Terpsichorean rites. As, however, I had to be up at three the next morning to catch the train for Marosvásárhely, I returned to my hotel, ate a hurried and very greasy supper, and, rolling myself in my railway-rug, was soon asleep.

The cold grey dawn of morning was just peeping in at my window, when I was awakened by the pretty 'slavey' in red-leather top-boots, and looking more than half-asleep as she brought me a tiny jug of hot water. I was soon dressed, had drunk some scalding coffee, gulped down a boiled egg, and found myself once more performing strange and involuntary acrobatic feats inside the hotel 'bus. I was treated just like a bottle of medicine, for the rule, 'to be well shaken before taken' (to the station), was carried out to the letter. Ultimately, however, I found myself in the train and on the journey.

Very soon after leaving Nagy-Várod a complete change seemed to come over the scenery. Instead of the monotony and unbroken flatness of the Alfold, I found rocky heights, which rose abruptly from the plain; grand, frowning gorges, down which sparkling streams emptied themselves into the valley; pretty winding brooks constantly disappearing and re-appearing; charming peeps of miniature waterfalls splashing over moss-covered stones: the whole reminding me very much of some parts of Wales. We were now fairly in the country called by the Romans Transylvania, or 'The land beyond the forests', and by the Hungarians Erdély, from '*erdö*, a forest', and by the Germans Siebenbürgen, or 'Seven Fortresses'. It is the most picturesque and romantic portion of Hungary.

This strange country, which was originally a part of Dacia, is inhabited by Magyars, Saxons, Wallachs, and Székelys. The Magyars inhabit the west, the Székelys the north and east, and the Saxons the south, with them the Wallachs – the descendants of the Dacians – being mixed in great numbers. The Székelys – who claim to be descended from Attila and the Huns – were found settled on the eastern frontier when the country was conquered by the Magyars, and the two races at once fraternised. This was in the eleventh century, and from that time till 1526 the country was nominally a part of Hungary, being governed by an official who was appointed by the kings of Hungary. To replace the waste of inhabitants in the constant wars of which Transylvania was the theatre, colonists were brought from Germany, and these colonists were the ancestors of the present Saxons of that country.

After the battle of Mohacs, which extinguished Hungarian independence, Transylvania fell into the hands of 'the unspeakable', who made it an independent principality under the protection of the Porte; the country being governed by princes who were elected by the people, subject to the approval of the Sultan.

Thus it was that when Hungary accepted an Austrian emperor as her king, Transylvania maintained her independence under Zápolya, but continued to pay tribute to the Porte. This, however, did not save her from the ruthless hand of the Moslem whenever he passed through her fair plains on his warlike expeditions to and from Hungary, as the frequent sacking of Kolozsvár and other frontier towns can testify. After the death of Zápolya, the province was governed by princes elected as before, but no Székely or Saxon was ever elected to this office, it being reserved for members of the Hungarian nobility. Of these princes the Bethlens, especially

Bethlen Gábor, did most to consolidate the country and raise her to independence.

The 'protection' of Turkey was finally withdrawn in 1699, after which Transylvania became the prey of perpetual war, during which, however, freedom was developed, and all classes, with the exception of the Wallachs and the Gipsies, obtained equal rights. During these wars, repeated attempts were made by the Austrian Emperor to infringe on those rights, and to gradually obtain possession of the country. At length, in 1791, the Emperor was elected prince of the province, the celebrated Diploma Leopoldi being forced down the throats of the inhabitants by Maria Theresa. Up to this time all the inhabitants of the country – Magyars, Székelys, and Saxons – had had an equal vote in the Diet. This was soon abolished; and the Diet was deprived altogether of the right of electing princes.

As Austria persistently evaded the fulfilment of her engagements with Transylvania, and frequently infringed on the rights of the country, a meeting of the inhabitants was held in 1834. On this occasion the Székelys and the Protestant Saxons did not fail to proclaim their grievances, and with such effect that Austria was brought to her senses, and the Diet was called together. Taking alarm, however, at the constitutional demands of this Diet under their leader, Baron Nicolas Wesselenyi, Austria again dissolved it, poured troops into the country, and declared martial law throughout the province.

Although the two countries, Hungary and Transylvania, have been nominally united since the ninth century, they were not really one until 1848 – that year of volcanic change and universal levelling down. In that year the Transylvanian Diet voluntarily merged into that of Hungary, sending sixty-nine delegates to Pesth. After the crushing of the rebellion, the countries were again separated, and, after various changes in the electoral law, were finally united at the coronation of King Francis Joseph in 1867.

Geographically, Transylvania is a land of mountains and valleys, and gives rise to the rivers which flow through Moldavia, Wallachia, and Hungary. The region which the train enters on leaving Nagy-Várod is the most western spur, which from here takes a south-easterly direction towards Brassó and the Wallachian frontier. . . .

The Wallachs belong chiefly to the Greek Church, and are grossly superstitious, while the Magyars and Székelys mostly profess the Roman Catholic faith. Very large revenues are enjoyed by the bishops of this latter religion. The annual income of the Bishop of Nagy-Várod is about 26,000*l.*, while that of the Prince Primate of Hungary is not less than 60,000*l.*

In 1525 the Protestant Church was founded in Hungary, and comprehended nearly all the magnates, and two thirds of the population. The Protestants were, however, successively deprived of their equal political and civil rights, and their churches, by concessions extorted from weak princes by Jesuit intriguers. Thus the Lutheran faith has suffered severely, both in numbers and prosperity. This has been assigned, by some writers, as one of the causes of the Protestants having taken part in the rising in 1848, which was exclusively Magyar.

The Székelys have played a very important part in the history of Hungary and Transylvania. They were recognised as kindred by the Magyars on their first entering Hungary, and the two races have remained allies ever since. The Székelys also received certain privileges in return for their having guarded the frontier towards Moldavia and 'Turkey-land'. They became also the guardians of the national language, for they speak the purest Hungarian. In the struggle for independence in 1848 they joined the national forces against the Austrians, and only yielded when Russian intervention rendered further resistance futile.

The Slav troops in the Austrian service on this occasion remained staunch to the Imperial cause, the wild Seressians and the Croatian border regiments particularly distinguishing themselves under Jellachich, the Ban of Croatia, who, after desperate fighting in the plains against the patriot cavalry, counter-marched just in time to join Prince Windischgrätz in the recapture of Vienna.

The word 'Ban' means 'Lord', and is applied to the civil and military Governor, or Lord-Lieutenant of a Banat or Province. Prior to the conquest of Hungary by the Turks, in the sixteenth century, there were several Banats along the Turkish frontier. The only one now remaining is that of Dalmatia and Croatia.

Yet, though they fought bravely, the Székelys do not appear to have been specially enthusiastic about the rebellion. An Hungarian officer once, on entering a village, asked a peasant if he was not delighted that the National Army had come. The bucolic answered, 'It is just the same to us: the Austrian army come, they eat, they drink, and pay nothing; the National Army come, they eat, they drink, and they pay no more.'

Nor do the peasants appear to have been altogether clear as to the causes of the rising, or the objects of those who took part in it. One of them, being asked what the fighting was all about, delivered himself of the following highly lucid and statesmanlike explanation:– 'We want,' he said, 'a Republic, and to choose the Archduke Stephen *as our King, with the kind permission of our Emperor!'*

On another occasion, a priest asked a peasant what fault he had to find with the new state of things. 'Why,' answered the wretch, whose wrongs (unlike those of the knife-grinder) had roused him to vengeance, 'if Kossuth had only followed my advice, he would have beheaded every Count and hanged every Bishop; then *I* should have been a Count, and you would have been a Bishop.'

The character of the Székelys seems to be a curious combination of the canny Scot and the imprudent Irishman. Like the former, they are plucky, industrious, and frugal. Like the latter, they are excitable, and, consequently, despondent under reverses.

They are a notoriously witty race. It is essential with them to mix some fun with their conversation. Very good talkers are to be found among them, and they possess the rare merit of never laughing at their own tales. . . .

The population of Transylvania is about 2,000,000, and of these some 1,200,000 are Wallachs, or, as they call themselves, Rummie. The Hungarians call them Oláhok. The Wallach has many points of resemblance to our friend Paddy. He is grossly superstitious, as the number of crosses by the roadside and on every eminence testify; and, like his prototype, he lives in abject terror of his priest, of whose powers he has the most exalted ideas. He believes that 'his rivirence' could turn him into a cow, or, as in Lover's famous anecdote, 'make him meander up and down in the form of an ould gander' for eternity, should he show any sign of having a will of his own. He is, too, a lazy, pleasant, good-natured, drunken, careless, improvident fellow; living like the grasshopper while the sun shines, and 'the divil may care for the morn.' His wife is, however, a marked contrast to him, and most emphatically his 'better' half, for she is never at rest, and does all the work, both in and out of the house; she is also very clever with her needle.

I have already described the Wallach costume, male and female; I will merely observe here that the women are very fond of show, and make themselves up, like any civilised lady of Western fashion. They rouge their cheeks, and paint their eyebrows; wear earrings and necklaces of beads and coins, and, when they can afford it, of gold and silver. These they hang sometimes down to the waist. They also embroider their chemises on the breast and sleeves with gaudy coloured threads. The girls wear netting on their heads' and the married women white cloths. The Wallach peasant is, of course, very fond of marrying early, and when asked why he marries, candidly replies 'to have somebody to work for him and to keep him clean.' He has one, or at most two rooms in his cottage, and here he and all his family live. He further resembles the Irish peasant in his hospitality to pigs, and his simplicity. *A propos* of the latter quality, I may as well here recount an old but very characteristic anecdote of this interesting people. Some peasants were one day working in a field near the banks of the Maros. Suddenly they saw a stranger rush frantically through the field, and precipitate himself headlong into the river; they pursued and dragged him out dripping; he departed, and they resumed their work. Shortly afterwards, he again appeared, and for the second time took a suicidal 'header'. Again the peasants snatched him from the raging torrent, and the jaws of the grim monarch, and returned to their work. Yet a third time they saw him enter the field, but on this occasion he did not make for the river, but climbing into a tree, deliberately proceeded to hang himself from one of the branches. This time his previous preservers did not interfere, and he drained the cup of his fate 'to the last drop'. Presently a crowd of the relations and friends of the deceased, from whose custody he had escaped, arrived, headed by the parish priest, and roundly abused the peasants for permitting the late lamented to perform 'the happy despatch'. The peasants naively replied, that they had pulled him out of the river twice, and as he was dripping wet, they thought he had merely *hung himself up to dry!*

There are other and darker shades in the Wallach character, and in these, alas! he much resembles his Hibernian prototype. He is much given to treacherous revenge, and is capable of the most awful atrocities when aroused. Proofs of this were given in 1784 and 1848, when the Wallachs joined the Saxons and Austrians against the Hungarians.

The diet of the Wallach peasants – when they are allowed to eat anything – is very simple. It consists principally of a porridge, made of the meal of maize, like the polenta of Italy, and called 'Mamaliga.'

Of this meal they also make a cake, which serves them as bread. They also eat vegetables, cheese, fruit, garlic and onions, and wash all this down with copious draughts of home-brewed brandy.

I have mentioned the priests. Being all of the peasant class, they are very little better than the people over whom they rule; indeed, their ignorance and superstition surpass all belief. They have no distinctive mark of their profession, and work in the fields like the humblest of their flock, or turn an honest penny by carrying messages to a neighbouring village. In many instances they can neither read nor write. They are obliged to marry, but are only allowed to do so once, and I am afraid that their moral character would not bear a very close or very critical examination. They can scarcely, however, fulfil the old adage, 'Who leads a good life is sure to live well,' for, by the rigid fasts of their church, they are denied all animal food for fully three quarters of the year.

This same ecclesiastical influence has something to do with the laziness of the Wallachian peasant. When we accuse him of idleness, we should remember that he is forbidden by his religion to work on feast-days or fast-days, and that, as these occupy the greater part of the year, his opportunities for work are a good deal limited. Moreover, he is less inclined and less able to work, as the continued fasting reduces his bodily strength to a point not much exceeding that of wet blotting-paper. All these, and many other, details connected with this interesting people, I learned from Count P——B——, as we whirled along through the clouds of dust into which the mud had now become converted.

From On the Track of the Crescent *(1885) pages 200–207, 233–235, 249–252.*

CHAPTER SEVEN

Transylvanian Superstitions

Emily de Laszowska Gerard

It is known that when Bram Stoker began preparing his vampire novel he was not looking beyond Styria as the place to site it, nor had he yet come across the historical Dracula to base it upon. If the introduction to Voyvode Dracula, courtesy of William Wilkinson, was Stoker's first major breakthrough, then stumbling across Emily Gerard's 'Transylvanian Superstitions' was the second.

Stoker's debt to Emily Gerard is immense. Hardly any of his other sources on Transylvania spared a sentence for the myths and superstitions of that wedge of land locked away within the horseshoe of the Carpathian mountains. It was Gerard who supplied them in lush detail. She had lived in Transylvania for two years as the English wife of a Hungarian cavalry brigade commander despatched to that province. She writes with the intrepid curiosity that was typical of a certain kind of Victorian woman adventurer. Not that she approached all aspects of her task with a mind as open as her eyes. Although she speaks of the indolent charm and drowsy poetry of Transylvania she is less tolerant of its superstitions, describing them as a crooked plant of delusion, an evil which every person with a well-balanced mind should wish to die out. This is the mesh through which we have to assess her observations.

It is through reading her article that so many of the questions pertaining to *Dracula*'s origins are answered. She presents Transylvania as the superstitious backwater of Europe, a place where belief in ghouls, goblins and vampires is accepted without question. This peculiar susceptibility to superstition is part due to history – the mixing of races and religions – and part due to remote geography. Surrounded on three sides by the rocky barrier of the Carpathians, and on its western approaches by one of Europe's most impenetrable forests, it is little wonder that 'Transylvania', when translated from the latin, means 'the land beyond the forest'. The stretching tentacles of the iron road were still opening up parts of Transylvania even as Stoker wrote *Dracula*. Some of the maps appended to his source books reveal the extent of railway development at the time. Stoker has Jonathan Harker take advantage of the train as far as Bistritz [sic], but from there through the Borgo Pass and on to Castle Dracula he must rely on horse-drawn transport.

But why should Stoker have alighted upon this particular location to house the most demonic character in English fiction? None of the travellers to Transylvania whose books he consulted ever journeyed through the Borgo Pass or left any descriptions. It seemed to be the remotest part of a remote country – a land beyond the land beyond the forest, you might say. We should also remember that Stoker describes Count Dracula as a Székler, whose race were traditional guardians of the frontier with Moldavia and the Ottoman Empire. The Borgo Pass actually connects Transylvania with Moldavia. And when we bear in mind Transylvania's geology – sulphuric springs, bottomless caverns, vertical precipices – we can see that Stoker had stumbled upon a perfect location for a lost world. Another writer might equally have used eastern Transylvania to discover dinosaurs: Stoker used it to bring to life a long-dead monster of human species.

To mention but a few of Gerard's observations that found their way into *Dracula*: the importance of St George's Eve as a time when all the forces of evil are let loose; the mysterious blue flame which guards the site of buried treasure; Thursday being a lucky day for marriage (Jonathan and Mina are married on that day). Gerard reminds Stoker that the name 'Drakul' means 'devil', as in 'Gania Drakuluj' (devil's mountain). She spells out the local belief in vampires, or *nosferatu* as they are otherwise known. Most important of all, she gives Stoker the idea for how Dracula could have originally turned into a vampire. High in the Carpathians above the town of Hermanstadt exists a mythical academy run by the devil . . .

Gerard's article appeared in *The Nineteenth Century* magazine in July 1885. Three years later the same material was spread over several chapters of her two-volume book *The Land Beyond the Forest*. Stoker makes no mention of this work, nor of her earlier novel set in southern Transylvania, *The Waters of Hercules*. 'Transylvanian Superstitions' is reproduced below, excluding the section on Saxon superstitions which is of less relevance to *Dracula*.

✻

Transylvanian Superstitions

Transylvania might well be termed the land of superstition, for nowhere else does this curious crooked plant of delusion flourish as persistently and in such bewildering variety. It would almost seem as though the whole species of demons, pixies, witches, and hobgoblins, driven from the rest of Europe by the wand of science, had taken refuge within this mountain rampart, well aware that here they would find secure lurking-places, whence they might defy their persecutors yet awhile.

There are many reasons why these fabulous beings should retain an abnormally firm hold on the soil of these parts; and looking at the matter closely we find here no less than three separate sources of superstition.

First, there is what may be called the indigenous superstition of the country, the scenery of which is peculiarly adapted to serve as background to all sorts of supernatural beings and monsters. There are innumerable caverns, whose mysterious depths seem made to harbour whole legions of evil spirits: forest glades fit only for fairy folk on moonlight nights, solitary lakes which instinctively call up visions of water sprites; golden treasures lying hidden in mountain chasms, all of which have gradually insinuated themselves into the minds of the oldest inhabitants, the Roumenians, and influenced their way of thinking, so that these people, by nature imaginative and poetically inclined, have built up for themselves out of the surrounding materials a whole code of fanciful superstition, to which they adhere as closely as to their religion itself.

Secondly, there is here the imported superstition! that is to say, the old German customs and beliefs brought hither seven hundred years ago by the Saxon colonists from their native land, and like many other things, preserved here in greater perfection than in the original country.

Thirdly, there is the wandering superstition of the gypsy tribes, themselves a race of fortune-tellers and witches, whose ambulating caravans cover the country as with a network, and whose less vagrant members fill up the suburbs of towns and villages.

Of course all these various sorts of superstition have twined and intermingled, acted and reacted upon each other, until in many cases it is a difficult matter to determine the exact parentage of some particular belief or custom; but in a general way the three sources I have named may be admitted as a rough sort of classification in dealing with the principal superstitions afloat in Transylvania.

There is on this subject no truer saying than that of Grimm, to the effect that 'superstition in all its manifold varieties constitutes a sort of religion, applicable to the common household necessities of daily life,'* and as such, particular forms of superstition may very well serve as guide to the characters and habits of the particular nation in which they are prevalent.

The spirit of evil (or, not to put too fine a point upon it, the devil) plays a conspicuous part in the Roumenian code of superstition, and such designations as the Gregynia Drakuluj (devil's garden), the Gania Drakuluj (devil's mountain), Yadu Drakuluj (devil's hell or abyss), &c, &c, which we frequently find attached to rocks, caverns, or heights, attest the fact that these people believe themselves to be surrounded on all sides by a whole legion of evil spirits.

The devils are furthermore assisted by witches and dragons, and to all of these dangerous beings are ascribed peculiar powers on particular days and at certain places. Many and curious are therefore the means by which the Roumenians endeavour to counteract these baleful influences, and a whole complicated study, about as laborious as the mastering of any unknown language, is required in order to teach an unfortunate peasant to steer clear of the dangers by which he considers himself to be beset on all sides. The bringing up of a common domestic cow is apparently as difficult a task as the rearing of any dear gazelle, and even the well-doing of a simple turnip or potato about as precarious as that of the most tender exotic plant.

Of the seven days of the week, Wednesday (Miercuri) and Friday (Vinire) are considered suspicious days, on which it is not allowed to use needle or scissors, or to bake bread; neither is it wise to sow flax on these days. Venus (called here Paraschiva), to whom the Friday is sacred, punishes all infractions of this rule by causing fires or other misfortunes.

Tuesday, however (Marti, named from Mars, the bloody god of war), is a decidedly unlucky day, on which spinning is totally prohibited, and even such seemingly harmless pursuits as washing the hands or combing the hair are not unattended by danger. On Tuesday evening about sunset, the evil spirit of that day is in its fullest force, and in many districts the people refrain from leaving

* *'Der Aberglaube in seiner Mannigfaltigkeit bildet gewissermassen eine Religion fur den ganzen niederen Hausbedarf.'*

their huts between sunset and midnight. 'May the *mar sara* (spirit of Tuesday evening) carry you off,' is here equivalent to saying 'May the devil take you!'

It must not, however, be supposed that Monday, Thursday, and Saturday are unconditionally lucky days, on which the Roumenian is at liberty to do as he pleases. Thus every well educated Roumenian matron knows that she may wash on Thursdays and spin on Saturdays, but that it would be a fatal mistake to reverse the order of these proceedings; and though Thursday is a lucky day for marriage,* and is on that account mostly chosen for weddings, it is proportionately unfavourable to agriculture. In many parishes it is considered dangerous to work in the fields on all Thursdays between Easter and Pentecost, and it is believed that if these days are not set aside as days of rest, ravaging hailstorms will be the inevitable punishment of the impiety. Many of the more enlightened Roumenian pastors have preached in vain against this belief, and some years ago the members of a parish presented an official complaint to the bishop, requesting the removal of their *curé*, on the ground that not only he gave bad example by working on the prohibited days, but had actually caused them serious material damage, by the hailstorms his sinful behaviour had provoked.

This respect of the Thursday seems to be the remains of a deeply ingrained, though now unconscious, worship of Jupiter (Zoi), who gives his name to the day.

To different hours of the day are likewise ascribed different influences, favourable or the reverse. Thus it is always considered unlucky to look at oneself in the glass after sunset; also it is not wise to sweep the dust over the threshold in the evening, or to give back a sieve or a whip which has been borrowed of a neighbour.

The exact hour of noon is precarious on account of the evil spirit *Pripolniza*,† and so is midnight because of the *midse nópte* (night spirit), and it is safer to remain within doors at these hours. If, however, some misguided peasant does happen to leave his home at midnight, and espies (as very likely he may) a flaming dragon in the

---

* This would seem to suggest a German (or Celtic) origin. Donar, as god of marriages, blesses unions with his hammer.

† This spirit corresponds to the Polednice of the Bohemians and the Poludnica of the Poles and Russians. Grimm, in speaking of the Russians, in his German Mythology, quotes from Boxhorn's *Resp. Moschr:* '*Dæmonem meridianum Moscovitæ et colunt.*' ['Even the Muscovites worship the southern spirit.']

sky, he need not necessarily give himself up as lost, for if he have the presence of mind to stick a fork into the ground alongside of him, the fiery monster will thereby be prevented from carrying him off.

The finger which ventures to point at a rainbow will be straightway seized by a gnawing disease, and a rainbow appearing in December is always considered to bode misfortune.

The Greek Church, to which the Roumenians exclusively belong, has an abnormal number of feast-days, to almost each of which peculiar customs and superstitions are attached. I will here only attempt to mention a few of the principal ones.

On New Year's Day it is customary for the Roumenian to interrogate his fate, by placing a leaf of evergreen on the freshly swept and heated hearthstone. If the leaf takes a gyratory movement he will be lucky, but if it shrivels up where it lies, then he may expect misfortune during the coming year. To ensure the welfare of the cattle it is advisable to place a gold or silver piece in the water-trough, out of which they drink for the first time on New Year's morning.

The feast of the Epiphany, or Three Kings (*Tre crai*) is one of the oldest festivals, and was solemnised by the Oriental Church as early as the second century, fully 200 years before it was adopted by the Latins. On this day, which popular belief regards as the coldest in the winter, the blessing of the waters, known as the feast of the Jordan, or *bobetasu* (baptism) feast, takes place. The priests, attired in their richest vestments, proceed to the shore of the nearest river or lake, and bless the waters, which have been unclosed by cutting a Greek cross some six or eight feet long in the surface of the ice. Every pious Roumenian is careful to fill a bottle with the consecreated water before the surface freezes over, and preserves it, tightly corked and sealed up, as an infallible remedy in case of illness.

Particularly lucky is considered whoever dies on that day, for he will be sure to go straight to heaven, the door of which is supposed to stand open all day, in memory of the descent of the Holy Ghost at the Baptism of Christ.

The feast of St Theodore, 11th of January (corresponding to our 23rd of January), is a day of rest for the girls, and whichever of them transgresses the rule is liable to be carried off by the saint, who sometimes appears in the shape of a beautiful youth, sometimes as a terrible monster.

The Wednesday in Holy Week is very important. The Easter

cakes and breads are baked on this day, and some crumbs are mixed up with the cow's fodder; woe to the woman who indulges in a nap today, for the whole year she will not be able to shake off her drowsiness. In the evening the young men in each home bind as many wreaths as there are members of the family: each of these is marked with the name of an individual and thrown up upon the roof. The wreaths which fall down to the ground indicate those who will die that year.

Skin diseases are cured by taking a bath on Good Friday, in a stream or river which flows towards the east.

In the night preceding Easter Sunday witches and demons are abroad, and hidden treasures are said to betray their site by a glowing flame. No God-fearing peasant will, however, allow himself to be tempted by the hopes of such riches, which he cannot on that day appropriate without sin. On no account should he presume to absent himself from the midnight church service, and his devotion will be rewarded by the mystic qualities attached to the wax candle he has carried in his hand, and which when lighted hereafter during a thunderstorm will infallibly keep the lightning from striking his house.

The greatest luck which can befall a mortal is to be born on Easter Sunday while the bells are ringing, but it is not lucky to die on that day. The spoon with which the Easter eggs have been removed from the boiling pot is carefully treasured up, and worn in the belt by the shepherd; it gives him the power to distinguish the witches who seek to molest his flock.

Perhaps the most important day in the year is St George's, the 23rd of April (corresponds to our 5th of May), the eve of which is still frequently kept by occult meetings taking place at night in lonely caverns or within ruined walls, and where all the ceremonies usual to the celebration of a witches' Sabbath are put into practice.

The feast itself is the great day to beware of witches, to counteract whose influence square-cut blocks of green turf are placed in front of each door and window.* This is supposed effectually to bar their entrance to the house or stables, but for still greater safety it is usual here for the peasants to keep watch all night by the sleeping cattle.

This same night is the best for finding treasures, and many people spend it in wandering about the hills trying to probe the earth for the

---

* This is also usual in Poland, Moldavia and the Bukowina.

gold it contains. Vain and futile as such researches usually are, yet they have in this country a somewhat greater semblance of reason than in most other parts, for perhaps nowhere else have so many successive nations been forced to secrete their riches in flying from an enemy, to say nothing of the numerous veins of undiscovered gold and silver which must be seaming the country in all directions. Not a year passes without bringing to light some earthern jar containing old Dacian coins, or golden ornaments of Roman origin, and all such discoveries serve to feed and keep up the national superstition.

In the night of St George's Day (so say the legends) all these treasures begin to burn, or, to speak in mystic language, to 'bloom' in the bosom of the earth, and the light they give forth, described as a bluish flame resembling the colour of lighted spirits of wine, serves to guide favoured mortals to their place of concealment. The conditions to the successful raising of such a treasure are manifold, and difficult of accomplishment. In the first place, it is by no means easy for a common mortal who has not been born on a Sunday nor at midday when the bells are ringing, to hit upon a treasure at all. If he does, however, catch sight of a flame such as I have described, he must quickly stick a knife through the swaddling rags of his right foot,* and then throw the knife in the direction of the flame he has seen. If two people are together during this discovery they must not on any account break silence till the treasure is removed, neither is it allowed to fill up the hole from which anything has been taken, for that would induce a speedy death. Another important feature to be noted is that the lights seen before midnight on St George's Day, denote treasures kept by benevolent spirits, while those which appear at a later hour are unquestionably of a pernicious nature.

For the comfort of less-favoured mortals, who happen neither to have been born on a Sunday, nor during bell-ringing, I must here mention that these deficiencies may be to some extent condoned and the mental vision sharpened by the consumption of mouldy bread; so that whoever has during the preceding year been careful to feed upon decayed loaves only, may (if he survives this trying *régime*) be likewise the fortunate discoverer of hidden treasures.

Sometimes the power of discovering a particular treasure is

---

* The Roumenian peasant does not wear shoes or stockings, but has his feet swaddled up in linen rags, which are kept in their place by a rough sandal made of a flat piece of leather.

supposed to be possessed only by members of some particular family. A curious instance of this was lately recorded in Roumenia relating to an old ruined convent, where, according to a popular legend, a large sum of gold is concealed. A deputation of peasants, at considerable trouble and expense, found out the last surviving member of the family supposed to possess the mystic power, and offered him, unconditionally, a very handsome sum merely for his assistance in the search. The gentleman in question, being old, and probably sceptical, declined the offer, to the great disappointment of the peasant deputation.

The feast of St George, being the day when flocks are first driven out to pasture, is in a special manner the feast of all shepherds and cowherds, and on this day only it is allowed to count the flocks and assure oneself of the exact number of sheep. In general, these numbers are but approximately guessed at, and vaguely designated. Thus the Roumenian shepherd, interrogated as to the number of his master's sheep, will probably inform you that they are as numerous as the stars of heaven, or as the daisies which dot the meadows.

The throwing up of wreaths on to the roofs, described above, is in some districts practised on the feast of St John the Baptist, the 24th of June (July 6th), instead of on the Wednesday in Holy Week. Fires lighted on the mountains this same night are supposed to protect the flocks from evil spirits.

The feast of St Elias, the 20th of July (August 1), is a very unlucky day, on which the lightning may be expected to strike.

If a house struck by lightning begins to burn, it is not allowed to put out the flames, because God has lit the fire and it would be presumption if man were to dare to meddle.* In some places it is believed that a fire lit by lightning can only be put out with milk.

An approved method for averting the danger of the dwelling being struck by lightning is to form a top by sticking a knife through a piece of bread, and spin it on the floor of the loft during the whole time the storm lasts. The ringing of bells is likewise very efficacious, provided, however, that the bell in question has been cast under a perfectly cloudless sky.

As I am on the subject of thunderstorms, I may as well here mention the *Scholomance*, or school supposed to exist somewhere in the heart of the mountains, and where all the secrets of nature, the

* Also believed in Poland.

language of animals, and all imaginable magic spells and charms are taught by the devil in person. Only ten scholars are admitted at a time, and when the course of learning has expired and nine of them are released to return to their homes, the tenth scholar is detained by the devil as payment, and mounted upon an *Ismeju* (dragon) he becomes henceforward the devil's aide-de-camp, and assists him in 'making the weather,' that is to say, preparing the thunderbolts.

A small lake, immeasurably deep, lying high up among the mountains to the south of Hermanstadt, is supposed to be the cauldron where is brewed the thunder, and in fair weather the dragon sleeps beneath the waters. Roumenian peasants anxiously warn the traveller to beware of throwing a stone into this lake lest it should wake the dragon and provoke a thunderstorm. It is, however, no mere superstition that in summer there occur almost daily thunderstorms at this spot, about the hour of midday, and numerous cairns of stones round the shores attest the fact that many people have here found their death by lightning. On this account the place is shunned, and no Roumenians will venture to rest here at the hour of noon.

Whoever turns three somersaults the first time he hears the thunder will be free from pains in the back during a twelvemonth, and the man who wishes to be ensured against headache has only to rub it against a stone or knock it with a piece of iron.

The Polish harvest custom of decking out a girl with a wreath of corn ears, and leading her in procession to the house of the landed proprietor, is likewise practised here, with the difference that instead of the songs customary in Poland, the girl is here followed with loud cries of *'Prihu! Prihu!'* or else *'Priku!'** and that whoever meets her on the way is bound to sprinkle the wreath with water. If this detail be neglected the next year's crops will assuredly fail. It is also customary to keep the wreaths till next sowing time, when the corn is shaken out, and mingled with the grain to be sowed will ensure a rich harvest.

The feast of St Spiridion, the 12th of December (corresponding to our 24th), is an ominous day, especially for housewives, and the saint often destroys those who desecrate his feast by manual labour.

---

* Archaeologists have derived this word from *Pri*, which in Sanscrit means fruitful, and *Hu*, the god of the Celtic deluge tradition, also regarded as a personification of fruitful nature.

That the cattle are endowed with speech during the Christmas night is a general belief, but it is not considered wise to pry upon them and try to overhear what they say, or the listener will rarely overhear any good.

This night is likewise favourable to the discovery of hidden treasures, and the man who has courage to conjure up the evil spirit will be sure to see him if he call upon him at midnight. Three burning coals placed upon the threshold will prevent the devil from carrying him off.

Christmas carols and dramas are also usual among the Roumenians, under the name of Kolinda, supposed to be derived from Kolinda, or Lada, goddess of peace.* Amongst the parts enacted in these games, are those of Judas, who stands at the door and receives the money collected, and that of the bull, called Turka or Tur,† a sort of vague monster fantastically dressed up, half bull, half bear, with a clattering wooden bill, and a dash of Herod about his character, in so far as he is supposed to devour little children, and requires to be propitiated by a copper coin thrust into his bill.‡ In many districts the personating of these characters is supposed to entail a certain amount of odium upon the actors, who are regarded as unclean or bewitched by the devil during a period of six weeks, and may not enter a church nor approach a sacrament till this time has elapsed.

A leaf of evergreen laid into a plate of water on the last day of the year when the bells are ringing will denote health, sickness, or death, during the coming year, according as it is found to be green, spotted, or black on the following morning.

The girl whose thoughts are turned towards love and matrimony has many approved methods of testing her fate on this night.

First of all she may, by cracking the joints of her fingers, accurately ascertain the number of her admirers, also a freshly laid egg broken into a glass of water will give much clue to the events in store for her by the shape it adopts. To form a conjecture as to the shape and build of her future husband, she is recommended to throw an armful of

---

* The Council of Constantinople, 869 A.D., forbade the members of the Oriental Church to keep the feast of the Pagan goddess, Kolinda, occurring on the shortest day.

† Called Turon by the Poles, who have many similar games.

‡ This detail would seem to bear some resemblance to Saturn devouring his children, and being cheated by stones thrown into his jaws.

firewood as far as she can from her; the piece which has gone furthest will be the image of her intended, according as the stick happens to be tall or short, broad or slender, straight or crooked. If these general indications do not suffice, and she wishes to see the reflection of his face in the water, she has only to step naked at midnight into the nearest lake or river. Very efficacious is it likewise to stand at midnight on the dunghill with a piece of Christmas cake in her mouth, and listen for the first sound of a dog's barking which reaches her ear. From whichever side it proceeds will also come the expected suitor.

Of the household animals, the sheep is the most highly prized by the Roumenian, who makes of it his companion, and frequently his counsellor, and by its bearing it is supposed often to give warning when danger is near.

The swallow is here, as elsewhere, a luck-bringing bird, and goes by the name of *galinele lui Dieu* (fowls of the Lord). There is always a treasure to be found near the place where the first swallow has been espied.

The crow, on the contrary, is a bird of evil omen, and is particularly ominous when it flies straight over the head of any man.*

The magpie perched upon a roof gives notice of the approach of guests,† but a shrieking magpie meeting or accompanying a traveller denotes death.

The cuckoo is an oracle to be consulted in manifold contingencies. This bird plays a great part in Roumenian poetry, and is frequently supposed to be the spirit of an unfortunate lover.

It is never permissible to kill a spider, as that would entail misfortune.

A toad taking up its residence in a cow-byre is assuredly in the service of a witch, and has been sent there to purloin the milk. It should therefore be stoned to death; but the same liberty must not be taken with the equally pernicious weasel, and if these animals be found to inhabit a barn or stable, the peasant must endeavour to render them harmless by diverting their thoughts into a safer channel. To this end a tiny threshing-flail must be prepared for the male weasel, and a distaff for his female partner, and laid at a place the animals are known to frequent.

* Likewise in Bavaria.

† Also believed by most Slav nations.

The skull of a horse placed over the gate of the courtyard,* or the bones of fallen animals, buried under the doorstep, are preservatives against ghosts.

The place where a horse has rolled on the ground is unwholesome, and the man who steps upon it will be speedily attacked by eruptions, boils, or other skin diseases.

Black fowls are always viewed with suspicion, as possibly standing in the service of a witch, and the Brahmaputra fowl is curiously enough considered to be the offspring of the devil with a Jewish girl.

If a cow has gone astray it will assuredly be eaten by the wolf, unless the owner remembers to stick a pair of scissors in the centre rafter of the dwelling-room.

As a matter of course, such places as churchyards, gallow-trees, and cross-roads are to be avoided, but even the left bank of a river may under circumstances become equally dangerous.

A whirlwind always denotes that the devil is dancing with a witch, and whoever approaches too near to this dangerous circle, may be carried off bodily, or at the very least will lose his head-covering.

But the Roumenian does not always endeavour to keep the evil one at arm's length; sometimes, on the contrary, he invokes the devil's assistance, and enters into a regular compact with him.

Supposing, for instance, that he wishes to ensure a flock, garden or field against thieves, wild beasts, or bad weather, the matter is very simple. He has only to repair to a cross-road, at the junction of which he takes up his stand, in the centre of a circle he has traced on the ground. Here, after depositing a copper coin as payment, he summons the demon with the following words: –

'Satan, I give thee over my flock (garden or field) to keep till – (such and such a term), that thou mayest defend and protect it for me, and be my servant till this time has expired—'

He must, however, be careful to keep within the circle he has traced, until the devil, who may very likely have chosen to appear in the shape of a goat, crow, toad, or serpent, has completely disappeared, otherwise the unfortunate wretch is irretrievably lost. He is equally sure to lose his soul if he die before the time of the contract has elapsed.

An apothecary of this town (Hermanstadt) told me that he was

* The original signification of this seems to have gone astray, but was probably based on former worship of the horse, long regarded as a sacred animal by Indians, Parsees, Arabs, and Germans.

Castle Dracula Panoramic view from the top of Poenari Fortress.

(Left) 'Then the mountains seemed to come nearer to us on each side and to frown down upon us; we were entering the Borgo Pass'. This is a view of the spectacular Bicaz Gorge, about eighty miles south-east of the Borgo Pass.

(Below) 'Straight in front of us and not far off – in fact so near that I wondered we had not noticed it before – came a group of mounted men hurrying along. In the midst of them was a cart, a long leiter-waggon, which swept from side to side, like a dog's tail wagging, with each stern inequality of the road'. This is a leiter-waggon, of the kind upon which Dracula, in his box of earth, is carried to his doom in the novel's climax.

frequently applied to for a magic potion called *spiridusch*, which is said to have the property of disclosing hidden treasures to its lucky possessor. Only a few weeks ago he received the following letter, published in one of the local papers, and which I have here translated as literally as possible.

> Worthy Sir, – I wish to ask you of something I have been told by others – that is, that you have got for sale a thing they call *spiridusch*, but which, to speak more plainly, is the devil himself. And if this be true, I beg you to tell me if it be really true, and how much it costs; for my poverty is so great and has brought me so far that I must ask the devil to help me. Those who told me this were weak, silly fellows, and were afraid, but I have no fear and have seen many things in my life before; therefore I beg you to write me this, and to take the greeting of an unknown man.–N. N.

Here, as elsewhere, thirteen is an ominous number.

It is unfortunate to meet an old woman or a Roumenian Pope; the meeting of a Protestant or Catholic clergyman is indifferent, and brings neither good nor evil.

It is bad luck if your path be traversed by a hare, but a fox or wolf crossing your road is a good omen.

Likewise, it is lucky to meet a woman with a jug full of water, while an empty jug is unlucky; therefore, the Roumenian maiden who meets you on the way back from the well will, smiling, display her brimming pitcher as she passes, with a pleased consciousness of bringing good luck; while the girl whose pitcher is empty will slink past shamefacedly, as though she had a crime to conceal.

Every orthodox Roumenian woman is careful to do homage to the water-spirit, the *wodna zena* or *zona*, which resides in each spring, by spilling a few drops on the ground, after she has emptied her jug. She will never venture to draw the water against the current, for that would strike the spirit home and provoke her anger.

The Roumenian in general avoids the neighbourhood of deep pools of water, especially whirlpools, for here resides the dreadful *balaur*, or the *wodna muz*, the cruel waterman who lies in wait for human victims.

Each forest has likewise its own particular spirit, its *mama padura*,* or forest mother. This fairy is in general supposed to be

---

* So in India the Matris, also known amongst the Egyptians, Chaldeans, and Mexicans. A corresponding spirit is likewise found in the Scandinavian and Lithuanian mythologies; in the latter under the name of *medziajna*.

good-natured, especially towards children who have lost their way in the wood. Less to be trusted is *Panusch* (surely a corruption of the Greek god Pan?), who haunts the forest glades and lies in wait for helpless maidens.

Ravaging diseases, like the pest, cholera, &c, are attributed to a spirit called the *dschuma*, to whom is sometimes given the shape of a fierce virgin, sometimes that of a toothless old hag. This spectre can only be driven away if a red shirt, which must be spun, woven, and sewed all in one night by seven old women, is hung out at the entrance of the afflicted village.*

The body of a drowned man can only be found again by sticking a lighted candle into a hollowed-out loaf of bread and setting it afloat at night on the river or lake. There where the light comes to a standstill will the corpse be found. Until this has been done the water will continue to rise and the rain to fall.

At the birth of a child each one present takes a stone, and throws it behind him, saying, 'This into the jaws of the Strigoi,' which custom would also seem to suggest Saturn and the swaddled-up stones. As long as the child is unbaptised, it must be carefully watched over, for fear of being changed or otherwise harmed by a witch. A piece of iron or a broom laid under its pillow will keep the evil charms away.

Even the Roumenian's wedding day is darkened by the shade of superstition. He can never be quite sure of his affection for his bride being a natural, spontaneous feeling, since it may or will have been caused by the evil influence of a witch. Also at church, when the priest offers the blest bread to himself and his new-made wife, he will tremblingly compare the relative sizes of the two pieces, for whoever chances to get the smaller one must inevitably be the first to die.

But nowhere does the inherent superstition of the Roumenian peasant find stronger expression than in his mourning and funeral ceremonies, which are based upon a totally original conception of death.

Among the various omens of approaching death are the ungrounded barking of a dog or the crowing of a black hen. The influence of the latter may, however, by annulled and the catastrophe averted if the bird be put in a sack and carried thrice round the house.

Roots dug up from the churchyard on Good Friday are to be given

* Also practised in Poland.

to people in danger of death. If, however, this and other remedies fail to save the doomed man, then he must have a burning candle put into his hand; for it is considered to be the greatest of all misfortunes if a man die without a candle – a favour the Roumenian durst not refuse to his most deadly enemy.

The corpse must be washed immediately after death, and the dirt, if necessary, scraped off with knives, because the dead man is more likely to find favour with God if he appear before Him in a clean state. Then he is attired in his best clothes, in doing which great care must be taken not to tie anything in a knot, for that would disturb his rest; likewise, he must not be allowed to carry away any particle of iron about his dress (such as buttons, boot nails, &c), for this would assuredly prevent him from reaching Paradise, the road to which is long, and is, moreover, divided off by several tolls or ferries. To enable the soul to pass through these a piece of money must be laid in the hand, under the pillow, or beneath the tongue of the corpse. In the neighbourhood of Fogaras, where the ferries or toll-bars are supposed to amount to twenty-five, the hair of the defunct is divided into as many plaits, and a piece of money secured in each. Likewise, a small provision of needles, pins, thread, &c are put into the coffin to enable the pilgrim to repair any damage his clothes may receive on the way.

The mourning songs, called *Bocete*, usually performed by paid mourners, are directly addressed to the corpse and sung into his ear on either side. This is the last attempt made by the survivors to wake the dead man to life, by reminding him of all he is leaving, and urging him to make a final effort to arouse his dormant faculties – the thought which underlies all these proceedings being, that the dead man hears and sees all that goes on around him, and that it only requires the determined effort of a strong will in order to restore elasticity to the stiffened limbs, and cause the torpid blood to flow again within the veins.

In many places two openings, corresponding to the ears of the deceased, are cut out in the wood of the coffin to enable him to hear the songs of mourning which are sung on either side of him as he is carried to the grave.

This singing into the ears has passed into a proverb, and when the Roumenian says, *i-a-cantat la wechia* (he has sung into his ears), it is tantamount to saying that prayer and admonition have been used in vain.

The *Pomana*, or funeral feast, is invariably held after the funeral, for much of the peace of the defunct depends upon the strict observance of this ceremony. At this banquet all the favourite dishes of the dead man are served, and each guest receives a cake (*colac*) and a jug (*ulcior*), also a wax candle, in his memory. Similar *Pomanas* are repeated after a fortnight, six weeks, and on each anniversary for the next seven years; also, whenever the defunct has appeared in dream to any member of the family, this likewise calls for another *Pomana*; and when these conditions are not exactly complied with, the soul thus neglected is apt to wander complaining about the earth, and cannot find rest. These restless spirits, called *Strigoi*, are not malicious, but their appearance bodes no good, and may be regarded as omens of sickness or misfortune.

More decidedly evil, however, is the vampire, or *nosferatu*, in whom every Roumenian peasant believes as firmly as he does in heaven or hell. There are two sorts of vampires – living and dead. The living vampire is in general the illegitimate offspring of two illegitimate persons, but even a flawless pedigree will not ensure anyone against the intrusion of a vampire into his family vault, since every person killed by a *nosferatu* becomes likewise a vampire after death, and will continue to suck the blood of other innocent people till the spirit has been exorcised, either by opening the grave of the person suspected and driving a stake through the corpse, or firing a pistol shot into the coffin. In very obstinate cases it is further recommended to cut off the head and replace it in the coffin with the mouth filled with garlic, or to extract the heart and burn it, strewing the ashes over the grave.

That such remedies are often resorted to, even in our enlightened days, is a well-attested fact, and there are probably few Roumenian villages where such has not taken place within the memory of the inhabitants.

First cousin to the vampire, the long exploded were-wolf of the Germans is here to be found, lingering yet under the name of the *Prikolitsch*. Sometimes it is a dog instead of a wolf, whose form a man has taken either voluntarily or as penance for his sins. In one of the villages a story is still told (and believed) of such a man, who driving home from church on Sunday with his wife, suddenly felt that the time for his transformation had come. He therefore gave over the reins to her, and stepped aside into the bushes, where, murmuring the mystic formula, he turned three somersaults over a ditch. Soon after this the woman, waiting in vain for her husband, was attacked by a furious dog, which rushed, barking, out of the bushes and succeeded in biting her severely, as well as tearing her dress. When, an hour later, this woman reached home alone she was met by her husband, who advanced smiling to meet her, but between his teeth she caught sight of the shreds of her dress which had been bitten out by the dog, and the horror of the discovery caused her to faint away.

Another man used gravely to assert that for more than five years he had gone about in the form of a wolf, leading on a troop of these animals, until a hunter, in striking off his head, restored him to his natural shape.

A French traveller relates an instance of a harmless botanist who, while collecting herbs on a hillside in a crouching attitude, was observed by some peasants at a distance and taken for a wolf. Before they had time to reach him, however, he had risen to his feet and disclosed himself in the form of a man; but this, in the minds of the Roumenians, who now regarded him as an aggravated case of wolf, was but additional motive for attacking him. They were quite sure that he must be a Prikolitsch, for only such could change his shape in such an unaccountable manner, and in another minute they were all in full cry after the wretched victim of science, who might have fared badly indeed, had he not happened to gain a carriage on the high road before his pursuers came up.

We do not require to go far for the explanation of the extraordinary tenacity of life of the were-wolf legend in a country like Transylvania, where real wolves still abound. Every winter here brings fresh proof of the boldness and cunning of these terrible animals, whose attacks on flocks and farms are often conducted with a skill which would do honour to a human intellect. Sometimes a whole village is kept in trepidation for weeks together by some particularly audacious leader of a flock of wolves, to whom the peasants not unnaturally attribute a more than animal nature, and one may safely prophesy that so long as the real wolf continues to haunt the Transylvanian forests, so long will his spectre brother survive in the minds of the inhabitants.

Many ancient Roumenian legends tell us that every new church or otherwise important building became a human grave, as it was thought indispensable to its stability to wall in a living man or woman, whose spirit henceforward haunts the place. In later times people having become less cruel, or more probably, because murder is now attended with greater inconvenience to the actors, this custom underwent some modifications, and it became usual in place of a living man to wall in his shadow instead. This is done by measuring the shadow of a person with a long piece of cord, or a ribbon made of strips of reed, and interring this measure instead of the person himself, who, unconscious victim of the spell thrown upon him, will pine away and die within forty days. It is an indispensable condition to the success of this proceeding that the chosen victim be ignorant of the part he is playing, therefore careless passers-by near a building place may often hear the warning cry 'Beware, lest they take thy shadow!' So deeply engrained is this superstition that not long ago there were still professional shadow-traders, who made it their business to provide architects with the necessary victims for securing their walls. 'Of course the man whose shadow is thus interred must die,' argues the Roumenian, 'but as he is unaware of his doom he does not feel any pain or anxiety, so it is less cruel than walling in a living man.'

From The Nineteenth Century *(July 1885) pages 128–144.*

CHAPTER EIGHT

'The World's Beautiful Woman'
(A Magyar Folk-Tale)

Translated by Rev W. Henry Jones and Lewis L. Kropf

The Folk-Tales of the Magyars, published in 1889, is dedicated to Professor Arminius Vambéry, the celebrated Hungarian linguist, scholar and traveller. Vambéry plays a vital yet disputed role in *Dracula*. Vital, because in the novel Van Helsing turns to 'my friend Arminius, of Buda-Pesth University' for all the background information he can throw on Dracula. Disputed, because it has been widely assumed that fact mirrored fiction, that the real-life Vambéry aided Stoker by shedding light on the real-life Dracula. The two men were acquainted, this much is clear from Stoker's *Personal Reminiscences of Henry Irving*. However, the fact that Vambéry never wrote about Vlad Dracula, and that all the information in the novel about Dracula and Transylvania can be traced to Stoker's named sources, discourages too much support for Vambéry's supposedly signal role in the origins of *Dracula*. Besides, the picture of Dracula attributed to Arminius by Van Helsing bears no resemblance to the known characteristics of the Impaler.

In his introduction to these Magyar folk-tales the Reverend Jones provides the most detailed written discussion available to Bram Stoker on the origins of the Székler people. The views of Arminius Vambéry feature prominently in this discussion. Jones also admits that in compiling and translating these tales he is not claiming to be presenting us with an insight into a totally alien culture. There is nothing particularly 'Magyaric' about his anthology, for the same themes can be found with only local variations in many human communities. All folk-tales are moralistic and blood-thirsty. Handsome princes are forever falling in love with angelic beauties. The stories necessarily divide the world up into good and evil. Good always wins.

Essentially, Magyaric folk-tales revolve around giants, fairies and witches. The giants live in castles upon lofty mountain crags.

Rumour has it that to this day 36 ruined battlements can still be found in Széklerland alone. So Stoker did not have to invent a castle for his demon: he was given plenty to choose from. These giants live to an interminable age, possess great physical strength, have buried vast stores of treasure, and have recourse to magical insight when necessary. This insight prevents any stranger from remaining undetected should he venture into the giant's domain. Legend insists that giants can only be killed with special weapons, such as a bullet that is fired at the first appearance of the new moon. Their downfall is usually attributable to the daring of a young knight, or other enterprising hero.

The Magyar fairies inhabit caves and caverns hidden deep under the castles of the giants, and come in every conceivable guise. The witches, likewise, appear in many forms. They have the power of transmutation into frogs or black cats. They are powerless at crossroads. In time of plague they will be dug up from their supposed resting places and turned face downwards. If this fails to stem the fatal tide their hearts will be cut out, divided into four, and each quarter ceremonially burnt. We learn that babies born with teeth or with any supernumerary – extra toe, nipple, or whatever – are automatically taken to be the offspring of witches. Sometimes these witches assume the form of roadside wanderers or grave dwellers, and should they touch or kiss a child the infant's doom is cast. Among the array of Catholic precautions against witches was the habit of some old women of not swallowing the consecrated wafer at communion, preferring to wrap it in a handkerchief and keep it in a drawer at home.

Of course, Bram Stoker was deeply immersed in folklore. He had published a collection of his own tales *Under the Sunset* in 1881, many of which dealt with similar motifs as those found in the Magyar tales. But *Dracula*, too, can be interpreted as a fairy tale on an epic scale. This is evident in humble Jonathan Harker's fateful confrontation with evil and his eventual slaying of his tormentor. In the process he acquires a fortune beyond his dreams and his fairy-princess wife gives birth to a divine child whose purpose is to usher in the light of the twentieth century.

The Magyar folk-tale here presented is 'The World's Beautiful Woman'. The similarity with the Sleeping Beauty is immediately obvious, and not just for the 'mirror mirror on the wall' passages. The image that death enhances beauty is emphasised both here and in *Dracula*. Is she dead, or merely sleeping or in trance? There is no dissolution or smell of death. Indeed, in this Magyar tale the victim is not really dead at all, but the victim of apparent death brought upon by the wiles of a wicked witch. She can therefore be saved by the hand that loves her.

✳

The World's Beautiful Woman

In the most beautiful land of Asia, where Adam and Eve may have lived, where all animals, including cows, live wild, where the corn grows wild, and even bread grows on trees, there lived a pretty girl, whose palace was built on a low hill, which looked over a pretty, a very pretty valley, from which one could see the whole world. In the same country there lived a young king who decided not to get married till he succeeded in finding the prettiest woman or girl in the world. The pretty maid lived with her old father, and with only two servant girls. The young king lived and enjoyed himself amongst the finest young aristocrats. One day it struck the young king that it would be a good thing to get married; so he instructed his aristocratic friends to go all over his vast realm, and to search about till they found the prettiest girl in the land: they had not to trouble whether she was poor or rich; but she must be the prettiest. Each of them was to remain in the town where he found the girl that he deemed was the prettiest and to write and let the king know, so that he might go and have a look at all of them and choose for himself the prettiest amongst all the beauties, the one he liked best. After a year he received letters from every one of his seventy-seven friends, and extraordinarily all the seventy-seven letters arrived from the same town, where, on a low hill above a pretty little valley; there stood a golden palace, in which there lived a young lady with a nice old man and two maids, and from the four windows of which palace the whole world could be seen. The young king started with a large retinue of wedding guests to the place where the prettiest girl in the world lived: he found there all his seventy-seven friends, who were all fever-stricken with love, and were lying about on the pavement of the palace, on hay which was of a very fine silk-like grass; there they lay every one of them. The moment the young king saw the beautiful girl he cried: 'The Lord has created you expressly for me; you are mine and I am yours! and it is my wish to find my rest in the same grave with you.'

The young lady also fell very much in love with the handsome king; in her fond passion she could not utter a word, but only took him round his slender waist* and led him to her father. Her old father wept tears of joy, that at last a man was found whom his daughter could love, as she had thought every man ugly hitherto. The ceremony of betrothal and wedding was very short; at his pretty wife's wish, the king came to live on the beautiful spot, than which there was not a prettier one in the whole world! By the side of the palace there was an earth-hut, in which lived an old witch who knew all the young lady's secrets, and who helped her with advice whenever she needed it. The old witch praised the young lady's beauty to all she met, and it was she who had gathered the seventy-seven young aristocrats into the palace. On the evening of the wedding she called upon 'the world's beautiful lady' and praised the young king to her, his handsomeness and riches, and after she had praised him for an hour or two she sighed heavily: the pretty young lady asked her what troubled her, as she had this very moment spoken of her husband as being a handsome, rich, and worthy man? 'Because, my pretty lady, my beautiful queen, if you two live sometime here, you will not long be the prettiest woman in the world; you are very pretty now, and your husband is the handsomest of all men; but should a daughter be born to you, she will be more beautiful than you; she will be more beautiful than the morning star – this is the reason of my sadness, my beautiful lady.' 'You are quite right, good old woman, I will follow any advice; if you tell me what to do, I will obey you. I will do anything to remain the most beautiful woman in the world.' This was what the old witch said to the beautiful lady: 'I will give you a handful of cotton wool; when your husband sleeps with you, put this wool on your lips, but be careful not to make it wet, because there will be poison on it. When your husband arrives at home all in perspiration from the dance, he will come to you and kiss you, and die a sudden death.' The young lady did as the witch told her, and the young king was found dead next morning; but the poison was of such a nature that the physicians were not able to find out what the king had died of.

The bride was left a widow, and again went to live with her maid and her old father, and made a solemn vow that she would never marry again. And she kept her word. As it happened, however, by some inexplicable circumstance, or by some miracle, after a few

* The great pride of the Hungarian youth is to have a slender waist.

months she discovered that she was with child; so she ran to the old witch and asked her what to do. The witch gave her a looking-glass and the following advice: 'Every morning you have to ask this mirror whether there is a more beautiful woman than yourself in existence, and if it says that there is not, there really won't be one for a long time, and your mind may be at ease; but should it say that there is one, there will be one, and I will see to that myself.' The beautiful lady snatched the mirror from the witch in great joy, and as soon as she reached her dressing-room she placed the little mirror on the window ledge and questioned it thus: 'Well, my dear little mirror, is there a more beautiful woman in the world than I?' The mirror replied: 'Not yet, but there will be one soon, who will be twice as handsome as you.' The beautiful woman nearly lost her wits in her sorrow, and informed the witch what the mirror had replied. 'No matter,' said the old hag, 'let her be born, and we shall soon put her out of the way.'

The beautiful lady was confined, and a pretty little daughter was born, and it would have been a sin to look at her with an evil eye. . . .

She spared her daughter till she was thirteen: the little girl grew more beautiful every day, so that the woman could not bear her daughter's beauty any longer, and handed her to the old witch to be killed. The witch was only too glad to avail herself of the opportunity, and took her into a vast forest, where she tied the girl's hands together with a wisp of straw, placed a wreath of straw on her head, and a girdle of straw round her waist, so that by lighting them she would burn to death the most beautiful masterpiece of the Lord. But all of a sudden a loud shouting was heard in the forest, and twelve robbers came running as swift as birds towards the place where the old witch and the pretty girl were standing. One of the robbers seized the girl, another knocked the old witch on the head, and gave her a sound beating. The witch shammed death, and the robbers left the wicked old wretch behind, carrying off the pretty girl (who had fainted in her fright) with them. After half an hour the old witch got up, and rushed to the castle where the beautiful woman lived, and said, 'Well, my queen, don't question your mirror any more, for you are now the most beautiful creature in the world, your beautiful daughter lies under ground.' The beautiful lady jumped for joy, and kissed the ugly old witch.

The pretty girl upon her recovery found herself in a nice little house, in a clean bed, and guarded by twelve men, who praised her beauty in whispers, which was such as no human eye had seen before. The innocent little thing, not thinking of any harm, looked at the men with their great beards, who stared at her with wide open eyes. She got up from her soft bed, and thanked the good men for having delivered her from the clutches of the awful old witch, and then inquired where she was, and what they intended to do with her; if they meant to kill her, she begged them do it at once, as she would die with pleasure, and was only afraid of being killed by that horrible old witch, who was going to burn her to death. None of the robbers could utter a word, their hearts were so softened by her sweet words: such words as they had never before heard from human lips, and her innocent look which would have tamed even a wild bull. At last one of the robbers, who was splendidly dressed, said:

'You pretty creature of the Lord, you are in the midst of twelve robbers, who are men of good hearts, but bad morals; we saved you from the hands of the ugly old witch whom I knocked down, and killed I believe; we would not kill you, for the whole world; but, on the contrary, would fight the whole world for you! Be the ornament of our house and the feast of our eyes! Whatsoever your eyes or your mouth may desire, be it wherever man exists, we will bring it to you! be our daughter, and we will be everything to you! your fathers! brothers! guardians! and, if you need it, your soldiers!'

The little girl smiled, and was very pleased: she found more happiness among the robbers than she ever did in her mother's palace; she shook hands with all, commended herself to their protection, and at once looked after the cooking. The chief of the robbers called three strong maidens, dressed in white, from a cave, and ordered them to carry out without delay the orders of their queen, and if he heard one word of complaint against any of them, they should die the death of a pig. The young girl spoke kindly to the three maids, and called them her companions.

The robbers then went out on to the highway in great joy – to continue their plundering – singing and whistling with delight, because their home and their band had the most beautiful queen in the world. The beautiful woman, the girl's mother, one day felt weary, and listless, because she had not heard any one praise her beauty for a very long time. So in her ennui she took her mirror and said to it: 'My dear, sweet little mirror, is there a more beautiful creature in all the world, than I?' The little mirror replied, 'You are very beautiful, but your daughter is a thousand times handsomer!'. . .

Upon this she called the old witch all kinds of bad names in her rage, and threatened her that if she did not kill her daughter outright she would betray her to the world, and accuse her of having led her to all her evil deeds; that it was she who induced her to kill her handsome husband, and that she had given her the mysterious mirror, which was the cause of her not being able to die in peace. The old hag made no reply, but went off in a boisterous manner: she transformed herself into a pretty girl and went straight into the house in which the young lady was dressing herself and falsely told her that she had been engaged by the robbers to wait always upon her while she dressed, because she had already been killed twice, once by a gipsy woman, and another time by a Jewess; and also that the robbers had ordered her not to do anything else but to help her in her toilet. The innocent girl believed all that the she-devil said. She allowed her to undo her hair and to comb it. The witch did her hair in accordance with the latest fashion, and plaited it and fastened it with all sorts of hair pins; while doing so she hid a hair-pin which she had brought with her among the girl's hair, so that it could not be noticed by anyone; having finished, the new lady's maid asked permission to leave her mistress for a moment, but never returned, and her young lady died, while all wept and sobbed most bitterly. . . .

Her mother was really delighted this time, because she kept on questioning the mirror for three or four days and it always replied to her heart's content. The robbers wailed and cried, and did not even enjoy their food; one of them proposed that they should not bury the girl, but that they should come to pray by the side of their dear dead; others again thought that it would be a pity to confide the pretty body to the earth, where it would be destroyed; others spoke of the terrible pang, and said that their hearts would break if they had to look at her dead beauty for any length of time. So they ordered a splendid coffin to be made of wrought gold. They wrapped her in purple and fine linen; they caught an elk and placed the coffin between its antlers, so that the precious body might not decompose underground: the elk quietly carried the precious coffin about, and took the utmost care to prevent it falling from its antlers or its back. This elk happened to graze in Persia just as the son of the Persian king was out hunting all alone. The prince was twenty-three years old; he noticed the elk and also the splendid coffin between its antlers, whereupon he took a pound of sugar from his bag and gave it to the elk to eat. Taking the coffin from its back the Persian king's son opened the gold coffin with fear and trembling, when, unfolding the fine linen, he discovered a corpse, the like of which he had never seen before, not even in his dreams.

He began to shake it to wake her: to kiss her, and at last went down upon his knees by her side to pray to God fervently to restore her to life, but still she didn't move. 'I will take her with me into my room,' he said, sobbing. 'Although it is a corpse that must have been dead for some time, there is no smell. The girl is prettier in her death than all the girls of Persia alive.' It was late at night when the prince got home, carrying the gold coffin under his cloak. He bewailed the dead girl for a long time and then went to supper. The king looked anxiously into his son's eyes, but did not dare to question him as to the cause of his grief. Every night the prince locked himself up, and did not go to sleep until he had, for a long time, bemoaned his dead sweetheart; and whenever he awoke in the night he wept again.

The prince had three sisters, and they were very good girls, and very fond of their brother. They watched him every night through the keyhole, but could see nothing. They heard, however, their brother's sobbing and were very much grieved by it. The Persian king had war declared against him by the king of the neighbouring country. The king, being very advanced in age, asked his son to go in his place to fight the enemy. The good son promised this willingly, although he was tortured by the thought of being obliged to leave his beautiful dead girl behind. As, however, he was aware that he would again be able to see and weep over his dear one when once the war was over, he locked himself in his room for two hours, weeping all the time, and kissing his sweetheart. Having finished, he locked his room and put the key in his sabretache.

The good-hearted princesses impatiently waited till their brother crossed the border with his army, and so soon as they knew that he had left the country they went to the locksmith of the castle and took away every key he had, and with these tried to unlock their brother's room, till at last one of the keys did fit. They ordered every servant away from the floor on which the room was situated and all three entered. They looked all round, and in all the cupboards, and even took the bed to pieces, and as they were taking out the planks of the bed they suddenly discovered the glittering gold coffin, and in all haste placed it on the table, and having opened it found the sleeping angel. All three kissed her; but when they saw that they were unable to restore life, they wept most bitterly. They rubbed her and held balsam under her nose, but without avail. Then they examined her dress, which was very far superior to their own. They moved her rings and breast-pins, and dressed her up like a pretty doll. The youngest princess brought combs and perfumed hair-oils in order to do the hair of the dear dead. They pulled out the hair-pins and arranged them in nice order, so as to be able to replace them as before. They parted her golden hair, and began to comb it, adorning each lock with a hair-pin. As they were combing the hair at the nape of the neck the comb stuck fast, so they looked at once for the cause of it, when they saw that a golden hair-pin was entangled in the hair, which the eldest princess moved with the greatest care. Whereupon the beautiful girl opened her eyes and her lips formed themselves into a smile; and, as if awakening from a long, long dream, she slightly stretched herself, and stepped from the coffin.

The girls were not afraid at all, as she, who was so beautiful in her death, was still more beautiful in life. The youngest girl ran to the old king and told him what they had done, and that they had found out the cause of their brother's grief, and how happy they were now. The old king wept for joy and hastened after his daughter, and on seeing the beautiful child exclaimed: 'You shall be my son's wife, the mother of my grandchildren!' And thereupon he embraced and kissed her, and took her into his room with his daughters. He sent for singing birds so that they might amuse his dear little new daughter. The old king inquired how she made his son's acquaintance and where she first met him. But the pretty princess knew nothing about it, but simply told him what she knew, namely, that she had two enemies who sooner or later would kill and destroy her; and she also told him that she had been living among robbers, to whom she had been handed over by an old witch who would always persecute her till the last moment of her life. . . .

The moment the prince arrived home in triumph, he jumped off his horse, and, not even taking time to greet his father, he unlocked his room and began to sob most violently, dragging out the coffin gently from under the bed, placing it on the bed with great care, and then opening the lid with tears; but he could only find a hair-pin. He rushed out of the room like a madman, leaving the coffin and the door open, crying aloud, and demanding what sacrilegious hand had robbed his angel from him. But his angel, over whom he had shed so many tears, stood smiling before him. The youth seized her and covered her with as many kisses as there was room for. He took his betrothed, whom Providence had given to him, to his father and told him how he had found the pretty corpse on the back of an elk; and the girl also told the whole story of her life; and the princesses confessed how they had broken into their brother's room, and how they restored his sweetheart to life again. The old king was intoxicated with joy, and the same day sent for a priest, and a great wedding feast was celebrated. The young folks whom Providence had brought together lived very happily, when one day the young queen, who was as beautiful as a fairy, informed her husband that she was being persecuted, and that while her mother lived she could never have any peace. 'Don't fear, angel of my heart,' said the young king, 'as no human or diabolic power can harm you while you are here. Providence is very kind to us. You seem to be a favourite and will be protected from all evil.' The young queen was of a pious turn of mind and believed the true words of her husband, as he had only spoken out her own thoughts.

About half a year had passed by and the beautiful woman of the world was still happy. Her mirror was covered with dust, as she never dreamt for a moment that her daughter was yet alive; but being one day desirous to repeat her former amusement she dusted her mirror, and, pressing it to her bosom, said: 'Is there a prettier living creature in the world than myself?' The mirror replied: 'You are very pretty, but your daughter is seventy-seven thousand times more beautiful than you.' The beautiful woman, on hearing the mirror's reply, fainted away, and they had to sprinkle cold water over her for two hours before she came round. Off she set, very ill, to the old witch and begged her, by everything that was holy, to save her from that hateful girl, else she would have to go and commit suicide. The old witch cheered her, and promised that she would do all that lay in her power.

After eight months had elapsed the young prince had to go to war again; and, with a heavy heart, took leave of his dear pretty wife, as – if one is obliged to tell it – she was *enceinte*. But the prince had to go, and he went, consoling his wife, who wept bitterly, that he would return soon. The young king left orders that as soon as his wife was confined a confidential messenger was to be sent without delay to

inform him of the event. Soon after his departure two beautiful boys
with golden hair were born and there was great joy in the royal
household. The old king danced about, like a young child, with
delight. The princesses wrapped the babies in purple and silk, and
showed them to everybody as miracles of beauty.

The old king wrote down the joyful news and sent the letter by a
faithful soldier, instructing him that he was not to put up anywhere
under any pretence whatever. The old soldier staked his moustache
not to call anywhere till he reached the young king.

While angels were rejoicing, devils were racking their brains and
planning mischief!

The old witch hid a flask full of spirits under her apron and hurried
off on the same road as the soldier, in order to meet him with his
letter. She pitched a small tent on the road-side using some dirty
sheets she had brought with her, and, placing her flask of spirits in
front of her, waited for the passers-by. She waited long, but no one
came; when all of a sudden a huge cloud gathered in the sky, and the
old witch was delighted. A fearful storm set in. As the rain poured
down, the old witch saw the soldier running to escape the rain. As he
ran past her tent, the wicked old soul shouted to him to come in and
sit down in her tent till the rain was over. The soldier, being afraid of
the thunder, accepted her invitation, and sat musingly in the tent,
when the old woman placed a good dose of spirits in front of him,
which the soldier drank; she gave him another drop, and he drank
that too. Now there was a sleeping-draft in it, and so the soldier fell
fast asleep, *and slept like a fur cloak*. The old woman then looked in his
bag for the letter, and, imitating *the old king's* hand-writing to great
perfection, informed the young prince that a great sorrow had fallen
upon his house, inasmuch as his wife had been delivered of two
puppies. She sealed the letter and woke the soldier, who began to run
again and did not stop until he reached the camp.

The young prince was very much upset by his father's letter, but
wrote in reply that no matter what sort of children his wife had borne
they were not to touch but to treat them as his own children until he
returned. He ordered the messenger to hurry back with his reply, and
not to stop anywhere; but the old soldier could not forget the
good glass of spirits he had, and so went into the tent again and had
some more. The witch again mixed it with a sleeping-draught and
searched the bag while the soldier slept. She stole the letter, and,
imitating the young prince's hand-writing, wrote back to the old

king that he was to have his wife and the young babes killed, because he held a woman who had puppies must be a bad person. The old king was very much surprised at his son's reply but said nothing to anyone. At night he secretly called the old soldier to him and had his daughter-in-law placed in a black carriage. The old soldier sat on the box and had orders to take the woman and her two children into the middle of the forest and brain them there. The carriage stopped in the middle of the forest, the old soldier got down and opened the door, weeping bitterly. He pulled out a big stick from under his seat and requested the young queen to alight. She obeyed his orders and descended holding her babes in her arms.

The old soldier tried three times to raise the stick, but could not do so; he was too much overcome by grief. The young queen implored him not to kill her, and told him she was willing to go away and never see anyone again. The old soldier let her go, and she took her two babes and sheltered in a hollow tree in the forest: there she passed her time living on roots and wild fruit.

The soldier returned home, and was questioned by the old king as to whether he had killed the young queen, as he didn't like to disappoint his son, who was to return from the camp next day. The old soldier declared on his oath that he had killed her and her babes too, and that he had thrown their bodies into the water. The young king arrived at home in great sorrow, and was afraid to catch sight of his unfortunate wife and her ugly babes.

The old king had left his son's letter upon his desk by mistake; the prince picked it up, and was enraged at its contents: 'This looks very like my writing,' he said, 'but I did not write it; it must be the work of some devil.' He then produced his father's letter from his pocket, and handed it to him. The old king was horrified at the awful lie which some devil had written in his hand. 'No, my dear son,' said the old father, weeping, 'this is not what I wrote to you; what I really did write was, that two sons with golden hair had been born to you.' 'And I,' replied the young king, 'said that whatsoever my wife's offspring was, no harm was to happen to them till I returned. Where is my wife? Where are my golden-haired children?' 'My son,' said the old king, 'I have carried out your orders; I sent them to the wood and had them killed, and the corporal belonging to the royal household had their bodies cast into the water.' The old soldier listened, through a crack in the door, to the conversation of the two kings, who both wept bitterly. He entered the room without being summoned, and said: 'I could not carry out your orders, my lord and king; I had not the heart to destroy the most beautiful creature in the world; so I let her go free in the forest, and she left, weeping. If they have not been devoured by wild beasts, they are alive still.'

The young king never touched a bit of supper, but had his horse saddled at once, and order his whole body-guard out. For three days and three nights they searched the wood in every direction without intermission: on the fourth night, at midnight, the young king thought he heard, issuing from a hollow tree, a baby's cry, which seemed as harmonious to him as the song of a nightingale. He sprang off his horse, and found his beautiful wife, who was more beautiful than ever, and his children, who were joyfully prattling in their mother's arms. He took his recovered family home, amidst the joyous strains of the band, and, indeed, a high festival was celebrated throughout the whole realm.

The young woman again expressed her fears with trembling, that, while her mother and that she-devil were alive, she could not live in peace.

The young king issued a warrant for the capture of the old witch; and the old soldier came, leading behind him, tied to a long rope, an awful creature, whose body was covered all over with frightful prickles, and who had an immense horn in the middle of her forehead. The young queen at once recognised her as the old witch, who had been captured in the act of searching the wood in order to find her, and slay her and her two babes. The young queen had the old witch led into a secret room, where she questioned her as to why she had persecuted her all her life.

'Because,' said the old witch, 'I am the daughter of your grandfather, and the sister of your mother! When I was yet but a suckling babe, your grandmother gave orders that I was to be thrown into the water; a devil coming along the road took me and educated me. I humoured your mother's folly because I thought she would go mad in her sorrow that a prettier creature than herself existed; but the Lord has preserved you, and your mother did not go mad till I covered her with small-pox, and her face became all pitted and scarred. Her mirror was always mocking her, and she became a wandering lunatic, roaming about over the face of the land, and the children pelting her with stones. She continually bewails you.'

The young queen informed her husband of all this, and he had the old witch strangled, strung up in a tree, and a fire made of brimstone lighted under her. When her soul (pára-animal soul) left her wicked body, a horse was tied to each of her hands and feet, and her body torn into four, one quarter of her body being sent to each of the points of the compass, so that the other witches might receive a warning as to their fate.

The 'most beautiful woman in the world' was now very ugly, and happened by chance to reach the palace where the pretty queen lived. Her daughter wept over her, and had her kept in a beautiful room, every day showing her through a glass door her beautiful children. The poor lunatic wept and tortured herself till one day she jumped out of the window and broke her neck. The young king loved his beautiful wife as a dove does its mate; he obeyed her slightest wish, and guarded her from every danger.

The two little sons with the golden hair became powerful and valiant heroes, and when the old king died he was carried to his vault by his two golden-haired grandchildren.

The young couple, who had gone through so many sad trials, are alive still, if they have not died since.

Abridged from The Folk-Tales of the Magyars *(1889) pages 163–181.*

CHAPTER NINE

Elizabeth Bathory and Werewolf Folklore

Sabine Baring-Gould

The idea that men and women can somehow turn into wolves prompts the obvious question. Why wolves? Why not bats, frogs, bears or even mice? In fact, according to superstition it is possible to transform into any animal – especially if it be dangerous or associated with magic powers. In the dense forests around the Carpathians it so happened that the greatest threat to life and limb was the wolf. The wolf posed the greatest terrors, therefore it was around the wolf that the myth of the man-wolf arose. Other communities, free from wolves, found something else to worry about. Were-bears, for example.

In the folklore of eastern Europe the vampire and the werewolf are often related. This involves no contradiction for the two disorders are complementary. Werewolfism – or lycanthropy to give it its proper name – is strictly an affliction for the living. Whether the result of undiagnosed mania or diabolical possession, the victim is very much alive at the time of his craving to assume a wolf's appearance. Some traditions speak of full transmutation: the man actually turns into a wolf. Others, less credulous, insist on a purely psychological association: the poor wretch merely behaves like a wolf, usually at the time of full moon. Either way, the curse of lycanthropy in life is widely presumed to lead directly to vampirism in death.

It was Stoker's intention that his demon combine the suave, sinister qualities of the literary vampire with the animalistic attributes prescribed by folklore. When Count Dracula is introduced it is evident to the reader, though not to Jonathan Harker, that he possesses peculiarly wolf-like features. Aside from his prominent canine teeth, Dracula is endowed with pointed ears, broad hands with squat fingers, and hairs in the centre of his palms.

Stoker lifted this description from Sabine Baring-Gould's *The Book of Were-Wolves*, which was among the very earliest works of that prolific author, and his first on a supernatural theme. Baring-Gould, of course, later wrote 'The Meaning of Mourning' which has already featured in the present study. In his introduction to *The Book of Were-Wolves* he states his aim of making it the first of a series, with a sequel on vampires to follow. Regrettably, he never fulfilled his pledge, turning his pen to all and sundry, but never to vampires. Stoker's débt to Baring-Gould nevertheless extends beyond being reminded of the ties between vampirism and lycanthropy. For in *The Book of Were-Wolves* Stoker was confronted with an account of real-life blood-drinking.

It has always struck critics as strange that having stumbled upon Voyvode Dracula, Stoker should then transport him from Wallachia to Transylvania, and change his title to 'Count'. Dracula was neither a Székler nor a Transylvanian nobleman. Bram Stoker makes him both. Why?

Perhaps the reference to Dracula in Wilkinson's *Account of Wallachia* was too fleeting to permit Stoker to draw fine distinctions between the nomenclature of Romanian and Hungarian nobilities. Perhaps the vitality of vampire superstition which he learned from Emily Gerard's 'Transylvanian Superstitions' prompted the switch from Wallachia. Perhaps Count Dracula was an amalgam of two people – combining the diabolism of the original Dracula with the bloody perversions of Elizabeth Bathory – who happened to be both Hungarian and a *Countess*.

Elizabeth Bathory was born in 1560 into one of the most powerful of Hungarian families. She was in her forties and middle age was beckoning when she embarked upon the torture and murder of so many young maidens that she has earned for herself the distinction of being the world's most prolific mass murderess, with over six hundred confirmed victims. It was to procure blood that she perpetrated these crimes, blood that she would drink, bathe in, or apply cosmetically for the intended purpose of regaining her lost youth and beauty. Similarly it is the rejuvenating power of blood that motivates Count Dracula. At the outset he is a tall old man with white hair. With each 'meal' he becomes younger, stronger, and his hair darkens.

More is known today about both Vlad Dracula and Elizabeth Bathory than was the case in Stoker's time. He was aware of the one, but what about the other? Only through knowing of Stoker's familiarity with Baring-Gould's *Book of Were-Wolves* can the question be answered. In the unexpected context of werewolves rather than vampires Baring-Gould relates briefly but in stark detail the grisly habits of Elizabeth —. Stoker would have had little difficulty in ascertaining the surname – assuming he was as interested in the perpetrator as in her crimes.

*

Elizabeth Bathory and Werewolf Folklore

'Elizabeth — was wont to dress well in order to please her husband, and she spent half the day over her toilet. On one occasion, a lady's-maid saw something wrong in her head-dress, and as a recompence for observing it, received such a severe box on the ears that the blood gushed from her nose, and spirted on to her mistress's face. When the blood drops were washed off her face, her skin appeared much more beautiful – whiter and more transparent on the spots where the blood had been.

'Elizabeth formed the resolution to bathe her face and her whole body in human blood so as to enhance her beauty. Two old women and a certain Fitzko assisted her in her undertaking. This monster used to kill the luckless victim, and the old women caught the blood, in which Elizabeth was wont to bathe at the hour of four in the morning. After the bath she appeared more beautiful than before.

'She continued this habit after the death of her husband (1604) in the hopes of gaining new suitors. The unhappy girls who were allured to the castle, under the plea that they were to be taken into service there, were locked up in a cellar. Here they were beaten till their bodies were swollen. Elizabeth not infrequently tortured the victims herself; often she changed their clothes which dripped with blood, and then renewed her cruelties. The swollen bodies were then cut up with razors.

'Occasionally she had the girls burned, and then cut up, but the great majority were beaten to death.

'At last her cruelty became so great, that she would stick needles into those who sat with her in a carriage, especially if they were of her own sex. One of her servant-girls she stripped naked, smeared her with honey, and so drove her out of the house.

'When she was ill, and could not indulge her cruelty, she bit a person who came near her sick bed as though she were a wild beast.

'She caused, in all, the death of 650 girls, some in Tscheita, on the neutral ground, where she had a cellar constructed for the purpose;

others in different localities; for murder and bloodshed became with her a necessity.

'When at last the parents of the lost children could no longer be cajoled, the castle was seized, and the traces of the murders were discovered. Her accomplices were executed, and she was imprisoned for life.' . . .

English folk-lore is singularly barren of were-wolf stories, the reason being that wolves had been extirpated from England under the Anglo-Saxon kings, and therefore ceased to be objects of dread to the people. The traditional belief in were-wolfism must, however, have remained long in the popular mind, though at present it has disappeared, for the word occurs in old ballads and romances. Thus in Kempion–

> O was it *war-wolf* in the wood?
> Or was it mermaid in the sea?
> Or was it man, or vile woman,
> My ain true love, that mis-shaped thee?

. . . In the popular mind the cat or the hare have taken the place of the wolf for witches' transformation, and we hear often of the hags attending the devil's Sabbath in these forms.

In Devonshire they range the moors in the shape of black dogs, and I know a story of two such creatures appearing in an inn and nightly drinking the cider, till the publican shot a silver batton over their heads, when they were instantly transformed into two ill-favoured old ladies of his acquaintance. On Heathfield, near Tavistock, the wild huntsman rides by full moon with his 'wush hounds'; and a white hare which they pursued was once rescued by a goody returning from market, and discovered to be a transformed young lady. . . .

If traditions of werewolves are scanty in England, it is quite the reverse if we cross the water.

In the south of France, it is still believed that fate has destined certain men to be lycanthropists – that they are transformed into wolves at full moon. The desire to run comes upon them at night. They leave their beds, jump out of a window, and plunge into a fountain. After the bath, they come out covered with dense fur, walking on all fours, and commence a raid over fields and meadows, through woods and villages, biting all beasts and human beings that

'The wind suddenly shifted to the north-east, and the remnant of the sea-fog melted in the blast; and then, *mirabile dictu* between the piers, leaping from wave to wave as it rushed at headlong speed, swept the strange schooner before the blast, with all sail set, and gained the safety of the harbour'. Contemporary view of Whitby harbour, where Dracula lands in England.

'The schooner paused not, but rushing across the harbour, pitched herself on that accumulation of sand and gravel washed by many tides and many storms into the south-east corner of the pier jutting under the East Cliff, known locally as Tate Hill Pier'. Site of Dracula's shipwreck, under the East Cliff, Whitby.

(Above) 'Between Whitby Abbey and the town there is another church, the parish one, round which is a big graveyard, all full of tombstones'. This is the scene of Dracula's first encounter with Lucy Westenra.

(Left) 'The steps are a grand feature of the place. They lead from the town up to the church; there are hundreds of them — I do not know how many — and they wind up in a delicate curve'. These are the steps up which Mina races, only to find Lucy's blood drained and Dracula escaped.

come in their way. At the approach of dawn, they return to the spring, plunge into it, lose their furry skins, and regain their deserted beds. Sometimes the loup-garou is said to appear under the form of a white dog, or to be loaded with chains; but there is probably a confusion of ideas between the werewolf and the church-dog, bar-ghest, pad-foit, wush-hound, or by whatever name the animal supposed to haunt a churchyard is designated.

In the Périgord, the were-wolf is called louléerou. Certain men, especially bastards, are obliged at each full moon to transform themselves into these diabolic beasts.

It is always at night that the fit comes on. The lycanthropist dashes out of a window, springs into a well, and, after having struggled in the water for a few moments, rises from it, dripping, and invested with a goatskin which the devil has given him. In this condition, the louléerous run upon four legs, pass the night in ranging over the country, and in biting and devouring all the dogs they meet. At break of day they lay aside their goatskins and return home. Often they are ill in consequence of having eaten tough old hounds, and they vomit up their undigested paws. One great nuisance to them is the fact that they may be wounded or killed in their louléerou state. With the first effusion of blood their diabolic covering vanishes, and they are recognized, to the disgrace of their families.

A werewolf may easily be detected, even when devoid of his skin; for his hands are broad, and his fingers short, and there are always some hairs in the hollow of his hand.

In Normandy, those who are doomed to be loups-garoux, clothe themselves every evening with a skin called their *hère* or *hure*, which is a loan from the devil. When they run in their transformed state, the evil one accompanies them and scourges them at the foot of every cross they pass. The only way in which a werewolf can be liberated from this cruel bondage, is by stabbing him three times in the forehead with a knife. However, some people less addicted to allopathic treatment, consider that three drops of blood drawn by a needle, will be sufficient to procure release.

According to an opinion of the vulgar in the same province, the loup-garou is sometimes a metamorphosis forced upon the body of a damned person, who, after having been tormented in his grave, has torn his way out of it. The first stage in the process consists in his devouring the cerecloth which enveloped his face; then his moans and muffled howls ring from the tomb, through the gloom of night, the earth of the grave begins to heave, and at last, with a scream, surrounded by a phosphorescent glare, and exhaling a foetid odour, he bursts away as a wolf.

In Le Bessin, they attribute to sorcerers the power of metamorphosing certain men into beasts, but the form of a dog is that principally affected by them.

In Norway it is believed that there are persons who can assume the form of a wolf or a bear (*Huse-björn*), and again resume their own; this property is either imparted to them by the Trollmen, or those possessing it are themselves Trolls.

In a hamlet in the midst of a forest, there dwelt a cottager named Lasse, and his wife. One day he went out in the forest to fell a tree, but had forgot to cross himself and say his paternoster, so that some troll or wolf-witch (*varga mor*) obtained power over him and transformed him into a wolf. His wife mourned him for many years, but, one Christmas-eve, there came a beggar-woman, very poor and ragged, to the door, and the good woman of the house took her in, fed her well, and entreated her kindly. At her departure the beggar-woman said that the wife would probably see her husband again, as he was not dead, but was wandering in the forest as a wolf. Towards night-fall the wife went to her pantry to place in it a piece of meat for the morrow, when, on turning to go out, she perceived a wolf standing before her, raising itself with its paws on the pantry steps, regarding her with sorrowful and hungry looks. Seeing this she exclaimed, 'If I were sure that thou wert my own Lasse, I would give thee a bit of meat.' At that instant the wolf-skin fell off, and her husband stood before her in the clothes he wore on the unlucky morning when she had last beheld him.

Finns, Lapps, and Russians are held in particular aversion, because the Swedes believe that they have power to change people into wild beasts. During the last year of the war with Russia, when Calmar was overrun with an unusual number of wolves, it was generally said that the Russians had transformed their Swedish prisoners into wolves, and sent them home to invest the country.

In Denmark the following stories are told:

A man, who from his childhood had been a werewolf, when returning one night with his wife from a merry-making, observed that the hour was at hand when the evil usually came upon him; giving therefore the reins to his wife, he descended from the vehicle, saying to her, 'If anything comes to thee, only strike at it with thine apron.' He then withdrew, but immediately after, the woman, as she was sitting in the vehicle, was attacked by a were-wolf. She did as the man had enjoined her, and struck it with her apron, from which it rived a portion, and then ran away. After some time the man returned, holding in his mouth the rent portion of his wife's apron, on seeing which, she cried out in terror, 'Good Lord, man, why, thou art a were-wolf!' 'Thank thee, wife,' said he, 'now I am free.' And from that time he was no more afflicted.

If a female at midnight stretches between four sticks the membrane which envelopes the foal when it is brought forth, and creeps through it, naked, she will bear children without pain; but all the boys will be were-wolves, and all the girls maras. By day the were-wolf has the human form, though he may be known by the meeting of his eyebrows above the nose. At a certain time of the night he has the form of a dog on three legs. It is only when another person tells him that he is a were-wolf, or reproaches him with being such, that a man can be freed from the ban. . . .

At Caseburg, on the isle of Usedom, a man and his wife were busy in the field making hay, when after some time the woman said to the man that she had no more peace, she could stay no longer, and went away. But she had previously desired her husband to promise, that if perchance a wild beast should come that way, he would cast his hat at it and then run away, and it would do him no injury. She had been gone but a short while, when a wolf came swimming across the Swine, and ran directly towards the haymakers. The man threw his hat at it, which the animal instantly tore to rags. But in the meantime a boy had run up with a pitchfork, and he stabbed the wolf from behind: in the same moment it became changed, and all saw that the boy had killed the man's wife.

Formerly there were individuals in the neighbourhood of Steina, who, by putting on a certain girdle, could transform themselves into were-wolves. A man of the neighbourhood, who had such a girdle, forgot one day when going out to lock it up, as was his wont. During his absence, his little son chanced to find it; he buckled it round him, and was instantaneously turned into an animal, to all outward appearance like a bundle of peat-straw, and he rolled about like an unwieldy bear. When those who were in the room perceived this, they hastened in search of the father, who was found in time to come and unbuckle the belt, before the child had done any mischief. The boy afterwards said, that when he had put on the girdle, he was seized with such a raging hunger, that he was ready to tear in pieces and devour all that came in his way.

The girdle is supposed to be made of human skin, and to be three finger-breadths wide.

In East Friesland, it is believed, when seven girls succeed each other in one family, that among them one is of necessity a werewolf, so that youths are slow in seeking one of seven sisters in marriage.

According to a curious Lithuanian story related by Schleicher in his *Litauische Märchen*, a person who is a werewolf or bear has to remain kneeling in one spot for one hundred years before he can hope to obtain release from his bestial form. . . .

Among the Bulgarians and Slovakians the were-wolf is called *vrkolak*, a name resembling that given it by the modern Greeks βρύκολακας. The Greek were-wolf is closely related to the vampire. The lycanthropist falls into a cataleptic trance, during which his soul leaves his body, enters that of a wolf and ravens for blood. On the return of the soul, the body is exhausted and aches as though it had been put through violent exercise. After death lycanthropists become vampires. They are believed to frequent battlefields in wolf or hyæna shapes, and to suck the breath from dying soldiers, or to enter houses and steal the infants from their cradles. Modern Greeks call any savage-looking man, with dark complexion, and with distorted, misshapen limbs, a βρύκολακας, and suppose him to be invested with power of running in wolf-form.

The Serbs connect the vampire and the were-wolf together, and call them by one name *vlkoslak*. These rage chiefly in the depths of winter: they hold their annual gatherings, and at them divest themselves of their wolf-skins, which they hang on the trees around them. If any one succeeds in obtaining the skin and burning it, the vlkoslak is thenceforth disenchanted.

The power to become a werewolf is obtained by drinking the water which settles in a foot-print left in clay by a wolf.

Among the White Russians the *wawkalak* is a man who has incurred the wrath of the devil, and the evil one punishes him by transforming him into a wolf and sending him among his relations, who recognize him and feed him well. He is a most amiably disposed were-wolf, for he does no mischief, and testifies his affection for his kindred by licking their hands. He cannot, however, remain long in any place, but is driven from house to house, and from hamlet to hamlet, by an irresistible passion for change of scene. This is an ugly superstition, for it sets a premium on standing well with the evil one.

The Slovakians merrily term a drunkard a *vlkodlak*, because, forsooth, he makes a beast of himself. A Slovakian household were-wolf tale closes this chapter.

The Poles have their were-wolves, which rage twice in the year – at Christmas and at midsummer.

According to a Polish story, if a witch lays a girdle of human skin on the threshold of a house in which a marriage is being celebrated, the bride and bridegroom, and bridesmaids and groomsmen, should they step across it, are transformed into wolves. After three years, however, the witch will cover them with skins with the hair turned outward; immediately they will recover their natural form. On one occasion, a witch cast a skin of too scanty dimensions over the bridegroom, so that his tail was left uncovered: he resumed his human form, but retained his lupine caudal appendage. . . .

I shall close this chapter with a Slovakian household tale given by T.T. Hanush in the third volume of *Zeitschrift für Deutsche Mythologie*.

The Daughter of the Vlkolak

'There was once a father, who had nine daughters, and they were all marriageable, but the youngest was the most beautiful. The father was a were-wolf. One day it came into his head: 'What is the good of having to support so many girls?" so he determined to put them all out of the way.

'He went accordingly into the forest to hew wood, and he ordered his daughters to let one of them bring him his dinner. It was the eldest who brought it.

' "Why, how come you so early with the food?" asked the woodcutter.

' "Truly, father, I wished to strengthen you, lest you should fall upon us, if famished!"

' "A good lass! Sit down whilst I eat." He ate, and whilst he ate he thought of a scheme. He rose and said: "My girl, come, and I will show you a pit I have been digging."

' "And what is the pit for?"

' "That we may be buried in it when we die, for poor folk will not be cared for much after they are dead and gone."

'So the girl went with him to the side of the deep pit. "Now hear," said the were-wolf, "you must die and be cast in there."

'She begged for her life, but all in vain, so he laid hold of her and cast her into the grave. Then he took a great stone and flung it in upon her and crushed her head, so the poor thing breathed out her soul. When the were-wolf had done this he went back to his work, and as dusk came on, the second daughter arrived, bringing him food. He told her of the pit, and brought her to it, and cast her in, and killed her as the first. And so he dealt with all his girls up to the last. The youngest knew well that her father was a were-wolf, and she was grieved that her sisters did not return; she thought, "Now where can they be? Has my father kept them for companionship; or to help him in his work?" So she made the food which she was to take him, and crept cautiously through the wood. When she came near the place where her father worked, she heard his strokes felling timber, and smelt smoke. She saw presently a large fire and two human heads roasting at it. Turning from the fire, she went in the direction of the axe-strokes, and found her father.

'"See," said she, "father, I have brought you food."

'"That is a good lass," said he. "Now stack the wood for me whilst I eat."

'"But where are my sisters?" she asked.

'"Down in yon valley drawing wood," he replied; "follow me, and I will bring you to them."

'They came to the pit; then he told her that he had dug it for a grave. "Now," said he, "you must die, and be cast into the pit with your sisters."

'"Turn aside, father," she asked, "whilst I strip off my clothes, and then slay me if you will."

'He turned aside as she requested, and then – tchich! she gave him a push, and he tumbled headlong into the hole he had dug for her.

'She fled for her life, for the were-wolf was not injured, and he soon would scramble out of the pit.

'Now she hears his howls resounding through the gloomy alleys of the forest, and swift as the wind she runs. She hears the tramp of his approaching feet, and the snuffle of his breath. Then she casts behind her her handkerchief. The were-wolf seizes this with teeth and nails, and rends it till it is reduced to tiny ribands. In another moment he is again in pursuit foaming at the mouth, and howling dismally, whilst his red eyes gleam like burning coals. As he gains on her, she casts behind her her gown, and bids him tear that. He seizes the gown and rives it to shreds, then again he pursues. This time she casts behind her her apron, next her petticoat, then her shift, and at last runs much in the condition in which she was born. Again the were-wolf approaches; she bounds out of the forest into a hay-field, and hides herself in the smallest heap of hay. Her father enters the field, runs howling about it in search of her, cannot find her, and begins to upset the different haycocks, all the while growling and gnashing his gleaming white fangs in his rage at her having escaped him. The foam flakes drop at every step from his mouth, and his skin is reeking with sweat. Before he has reached the smallest bundle of hay his strength leaves him, he feels exhaustion begin to creep over him, and he retires to the forest.

'The king goes out hunting every day; one of his dogs carries food to the hay-field, which has most unaccountably been neglected by the hay-makers for three days. The king, following the dog, discovers the fair damsel, not exactly "in the straw," but up to her neck in hay. She is carried, hay and all, to the palace, where she becomes his wife, making only one stipulation before becoming his bride, and that is, that no beggar shall be permitted to enter the palace.

'After some years a beggar does get in, the beggar being, of course, none other than her were-wolf father. He steals upstairs, enters the nursery, cuts the throats of the two children borne by the queen to her lord, and lays the knife under her pillow.

'In the morning, the king, supposing his wife to be the murderess, drives her from home, with the dead princes hung about her neck. A hermit comes to the rescue, and restores the babies to life. The king finds out his mistake, is reunited to the lady out of the hay, and the were-wolf is cast off a high cliff into the sea, and that is the end of *him*. The king, the queen, and the princes live happily, and may be living yet, for no notice of their death has appeared in the newspaper.'

The passages on Elizabeth Bathory are to be found in The Book of Were-wolves *(1865) pages 139–141. The material on werewolf folklore is an abridgement of pages 100–129.*

CHAPTER TEN

The Habits and Instincts of Bats

Sarah Lee

Animals feature in *Dracula* over and above their purpose of animalising the feral Count. Several passages in the book contain detailed animal scenes. There is the episode of Bersicker the wolf, freed from his cage in London zoo by Dracula in order to effect entry into the house of Lucy Westenra. (*Dracula* Chapter 11) Bersicker, a Norwegian grey wolf named after the fierce legendary Scandinavian warriors 'Berserkers', leaps through a garlic-bedecked window to free the way for his master. The job done, the wolf returns of his own accord to the zoo, Dracula having no more use for him.

Then there is the business of the rats in the chapel at Carfax, where Dracula had been hiding out. (*Dracula* Chapter 19) Rats were a favourite subject for Bram Stoker. This is hardly surprising: rats are part of the horror writer's stock-in-trade. Stoker had made use of them, to good effect, in several of his short stories. As with wolves, rats are widely regarded as lower, meaner specimens of the animal kingdom, and are therefore fitting associates for evil-doers.

Dracula commands wolves and rats to do his bidding as if they were part of his animal slave-world. However, when needing to disguise himself in England he does not transform himself into a wolf or a rat, for a wolf would have been too conspicuous and a rat too vulnerable, and Dracula is too shrewd to take unnecessary risks. When bounding ashore at Whitby from the stricken *Demeter*, Dracula assumes the form of a huge dog. (*Dracula* Chapter 7) In Britain, as he presumably knows, dogs attract affection, not stones, and Dracula's only problem is with another, smaller dog, whose throat he slashes.

Dracula's other preferred disguise is as a bat. Today, the association between bats and vampires is so deep-seated, due mainly to the cinema, that it is difficult to conceive of the one without the other. This was not the case in Stoker's day. It was *Dracula* which can be said to have most successfully exploited the bat as an aid to the literary vampire, although bats have no part to play in vampire folklore. Societies mythologize animals which threaten them, as instanced by werewolves proliferating in regions terrified of wolves. But vampire bats are not native to Europe, being found only in Central and South America. Consequently, the bat found itself annexed to a vampire-myth already in existence.

Of course, while the vampire bat is unknown to Europe its harmless cousins are not. All creatures that can operate at night find themselves the subject of dark rumours, and bats' habits of occupying buildings and flitting eerily from house to house or tree to tree with those peculiar membrane wings lend them a natural allegiance to the powers of evil. The introduction of the vampire bat, where artists and film-makers were concerned, was eagerly capitalised upon, and has subsequently served to underline the public's existing fear of bats.

Stoker has left us at least two sources for his information on animal behaviour. His notes contain a reference to observations he made at London zoo. They also refer to Sarah Lee's *Anecdotes of Habits and Instincts of Birds*. When this reference is checked it transpires that Mrs Lee (formerly Mrs Bowdich) compiled two volumes of anecdotes, one on birds, reptiles and fishes, the other on animals. It is surely the one on animals which Stoker consulted. It contains accounts of the behaviour of around thirty mammals – including rats, bats and wolves.

The chapter on wolves notes their powerful physique, their cunning which makes them popularly despised, and offers several accounts of 'tamed' wolves which might have assisted Stoker with his Bersicker episode. The section on bats (reproduced below) is even more significant, for it is almost entirely concerned with the blood-sucking variety, and provides instances of the vampire bat attaching itself to horses in South America. Perhaps this is the source for Quincey Morris's recollections in *Dracula*:

> I have not seen anything pulled down so quick since I was on the Pampas and had a mare that I was fond of go to grass all in a night. One of those big bats that they call vampires had got at her in the night, and, what with his gorge and the vein left open, there wasn't enough blood in her to let her stand up, and I had to put a bullet through her as she lay. (*Dracula* Chapter 12)

✢

The Habits and Instincts of Bats

A race of beings, to which the epithet mysterious may be with some truth applied, affords more interest from its peculiar habits, than from any proof which can be given of its mental powers; and its place in this work is due to the marvellous histories which have been related concerning it, and which have made it an object of superstitious alarm.

Bats, or Cheiroptera, are particularly distinguished from all other creatures which suckle their young, by possessing the power of flight. A Lemur Galeopithecus, which exists in the eastern part of the globe, takes long sweeps from tree to tree, and owes this faculty to the extension of its skin between its fore and hind limbs, including the tail; but it cannot be really said to fly. The bats, then, alone enjoy this privilege; and the prolongation of what, in common parlance, we should call the arms and fingers, constitutes the framework which supports the skin, or membrane forming the wings. The thumbs, however, are left free, and serve as hooks for various purposes. The legs, and tail (when they have any), generally help to extend the membrane of the wing; and the breast-bone is so formed as to support the powerful muscles which aid their locomotive peculiarities. They climb and crawl with great dexterity, and some will run when on the ground; but it is difficult for most of them to move on a smooth, horizontal surface, and they drag themselves along by their thumbs. A portion of the Cheiroptera feeds on insects, and another on fruits; one genus subsists chiefly on blood. The first help to clear the atmosphere of those insects which fly at twilight; the second are very destructive to our gardens and orchards; the last are especially the object of that superstitious fear to which I have already alluded. They are all nocturnal or crepuscular, and during the day remain suspended by the sharp claws of their feet to the under-branches of trees, the roofs of caves, subterranean quarries, or old ruins, hanging with their heads downwards; multitudes live in the tombs of Egypt.

The appearance of bats is always more or less grotesque; but this term more aptly applies to those which live on animal food, in consequence of the additions made to the nose and ears, probably for the sake of increasing their always acute senses of smell and hearing. The ears are frequently of an enormous size, and are joined together at the back of the head; besides which they have leaf, or lance-shaped appendages in front. A membrane of various forms is also often attached to the nose, in one species the shape of a horse-shoe. The bodies are always covered with hair, but the wings consist of a leathery membrane. Another singularity in one genus is the extremity of the spine being converted into two jointed, horny pieces, covered with skin, so as to form a box of two valves, each having an independent motion. The large bats of the East Indies measure five feet from the tip of one wing to that of the other, and they emit a musky odour. The skin of the Nyeteris Geoffroyi is very loose upon the body; and the animal draws air through openings in the cheek pouches, head, and back, and swells itself into a little balloon; the openings being closed at pleasure by means of valves. The bite of all is extremely sharp; and we seldom hear of an instance of one being tamed. They try to shelter themselves from chilly winds, and frequent sheltered spots, abounding in masonry, rocks, trees, and small streams.

About the Vampire, or the blood-sucker, there are different opinions: that of the East is said to be quite harmless; but it is asserted that the South American species love to attach themselves to all cattle, especially to horses with long manes, because they can cling to the hair while they suck the veins, and keep their victim quiet by flapping their wings over its head; they also fasten themselves upon the tail for the first reason, and a great loss of blood frequently ensues. Fowls are frequently killed by them as they roost upon their perches, for so noiseless and gentle are they in their flight and operations, that animals are not awakened out of their sleep by their attacks. The teeth are so disposed that they make a deep and triple puncture, and one was taken by Mr Darwin in the act of sucking blood from the neck of a horse. This able naturalist and accurate observer is of opinion, that horses do not suffer from the quantity of blood taken from them by the Vampire, but from the inflammation of the wound which they make, and which is increased if the saddle presses on it. Horses, however, turned out to grass at night, are frequently found the next morning with their necks and haunches covered with blood; and it is known that the bat fills and disgorges itself several times. Dr Carpenter is of the same opinion as Mr Darwin, and also disbelieves that these creatures soothe their victims by fanning them with their wings.

Captain Stedman, who travelled in Guiana, from 1772 to 1777, published an account of his adventures, and for several years afterwards, it was the fashion to doubt the truth of his statements. In fact, it was a general feeling, up to a much later period than the above, that travellers were not to be believed. As our knowledge, however, has increased, and the works of God have been made more manifest, the reputation of many a calumniated traveller has been restored, and, among others, that of Captain Stedman. I shall, therefore, unhesitatingly quote his account of the bite of the vampire:

> On waking, about four o'clock this morning, in my hammock, I was extremely alarmed at finding myself weltering in congealed blood, and without feeling any pain whatever. Having started up and run to the surgeon, with a firebrand in one hand, and all over besmeared with gore, the mystery was found to be, that I had been bitten by the vampire or spectre of Guiana, which is also called the flying dog of New Spain. This is no other than a bat of monstrous size, that sucks the blood from men and cattle, sometimes even till they die; knowing, by instinct, that the person they intend to attack is in a sound slumber, they generally alight near the feet, where, while the creature continues fanning with his enormous wings, which keeps one cool, he bites a piece out of the tip of the great toe, so very small indeed, that the head of a pin could scarcely be received into the wound, which is consequently not painful; yet, through this orifice, he contrives to suck the blood, until he is obliged to disgorge. He then begins again, and thus continues sucking and disgorging till he is scarcely able to fly, and the sufferer has often been known to sleep from time into eternity. Cattle they generally bite in the ear, but always in those places where the blood flows spontaneously. Having applied tobacco-ashes as the best remedy, and washed the gore from myself and my hammock, I observed several small heaps of congealed blood all around the place where I had lain, upon the ground; upon examining which, the surgeon judged that I had lost at least twelve or fourteen ounces during the night. Having measured this creature (one of the bats), I found it to be, between the tips of the wings, thirty-two inches and a half; the colour was a dark brown, nearly black, but lighter underneath.

Mr Waterton, whom all the world recognizes as a gentleman, and consequently a man of truth, laboured at one time under the same stigma of exaggeration as Captain Stedman, and many other illustrious travellers; and he confirms the bloodsucking in the following terms:

> Some years ago, I went to the river Paumarau, with a Scotch gentleman. We hung our hammocks in the thatched loft of a planter's house. Next morning I heard this gentleman muttering in his hammock, and now and then letting fall an imprecation or two, 'What is the matter, Sir,' said I softly, 'is anything amiss?' 'What is the matter!' answered he surlily,

'why the vampires have been sucking me to death.' As soon as there was light enough, I went to his hammock, and saw it much stained with blood. 'There,' said he, thrusting his foot out of the hammock, 'see how these imps have been drawing my life's blood.' On examining his foot, I found the vampire had tapped his great toe. There was a wound somewhat less than that made by a leech. The blood was still oozing from it, and I conjectured he might have lost from ten to twelve ounces of blood.

Mr Waterton further tells us, that a boy of ten or eleven years of age was bitten by a vampire, and a poor ass, belonging to the young gentleman's father, was dying by inches from the bites of the larger kinds, while most of his fowls were killed by the smaller bats.

The torpidity in which bats remain during the winter, in climates similar to that of England, is well known; and, like other animals which undergo the same suspension of powers, they have their histories of long imprisonment in places which seem inimical to life. There are two accounts of their being found in trees, which are extremely curious, and the more so, because the one corroborates the other. In the beginning of November, 1821, a woodman, engaged in splitting timber for rail-posts, in the woods close by the lake at Haining, a seat of Mr Pringle's, in Selkirkshire, discovered, in the centre of a large wild-cherry tree, a living bat, of a bright scarlet colour, which, as soon as it was relieved from its entombment, took to its wings and escaped. In the tree there was a recess sufficiently large to contain the animal; but all around, the wood was perfectly sound, solid, and free from any fissure through which the atmospheric air could reach the animal.

A man engaged in splitting timber, near Kelsall, in the beginning of December, 1826, discovered, in the centre of a large pear-tree, a living bat, of a bright scarlet colour, which he foolishly suffered to escape, from fear, being fully persuaded (with the characteristic superstition of the inhabitants of that part of Cheshire), that it was 'a being not of this world'. The tree presented a small cavity in the centre, where the bat was enclosed, but was perfectly sound and solid on each side. The scarlet colour of each of these prisoners seems at present to be inexplicable, and makes these statements still more marvellous.

Professor Bell, in his admirable work on British Quadrupeds speaks of a long-eared bat which fed from the hand; and if an insect were held between the lips, it would settle on its master's cheek, and take the fly from his mouth with great quietness. So accustomed was it to this, that it would seek his lips when he made a buzzing noise. It folded its beautiful ears under its arm when it went to sleep, and also during hibernation. Its cry was acute and shrill, becoming more clear and piercing when disturbed. It is most frequently seen in towns and villages. This instance of taming to a certain extent might, perhaps, be more frequently repeated, if bats were objects of more general interest.

From Anecdotes of Habits and Instincts of Animals *(1853) pages 33–40.*

CHAPTER ELEVEN

Credulities of the Sea and of Seamen

William Jones

The magic of the sea is a familiar theme in Bram Stoker's fiction. This was a reflection of the deep fascination which it evidently held for him. The seascape at Cruden Bay in Scotland where Stoker holidayed annually from 1893 was a source of particular inspiration. Several of his short stories and novels are set in Cruden Bay and its environs, among them *The Watter's Mou* and *The Mystery of the Sea*.

Dracula's two central locations – Transylvania and London – should not detract from the prominent role Stoker gives to the sea. The chapters dealing with the Count's journey from Varna to Whitby aboard the Russian vessel *Demeter* and its subsequent shipwreck are among the most vivid of the whole novel. The superstitious crew become aware of 'It', hidden down in the hold, which is responsible for mysteriously reducing their numbers one by one, till only the captain remains. Meanwhile, Lucy's conversations with old Mr Swales upon the Whitby clifftops provide Stoker the opportunity to reveal his intimate knowledge of seafarers and their world.

Seafolk are the most superstitious of people – and the most conservative, clinging unshakably to the beliefs of their forebears. With just a thin wooden hull and flimsy sail to protect them from the hereafter, omens assumed a prescient power in the minds of sailors. Meteorology being an infant and imprecise science, the causes of storms were more satisfactorily attributed to malevolent spirits than to atmospheric pressure.

If the vastness of outer space can excite the fancies of science fiction, what of the thoughts of sailors tossing about in a frail vessel in the midst of a boundless and unfathomable ocean? Winds, clouds, waves, sun, moon, stars, fog, sea monsters, and spectres were all taken to possess hidden powers with good or ill intent. Not until the coming of iron ships powered by steam did vulnerability to the elements greatly recede, and with the passing of sail went the passing of sailing lore. Bassett, writing in 1885, accounts for the demise of naval superstition with a tinge of regret:

> The old type of sailor, who believed in the mermaid, the sea-snake, and the phantom ship, is fast disappearing, and, with the gradual substitution of the steamship for the sailing-vessel, he is being replaced by the mechanical seaman, who sees no spectre in the fog, or sign of disaster in the air, or beneath the wave. Scientific progress has demonstrated the non-existence of imaginary creatures beneath the waves; better meteorological knowledge has banished the spectres of the air, and shown the unreliability of weather-indicators, and the decay of priestly influence has caused the abandonment of sacrifices and offerings to the sea, its deities or its saints.
>
> (*Legends and Superstitions of the Sea*, preface)

Stoker's enthusiasm for naval folklore is reflected in his source notes. During his visits to Whitby he recorded conversations with fishermen and coastguards and took note of several shipwrecks, including that of the Russian schooner *Dimetry* in 1885. He records the Beaufort windscale and other meteorological information taken from Robert Scott's *Fishery Barometer Manual*. This serves to make Stoker's shipwreck scenes convincingly authentic.

About a quarter of Stoker's named sources are connected with the legends and superstitions of the sea. These include Henry Lee's *Sea Fables Explained* and *Sea Monsters Unmasked*; Fletcher S. Bassett's *Legends and Superstitions of the Sea and of Sailors – In all Lands and at all Times*; and William Jones' *Credulities Past and Present*. Of particular interest regarding the origins of *Dracula* are the legends of the Phantom Ship, for these are related to the Wandering Jew and the Flying Dutchman, both of which being archetypal myths bound up with Dracula's eternal damnation for his commerce with the devil. Jonathan Harker was due to see a performance of *The Flying Dutchman* prior to his meeting with Dracula, although this scene was excised from the finished novel.

The extracts that follow are taken from Jones' *Credulities Past and Present* (1880). They deal with the legend of the Flying Dutchman, and also with storm-raising, apparitions, and superstitions pertaining to dead bodies found on ships.

*

Credulities of the Sea and of Seamen
It was a belief among the ancients that certain persons had the power

of raising tempests. Pomponius Mela, who wrote in the reign of the Emperor Claudian, mentions a set of priestesses, in the Island of Sena (*Ile des Saints*), on the coast of Gaul, who were said to control the winds and the waves by their enchantments. Eolus is stated in the *Odyssey* to have possessed these powers. Calypso in the same work is said to have been able to control the winds.

A strong belief in human agency to influence the ocean, prevailed in the fifteenth century. Witches were supposed to possess this attribute. A curious confession was made in Scotland about the year 1591, by one Agnes Sampson, a reputed witch, who seemed to have a ready imagination, quickened most probably by the application of torture. She vowed that

At the time his majesty (James VI.) was in Denmark, she took a cat and christened it, and afterwards bound to each part of that cat the chiefest parts of a dead man, and several joints of his body; and that in the night following, the said cat was conveyed into the midst of the sea, by herself and other witches, sailing in their riddles, or crieves, and so left the said cat right before the town of Leith, in Scotland. This done, there arose such a tempest in the sea, as a greater hath not been seen, which tempest was the cause of the perishing of a boat or vessel coming over from the town of Brunt Island to the town of Leith, wherein were sundry jewels and rich gifts, which should have been presented to the new Queen of Scotland, at her majesty's coming to Leith. Again, it is confessed that the said christened cat was the cause of the king's majesty's ship, at his coming forth of Denmark, having a contrary wind to the rest of the ships then being in his company, which thing was most strange and true, as the king's majesty acknowledgeth.

Supposing that the miserable old beldame really did perform her satanic operations, such an outrage on the majesty of the sea was quite enough to excite its indignation, though not in the partial manner described.

Agnes Sampson mentioned another frolic that she and her sister witches had enjoyed during a sea-journey performed in *sieves*. The Evil One, who condescended to amuse them, rolled upon the waves beside them, resembling a huge haystack in size and appearance. These agreeable old women went on board of a foreign ship richly laden with wines; where, invisible to the crew, they feasted until the sport became tiresome, and then Satan sunk the vessel, and all on board – the weird sisters of course excepted.

King James in his *Dæmonology* says that 'Witches can raise stormes and tempestes in the aire, either on sea or land.'

Scot, in his *Discoverie of Witchcraft*, observes:

No one endued with common sense but will deny that the elements are obedient to witches, and at their commandment, or that they may at their pleasure send hail, rain, tempest, thunder and lightning, when she being but an old doting woman casteth a flint stone over her left shoulder toward the west, or hurleth a little sea-sand up into the element, or wetteth a broom-sprig in water and sprinkleth the same into the air, or diggeth a pit in the earth, and putting water therein, stirreth it about with her finger; or boileth hog's bristles, or layeth sticks across upon a bank where never a drop of water is, or buryeth sage until it be rotten; all which things are confessed by witches, and affirmed by writers to be the means that witches use to raise extraordinary tempests and rain.

Reginald Scot has the advantage of his royal master, 'the British Solomon', on this subject, and his book (published in 1584) was designed to demonstrate the absurdity of the prevalent belief in witchcraft. This excited the fury of King James, who wrote his *Dæmonology* against 'the damnable opinions of Scot, who is not ashamed in public print to deny there can be such a thing as witchcraft.'

A hazy kind of belief in the power of witches to control the winds and sea existed in the eighteenth century. A tale was imposed upon the public by John Dunton, 'a man of scribbling celebrity' (as he is described by Sir Walter Scott), which was called the *Apparition Evidence*. In this story many incredible matters are related of an old lady named Leckie, who resided at Minehead in Somersetshire, with one son and a daughter. Mrs Leckie, who made herself so agreeable that her friends used to say to her, and to each other, it was a thousand pities such an excellent gentlewoman must from her age be soon lost to her friends. To this Mrs Leckie would reply: 'Although you appear to like me now, you will but little care to see or speak to me after my death, though I believe you may have that satisfaction.' These were strange words, but die, however, she did, and after her funeral she was repeatedly seen in her earthly likeness, at home and abroad, by night and by day. The resemblance, however, was in feature only, for the conduct of the ghost was the antipodes to respectable. Mischief and wickedness seemed the prevailing instincts of the spectre. It would appear at noonday upon the quay at

Minehead and cry, 'A boat! a boat, ho!' and if any boatmen or seamen were in sight, and did not come, they would be sure to be cast away, as, indeed, they would have been had they obeyed the summons. It was equally dangerous to please or displease her. Her son had several ships trading between England and Ireland; no sooner did they make land and come in sight of England, but this ghost would appear in the same garb and likeness as when she was alive, and standing at the mainmast, would blow with a whistle, and though it were never so great a calm, yet immediately there would arise a dreadful storm, that would break, wreck, and drown the ship and goods; only the seamen would escape with their lives, the evil spirit had no permission to take them away. At this rate, by her frequent apparitions and disturbances, she ruined her son, and he that was once worth thousands was reduced to penury.

So deep, we are told, was the impression made by this story on the inhabitants of Minehead, that the mariners belonging to the port often believed in stormy weather they heard the whistle of the horrible old lady, who tormented even her own family.

At Peel, in the Isle of Man, there is a tradition that a witch, with a basin of water, said that the herring-fleet would never return. Every ship was lost, and she was put in a barrel with spikes, and rolled down the hill. The place of this horrible punishment was before covered with grass, but it has never grown since.

The Evil One was supposed to have a direct influence on the winds and waves. 'Our sailors,' writes Dr Pegge in 1763, 'I am told at this very day – I mean the vulgar sort of them – have a strange opinion of satanic power and agency in stirring up winds, and that is the reason why they so seldom whistle on shipboard, esteeming it to be a mockery, and consequently an enraging of the devil. And it appears that even Zoroaster himself imagined that there was an evil spirit called *Vato*, that could excite storms of wind.'

Various practices were adopted to influence the winds, and ensure prosperous passages to seamen. The good wives of Winchelsea, in former days, hit upon an ingenious plan of their own for this purpose; in the success of which they, no doubt, implicitly believed. The Kentish perambulator, Lambarde, alluding to Winchelsea, says:

And because our portes men traded the sea, and lived by quicke returne, they were not unprovided with an Æolus also, that might directe the winde for their desire. For within memorie, there were standyng in Winchelsey three parish churches – St. Lennard, St. Giles, and St. Thomas; and in that of St. Lennard there was erected the picture of St. Lennard, the patrone of the place, holding a fane (or Æolus-scepter) in his hand, which was moovable at the pleasure of any that would turne it to such pointe of the compasse, as best fitted the return of the husband, or other friend, whom they expected.

This was, at least, an innocent method of working the winds. The women of Roscoff, in Brittany, after mass, sweep out the chapel *de la Sainte Union*, and blow the dust towards that side of the coast, by which their lovers and husbands should come to them; and they do this for the purpose of obtaining a favourable wind for the objects of their affection.

One would scarcely expect that the mere turning of a stone was supposed to have a sensible effect in procuring favourable breezes, yet we learn that the inhabitants of Fladda Chuan, in the Western Islands, had implicit faith in this charm. In a chapel on the island, there was a blue stone, fixed in the altar of a round form, which was always moist. It was an ordinary custom with any fishermen who were detained in the island by contrary winds, to wash this blue stone with water, expecting thereby to obtain a favourable wind. So great was the regard paid to this stone, that any oath sworn before it could never be broken. Another mode of these primitive islanders to secure auspicious winds, consisted in hanging a he-goat to the mast-head.

A similar feeling with regard to the efficacy of stones, though for another purpose, existed among the fishermen of Iona. This took the shape of a pillar, and the sailor who stretched his arm along it three times in the name of the Trinity, could never err in steering the helm of a vessel.

On the island of Gigha is a well with some stones in it; and it is affirmed that if the stones be taken out of it, a great storm will arise.

The Finlanders are said to have used a cord, tied with three knots, for raising the wind. When the first was loosed, they would expect a good wind; with the second, a stronger; on the third being loosed, such a storm would arise that the sailors would not be able to direct the ship, or avoid rocks, or to stand upon the decks.

In a *History of Kintyre* by Peter McIntosh (Campbeltown, 1870), we find:

Old John McTaggart was a trader between Kintyre and Ireland.

Wishing to get a fair wind to waft his bark across to the Emerald Isle, he applied to an old woman who was said to be able to give this. He received from her two strings, on each being three knots. He undid the first knot, and there blew a fine breeze. On opening the second, the breeze became a gale. On nearing the Irish shore he loosed the third, and such a hurricane arose, that some of the houses on shore were destroyed. On coming back to Kintyre, he was careful to loose only two knots on the remaining string.

The French seamen, in former days, had a comical notion that the spirit of the storm was to be propitiated by flogging unfortunate middies at the mainmast.*

St Gregory of Tours assures us that one of the nails of the cross on which Christ was crucified was thrown into the Adriatic by the Empress Helena during a storm (perhaps on her homeward passage from the East), in consequence of which sailors entered upon that sea as sanctified, with fastings, prayers, and singing hymns, even to his own day.

One of Baxter's tales is of 'an old *reading* parson, named Jewis, not far from Framlingham, that was hanged; who confessed that he had two imps, and that one of them was always putting him on doing mischief; and he being near the sea, as he saw a ship under sail, it moved him to send him to sink the ship, and he consented, and saw the ship sink before him.' The clergyman was four-score years old, and his confession was obtained after undergoing the ordeal of swimming, and made to walk incessantly for several days and nights by the infamous Hopkins, the witch-finder, and his gang.

According to Hallywell, who follows 'Marcus the Eremite, a skilful dæmonist,' there are six kinds of demons, the fourth of which 'are aquatic or watery, keeping their haunts about rivers, lakes, and springs, drowning men often, raising storms at sea, and sinking ships.'

Cassas mentions a belief that the hurricanes so frequent in the

---

* This brings to mind a paragraph in Galignani's newspaper (May, 1856), relative to the inhabitants of Constantina, in Africa, who, during a great drought, had recourse to what they consider an infallible means of obtaining rain, the ceremony of ducking, with religious forms, in the nearest water, the half-witted creatures called Marabouts. Five or six of these men were conveyed in procession to the Roumel, and there plunged in succession several times into the water, midst singing and shouting. One of them who was unwilling to undergo the ordeal, was thrown into the water by force, and when he came out, declared, in a passion, that no rain should fall for a year. Rain it did, however, on the next day.

Gulf of Carnero were occasioned by sorcerers, who, when offended, kindled great fires in their caverns in the mountains; and that the earth, enraged with the pain which this occasioned, raised such commotions in the air as to cause the destruction of those against whom the sorcerers were wroth. . . .

The Phantom Ship has long been a favourite subject with story-writers, and a belief in the appearance of this supernatural phenomenon prevailed among seamen of various countries for a considerable period. The Dutch claim the origin of the superstition, and the *Flying Dutchman* had no firmer votaries in favour of its existence than English sailors. There were few ships that 'doubled the Cape,' but had among the crews some who had seen this marvel. Sir Walter Scott alludes to it as a harbinger of woe. . . .

The legend of the *Flying Dutchman* runs, that she is supposed to be seen about the latitude of the Cape of Good Hope, and is distinguished from earthly vessels by bearing a press of sail, when all others are unable, from stress of weather, to show an inch of canvas. The cause of her wandering is not at all certain, but the general account is, that she was originally a vessel loaded with great wealth, on board of which some horrid act of murder and piracy had been committed; that the plague broke out among the wicked crew who had perpetrated the crime, and that they sailed in vain from port to port, offering, as the price of shelter, the whole of their ill-gotten wealth; that they were excluded from every harbour, for fear of the contagion which was devouring them; and that, as a punishment of their crimes, the apparition of the ship still continues to haunt those seas in which the catastrophe took place, and is considered by the mariners as the worst of all possible omens.

The Phantom Ship was an object of firm belief to the Norman fishermen. If the prayers offered for the souls in purgatory of those who had been shipwrecked had not been efficacious, the result is said to have been as follows: a tempest would arise, and a ship be seen at sea, struggling with the winds and waves. Suddenly the vessel would be driven with lightning rapidity towards the port, and on entering, the horrified spectators on the quay would recognise in the ship those who had been reported lost at sea years before. Assistance would be given to bring the ship into a safe place; ropes were thrown on board, which were caught by the crew, and the vessel was attached to the quay. The news would spread, and the widows, and children, and friends of the seamen who were supposed to have been drowned, would rush to the spot. The cries of recognition would arise, 'There is my father, my brother, or my lover.' No answer, however, would be heard from the vessel; not one cry from the crew, although the figures might be seen; not a lip moved, nor was any sign of recognition heard. At length the bells would sound the hour of midnight; a fog would steal over the sea, and on clearing off after a few moments, the vessel had disappeared. Amidst the sobs and the heart-rending bitterness of the spectators of the Phantom Ship, the warning voice of a priest would be heard, 'Pay your debts; pray for the lost souls in purgatory!'

There is a legend of a Herr von Falkenbeg, who is condemned to beat about the ocean until the day of judgment, on board a ship without a helm, or steersman, playing at dice for his soul with the devil. Seamen traversing the German Ocean often, it is said, met with the infernal vessel. It was probably no uncommon occurrence in early times for seafarers to fall in with ships abandoned to the winds and waves, with corpses on board, and out of such encounters may have grown this legend of Falkenbeg, that of the *Flying Dutchman*, and others of the same kind.

Mr Hunt relates the following Cornish tradition of the 'Spectre Ship:'

Years long ago, one night a gig's crew was called to go off to a 'hobble' to the westward of St Ive's Head. No sooner was one boat launched, than several others put off from the shore, and a stiff chase was maintained, each one being eager to get to the ship, as she had the appearance of a foreign trader. The hull was clearly visible; she was a schooner-rigged vessel, with a light over her bows.

Away they pulled, and the boat which had been first launched still kept ahead by dint of mechanical power and skill. All the men had thrown off their jackets to row with more freedom. At length the helmsman cried out: 'Stand ready to board her.' The sailor rowing the bow oar slipped it out of the row-lock, and stood on the forethought, taking his jacket on his arm, ready to spring aboard. The vessel came so close to the boat, that they could see the men, and the bow-oar man made a grasp at the bulwarks. His hand found nothing solid, and he fell, being caught by one of his mates, back into the boat, instead of into the water. Then ship and lights disappeared. The next morning the *Neptune* of London, Captain Richard Grant, was wrecked at Gwithian, and all perished. The captain's body was picked up after a few days, and that of his son also. They were both buried in Gwithian churchyard.

In Coleridge's splendid 'Rime', the ancient mariner beholds a sign in the element afar off, prefiguring the death of himself and his comrades. It is a 'spectre ship', in which Death and Life-in-death dice for the crew, and she wins the mariner:

> Her lips were red, her looks were free,
> Her locks were yellow as gold;
> Her skin was white as leprosy,
> The night-mare Life-in-death was she,
> Who thicks man's blood with cold.

After the death of the crew, their bodies are animated by 'a troop of spirits blest,' who leave them every morning, not visibly, but in music:

> For when it dawn'd – they dropped their arms,
>   And cluster'd round the mast;
> Sweet sounds rose slowly through their mouths,
>   And from their bodies pass'd.
>
> Around, around, flew each sweet sound,
>   Then darted to the sun;
> Slowly the sounds came back again,
>   Now mixed, now one by one.
>
> Sometimes adropping from the sky,
>   I heard the sky-lark sing,
> Sometimes all little birds that are,
> How they seemed to fill the sea and air
>   With their sweet jargoning!
>
> And now 'twas like all instruments,
>   Now like a lonely flute;
> And now it is an angel's song
>   That makes the heavens be mute.

One of the most beautiful conceptions of a saintly apparition at sea, is given by Dante. The translation, by the late Leigh Hunt, is worthy the original. Dante and his guide Virgil have just left the infernal regions, and are lingering on a solitary seashore in purgatory:

> That solitary shore we still kept on,
>   Like men, who musing on their journey, stay

At rest in body, yet in heart are gone;
When lo! at the early dawn of day,
    Red Mars looks deepening through the foggy heat,
    Down in the west, far o'er the watery way;
So did mine eyes behold (so may they yet)
    A light which came so swiftly o'er the sea,
    That never wing with such a fervour beat.
I did but turn to ask what it might be
    Of my sage leader, when its orb had got
    More large meanwhile, and came more gloriously;
And by degrees I saw I knew not what
    Of white about; and beneath the white
    Another. My great master uttered not
One word till those first issuing candours bright
    Fanned into wings; but soon as he had found
    Who was the mighty voyager now in sight,
He cried aloud, 'Down, down, upon the ground,
    It is God's Angel.'

Apparitions have been always a fruitful source of terror to seamen. In the *New Catalogue of Vulgar Errors* (1767), we read:

> I look upon our sailors to care as little what becomes of themselves, as any set of people under the sun; yet no persons are so much terrified at the thought of an apparition. Their sea-songs are full of them; they firmly believe their existence, and honest Jack Tar shall be more frightened at the glimmering of the moon upon the tackling of the ship, than he would be if a Frenchman were to place a blunderbuss at his head.

About half-a-dozen sailors on board a man-of-war, took it in their heads that there was a ghost in the ship; and being asked by the captain what reason they had to apprehend such a thing, they said they were sure of it, because *they smelt him*. The captain laughed at them, and called them a parcel of lubbers. One night they came again to the captain, and said that the ghost was behind the beer-barrels. The captain, enraged at their folly, ordered the boatswain's mate to give them a dozen lashes, which entirely cleared the ship of the ghost during the remainder of the voyage. However, when the barrels were removed some time after, a dead rat was found which had given rise to the story.

Brand mentions that the cook of a vessel belonging to Newcastle-upon-Tyne, died on a homeward passage. The man had one of his legs shorter than the other, which gave him a peculiarity of gait when he walked. A few nights after the body had been committed to the deep, the captain was alarmed by the mate assuring him that the man was walking before the ship, and all the crew came on deck to see him. On coming forward, the captain certainly saw something that seemed to move as the cook was accustomed to walk, and he ordered the ship to be steered towards the object. The crew were in a panic. It was found, however, on a near approach, that the ridiculous cause of all this terror was part of a maintop, the remains of some wreck, floating before them.

A ghost story, with a more tragical result, is related by Sir Walter Scott, in his *Demonology and Witchcraft*. A sailor had in his youth become mate in a slave vessel from Liverpool, of which town he was a native. The captain of the ship was a man of variable temper, sometimes kind and courteous to his men, but subject to fits of humour, dislike, and passion, during which he was very violent, tyrannical, and cruel. He took a particular dislike to one seaman on board, an elderly man, called Bill Jones, or some such name. He seldom spoke to the person without threats and abuse, which the old man, with the license which sailors take in merchant vessels, was very apt to return.

On one occasion, Bill Jones appeared slow in getting on the yard. The captain, according to custom, abused the seaman as a lubberly rascal, who got fat by leaving other people to do his duty. The man made a saucy answer, almost amounting to mutiny, on which, in a towering passion, the captain ran down to his cabin, and returned with a blunderbuss loaded with slugs, with which he took deliberate aim at the supposed mutineer, fired, and mortally wounded him. The man was carried down from the yard, and stretched on the deck, evidently dying. He fixed his eyes on the captain, and said: 'Sir, you have done for me, *but I will never leave you.*'

The captain, in return, swore at him for a fat lubber, and said he would have him thrown into the slave-kettle, where they made food for the negroes, and see how much fat he had got. The man died, and his body was actually thrown into the slave-kettle, and the sailor who related this story observed, with a *naïveté* which confirmed the extent of his own belief in the truth of what he told, 'there was not much fat about him after all.'

The captain told the crew they must keep absolute silence on the subject of what had passed; and as the mate was not willing to give an explicit and absolute promise, he ordered him to be confined below.

A day or two afterwards the captain came to the mate, and demanded if he had an intention to deliver him up for trial when the vessel reached home. The mate, who was tired of close confinement in that sultry climate, spoke his commander fair, and obtained his liberty. When he mingled among the crew once more, he found them impressed with the idea, not unnatural in their position, that the ghost of the dead man appeared amongst them when they had a spell of duty, especially if a sail was to be handled, on which occasion the spectre was sure to be out upon the yard before any of the crew. The narrator had seen the apparition frequently; he believed the captain saw it also, but he took no notice of it for some time, and the crew, terrified at the violent temper of the man, dared not call his attention to it. Thus they held on their course homeward, with great fear and anxiety.

At length, the captain invited the mate, who was now in a sort of favour, to go down to the cabin and take a glass of grog with him. In this interview he assumed a very grave and anxious aspect. 'I need not tell you, Jack,' he said, 'what sort of hands we have got on board with us; *he* told me he would never leave me, and *he has kept his word. You* only see him now and then, but he is always at my side, and never out of sight. At this very moment I see him. I am determined to bear it no longer, and I have resolved to leave you.'

The mate replied that his leaving the vessel while out of sight of any land was impossible. He suggested that if the captain apprehended any danger or bad consequences from what had happened, he should run for the west of Ireland, or France, and there go ashore, and leave him, the mate to carry the vessel to Liverpool. The captain only shook his head gloomily, and reiterated his determination to leave the ship. At this moment the mate was called to the deck for some purpose or other; and the instant he got up the companion-ladder, he heard a splash, and, looking over the ship's side, he saw that the captain had thrown himself into the sea from the quarter-gallery, and was swimming astern at the rate of six knots an hour. When just about to sink, he seemed to make a last exertion – sprang half out of the water, and clasped his hands towards the mate, exclaiming, 'Bill is with me now!' and then sank, to be seen no more.

This story leads to the inference that the naturally superstitious minds of the seamen would readily conjure up an apparition following a deed so truly horrible, in which the perpetrator would share, and madness or remorse would lead to the final catastrophe.

In *Blackwood's Magazine* for 1840, there is a letter which contains the following statement:

> The *Hawk* being on her passage from the Cape of Good Hope towards the island of Java, and myself having the charge of the middle-watch, between one and two in the morning I was taken suddenly ill, which obliged me to send for the officer next in turn. I then went down on the gun-deck, and sent my boy for a light. In the meanwhile I sat down on a chest in the steerage, under the after-grating, when I felt a gentle squeeze by a very cold hand. I started and saw a figure in white. Stepping back, I said, 'God's my life! – who is that?' It stood and gazed at me a short time, stooped its head to get a more perfect view, sighed aloud, repeated the exclamation, 'Oh!' three times, and instantly vanished. The night was fine, though the moon afforded through the gratings but a weak light, so that little of feature could be seen, only a figure rather tall than otherwise, and white-clad. My boy returning now with a light, I sent him to the cabins of all the officers, when he brought me word that not one of them had been stirring. Coming afterwards to St Helena, homeward-bound, hearing of my sister's death, and finding the time so nearly coinciding, it added much to my painful concern; and I have only to thank God that, when I saw what I verily believe to have been her apparition (my sister Ann), I did not then know the melancholy occasion of it.

As in all similar cases, we see the effect of superstitious feelings acting, no doubt, on a nervous temperament.

In Sandys's *Ovid* we find a curious story of the power of superstition, with, unfortunately, barbarous results:

> I have heard of seafaring men, and some of Bristol, how a quartermaster in a Bristol ship, then trading in the Streights, going down into the hold, saw a sort of women, his knowne neighbours, making merry together, and taking their cups liberally; who, having espied him, and threatening that he should repent their discovery, vanished suddenly out of sight, who thereupon was lame for ever after. The ship having made her voyage, nowe homeward-bound, and neere her harbour, stuck fast in the deepe sea, before a fresh gaile, to their no small amazement; nor for all they could doe, together with the helpe that came from the shoare, could they get her loose, until one (as *Cymothoe*, the Trojan ship) shoved her off with his shoulder (perhaps one of those whom they vulgarly call Wisemen, who doe good a bad way and undoe the enchantments of others). At their arrivall, the quarter-master accused these women, who were arraigned and convicted by their owne confession, for which five-and-twenty were executed.

'Lord Byron,' says Moore in his *Life* of the poet,

used sometimes to mention a strange story which the commander of the packet, Captain Kidd, related to him on the passage. This officer stated that, being asleep one night in his berth, he was awakened by the pressure of something heavy on his limbs, and, there being a faint light in the room, could see, as he thought, distinctly the figure of his brother, who was at that time in the same service, in the East Indies, dressed in his uniform, and stretched across the bed. Concluding it to be an illusion of his senses, he shut his eyes, and made an effort to sleep. But still the same pressure continued; and still, as often as he ventured to take another look, he saw the figure lying across him in the same position. To add to the wonder, on putting his hand forth to touch this form, he found the uniform in which it appeared to be dressed, *dripping wet*. On the entrance of one of his brother officers, to whom he called out in alarm, the apparition vanished; but in a few months afterwards, he received the startling intelligence that on that night his brother had been drowned in the Indian seas. Of the supernatural character of this appearance, Captain Kidd himself did not appear to have the slightest doubt.

Carrying dead bodies in ships has always been a sore point with sailors, who regard the omen derived from thence as disastrous. In the travels of Boullaye le Gouz (published in 1657), he says:

I had among my baggage the hand of a syren, or fisherwoman, which I threw, on the sly, into the sea, because the captain, seeing that we could not make way, asked me if I had not got some mummy or other in my bags which hindered our progress, in which case we must return to Egypt to carry it back again. Most of the Provençals have the opinion that vessels which transport the mummies from Egypt have great difficulty in arriving safe at port; so that I feared, lest coming to search among my goods, they might take the hand of this fish for a mummy's hand and insult me on account of it.

Fuller, in his *Holy Warre*, says of St Louis: 'His body was carried into France, there to be buried, and was most miserably tossed; it being observed that the sea cannot digest the crudity of a dead corpse, being a due debt to be interred where it dieth, *and a ship cannot abide to be made a bier of*.'

From Credulities Past and Present *(1880) pages 66–72, 82–91.*

CHAPTER TWELVE

The Influence of the Mind upon the Body

Thomas Pettigrew

The war against Dracula is waged on several fronts. Jonathan Harker and Van Helsing, lawyers both, provide the legal expertise – or, more exactly, the wherewithal to circumvent legal interference. Into Van Helsing's shaman-like hands is invested control of matters divine; crosses, holy wafer and indulgences. And should they fail he is not slow to apply the textbook teachings of superstition; garlic, stakes and decapitation.

But the ubiquitious Dutch professor is also a doctor. So is Seward. More particularly, they both specialise in disorders of the mind. When the victims of Dracula's assault are described as 'diseased', 'infected' and 'poisoned', Stoker is not speaking entirely figuratively. Lucy's malaise is treated first by a conventional doctor, Seward, and only when he fails to make progress does he summon the witch-doctor, Van Helsing – thereby reversing the assumed pecking order, according to western perceptions of rationality.

Three of Stoker's brothers were medical men, his eldest, William, becoming President of the Royal College of Surgeons in Ireland. From him Bram acquired the technical details necessary to describe the trephining operation performed on Renfield after Dracula's murderous attack.

For an understanding of the psychological aspects of illness Stoker turned to books written by two surgeons. One of them, Herbert Mayo, features elsewhere in these pages. The other was Thomas Pettigrew, sometime surgeon to the Duchess of Kent and to the Asylum for Female Orphans. Some of Pettigrew's earlier books would have intrigued Stoker, for their subjects include hydrophobia and cholera – both of which are held to produce symptoms likened to those of vampirism. He also left a history of Egyptian mummies. Egyptology was to feature in Stoker's later supernatural thriller *The Jewel of Seven Stars*.

But for the purposes of researching *Dracula* Stoker was attracted by Pettigrew's *On Superstitions connected with the History and Practice of Medicine and Surgery*, dating back to 1844. Pettigrew reminds us that because good health is a prerequisite for all other happiness, those who specialise in the fight against disease and pain are accorded special, almost venerated, status. (Like Van Helsing). Psychology is bound up in the treatment of all ailments. To reassure the patient that all will be well is to put him half-way on the road to recovery. Unfortunately, physicians' esteemed place in society sometimes encourages them to expound theories which go beyond strict medical boundaries. Paracelsus, for example, boasted of his power to bestow immortality, and Van Helsing believes vampires exist in London in the 1890s.

These supernatural claims should not occasion surprise. In 'savage' nations physicians are necessarily conjurers and wizards. Didn't Pliny describe magic as the offspring of medicine? As all medical knowledge was assumed to be divinely granted it was understandably thought to be concentrated in the hands of priests, or other intermediaries with the Almighty. Until comparatively recently disease and pestilence were regarded as divine disfavour, and therefore cure took the form of repentence and appeasement.

The use of crucifixes and garlic necklaces to ward off evil acknowledges ancient forms of protection, as sought from talismans, charms and amulets – between which Pettigrew draws clear distinctions. He may have been responsible for Stoker's idea of draining the colour from Harker's hair and transferring it to the Count. Fear can produce marked physiological effects upon the body, such as turning the hair white, and even removing toothache when the dental appointment draws near.

Pettigrew's laboured distinction between the mind and the body, with its suggestion that illness is often psychosomatic in nature, pays homage to Descartes' ghost in the machine and would be questioned on modern, holistic grounds. Nevertheless it is useful for outlining the climate of medical opinion considered orthodox in Stoker's day. Pettigrew is particularly interesting for his insistence on the power of suggestion as the key to cure. Faith is of the essence if the patient is to become well. Van Helsing knew as much. And suggestibility opens the door to hypnosis. . .

*

The Influence of the Mind upon the Body

As the possession of medical knowledge was considered to be
received through the direct agency of heaven, it is natural to conceive
the exercise of it to have originated with the priests.   In early and
superstitious ages, as already shown, diseases were regarded as
inflictions of the divine vengeance; and means were therefore sought
to appease the anger of the gods, and mitigate the celestial wrath.
Appeals to the oracles, divination, and magic henceforth became
connected with medicine. Hippocrates was the first physician to
relieve medicine from the trammels of superstition and the delusions
of philosophy.

Nothing could tend more to retard the progress of medicine, and
paralyse all efforts for its improvement, than the opinion, once so
generally entertained, of the celestial origin of disease, which, if
admitted, appears necessarily to demand divine interposition for its
relief. Religion and medicine were both brought into contempt by
the adoption of sacrifices and incantations, and the mercenary
practices of the priests to ensure intercession with the gods.
Hippocrates resisted this folly and wickedness, and boldly declared
that no disease whatever came from the gods, but owed its origin to
its own natural and manifest cause. Even the learned Celsus, whose
works are universally read and admired at the present day, whose
writings are considered as forming a conspicuous portion of our
standard medical literature, was not free of the prejudices of his time,
with regard to the origin of disease. . . .

Medicine took its rise in the East, passed into Egypt, thence into
Greece, and so was disseminated throughout the civilized world. All
knowledge being in the earliest times confined to the priests, and the
art of healing being traced to a celestial origin, it is easy to
comprehend its connexion with the ceremonials of religion, and in
what manner, therefore, the superstitions, in relation to it, were
cherished and monopolized by the priesthood. To their class
application was of course made to invoke celestial aid, to appease the
offended divinities, and to insure the restoration of health. Magic
and divination were indeed looked upon as belonging to their sacred
function, and regarded as the highest branches of the medical
profession.

'Magic, according to the Greeks,' says Psellus, 'is a thing of a very
powerful nature. They say that this forms the last part of the
sacerdotal science. Magic, indeed, investigates the nature, power,

and quality of everything sublunary; viz, of the elements and their parts, of animals, all various plants and their fruits, of stones, and herbs; and, in short, it explores the essence, and power of everything. From hence, therefore, it produces its effects. And it forms statues which procure health, makes all various figures, and things which become the instruments of disease. It asserts, too, that eagles and dragons contribute to health; but that cats, dogs, and crows are symbols of vigilance, to which, therefore, they contribute. But for the fashioning of certain parts, wax and clay are used. Often, too, celestial fire is made to appear through magic; and these statues laugh, and lamps are spontaneously enkindled.' The Council of Laodicea, A.D. 366, wisely forbade the priesthood the study and practice of enchantment, mathematics, astrology, and the binding of the soul by amulets.

There is reason to fear that the purposes of medicine were converted by the monks to the basest uses, and that the authority of the physician superadded to the terrors of the church, exercised over those in whom the mind was enfeebled by disease and incapable of exerting its power, were employed in the extortion of money and the indulgence of rapacity. Want of knowledge was supplied by mystery, and faith usurped the place of effectual prescription. Hence arose the employment of charms, amulets, relics, &c. The ignorance and the cupidity of the monks caused the Lateran Council, under the pontificate of Calistus II, A.D. 1123, to forbid the attendance of the priests and monks at the bedside of the sick, otherwise than as ministers of religion. Still, however, it was secretly followed, and Pope Innocent II, in a council at Rheims, A.D. 1131, enforced the decree prohibiting the monks frequenting schools of medicine, and directed them to confine their practice to the limits of their own monastery. Some, however, continued to pursue it, and some of the secular clergy practised it as generally as before, so that the decrees were found inefficient in the accomplishment of their object; and a Lateran Council, in A.D. 1139, threatened all who neglected its orders with the severest penalties and suspension from the exercise of all ecclesiastical functions; denouncing such practices as a neglect of the sacred objects of their profession in exchange for ungodly lucre. . . .

When the priests ascertained that they could no longer confine the practice of medicine to themselves it was stigmatized and denounced. At the Council of Tours, held in 1163 by Pope Alexander

III, it was maintained that the devil, to seduce the priesthood from the duties of the altar, involved them in mundane occupations, which, under the plea of humanity, exposed them to constant and perilous temptations. They were accordingly prohibited the study of medicine, and that of the law, and every ecclesiastic who should infringe the decree was threatened with excommunication. In 1215 Pope Innocent III fulminated an anathema specially directed against surgery, by ordaining, that as the church abhorred all cruel or sanguinary practices, no priest should be permitted to follow surgery, or to perform any operations in which either instruments of steel or fire were employed; and that they should refuse their benediction to all those who professed and pursued it.

Stringent as these measures were, they were found inadequate to effect the purpose intended, and it was only at length accomplished by a special bull procured from the Pope, which, by permitting physicians to marry, effectually divorced medicine from theology.

In many catholic countries, however, the saints have proved sad enemies to the doctors. The priests, in some parts of Italy, still hold their medical influence. An ingenious young physician, travelling in that country in 1838, met with several instances during his stay in Naples. In one case he was asked by the parents of a poor girl to visit their child who was ill of a fever. He accompanied them to their miserable cabin, and found her in an advanced stage of typhus, yet not, he thought, hopelessly beyond the reach of art. He prescribed for her, and laid down strict injunctions to be followed during his absence. Upon visiting her again, he was surprised to find that his directions had not been followed, nor the treatment he directed pursued. She was now *in articulo mortis*. As he had not intruded his advice, this conduct on the part of the parents at first seemed inexplicable; but he soon found an explanation in the appearance of a priest, who, regardless of his presence, advanced to the bedside, and, inquiring whether his medicine had been administered, unfolded a paper containing a black salve, a minute portion of which he placed upon her tongue, and then harangued in a most intemperate manner upon the abomination the parents had been guilty of in seeking assistance from a heretic, who, he said, would be sure to administer poison in place of balm to their ills. In other cases the physician met with similar conduct.

At the time of the prevalence of the cholera in Canada, a man named Ayres, who came out of the States, and was said to be a graduate of the University of New Jersey, was given out to be St Roche, the principal patron saint of the Canadians, and renowned for his power in averting pestilential diseases. He was reported to have descended from heaven to cure his suffering people of the cholera, and many were the cases in which he appeared to afford relief. Many were thus dispossessed of their fright in anticipation of the disease, who might, probably, but for his inspiriting influence, have fallen victims to their apprehensions. The remedy he employed was an admixture of maple sugar, charcoal, and lard.

Miraculous cures are attested by monks, abbots, bishops, popes, and consecrated saints. St Martin's shrine alone is said to have restored fifty blind people to the blessing of sight; stories related no less at variance with the sentiments and characters of the men than contradicted by the laws of nature. Pilgrimages and visits to holy shrines have usurped the place of medicine, and, as in many cases at our own watering places, by air and exercise, have unquestionably effected what the employment of regular professional aid had been unable to accomplish. . . .

Medical observers constantly meet with extraordinary changes produced upon the body from passions of the mind or sudden emotions. Jaundice has been known to occur almost instantaneously upon a violent fit of anger, or within twenty-four hours of the receipt of bad intelligence or the occurrence of unexpectedly severe losses. The hair which was jet black shall in a few hours lose its colour, be deprived of its natural secretion, and turn gray or white, and this may be either partial or general.

> For deadly fear can time outgo,
> And blaunch at once the hair.
>
> (*Marmion.*)

Some remarkable instances of this kind are to be found in Schenckius. One of a noble Spaniard, Don Diego Osorio, who being in love with a young lady of the court, had prevailed with her for a private conference within the gardens of the king; but by the barking of a little dog their privacy was betrayed, the young gentleman seized by the king's guard and imprisoned. It was capital to be found in that place, and therefore he was condemned to die. He was so terrified at hearing this sentence, that one and the same night saw the same person young and old, being turned grey, as in those stricken in years. The gaoler, moved at the sight, related the accident to King Ferdinand as a prodigy, who thereupon pardoned him, saying, he had been sufficiently punished for his fault. A nobleman of the Roman court was also detected in an intrigue, cast into prison, and sentenced to be decapitated on the morrow. When brought before the Emperor Caesar he was so altered by the apprehension of death that his identity was questioned; the comeliness and beauty of his face being vanished, his countenance like a dead man's, his hair and beard turned grey, and in all respects so changed that the emperor caused strict examination of him to be made, and to ascertain whether his hair and beard had not been changed by art; this, however, being satisfactorily proved not to be the case, the emperor moved to pity, graciously pardoned him. The Hon Robert Boyle mentions partial cases which occurred during the Irish rebellion. Borelli gives an instance of a French gentleman, who upon being thrown into prison was so powerfully affected by fear, that his hair changed completely to a grey in the course of the night. He was released and the hair recovered its colour.

The effects of fear upon the body are apparent in many other ways. An approach to the door of a dentist by one labouring under toothache has often been found a sure means of banishing violent pain. Fright has frequently cured ague and other disorders of a periodical character; even fits of the gout have been terminated in the same manner. Paralysed muscles, and limbs that were useless have suddenly been thrown into action, and haemorrhages have as instantaneously been checked. The same causes productive of disease have been found also to effect their cure. Dr Pfeuffer knew a girl in the vicinity of Wurzburg, who, after being deaf for several years, instantly regained her hearing upon being made acquainted with the sudden death of her father. Every one has heard of the treatment proposed by the celebrated Boerhaave, to restrain imitative epilepsy by branding the next who should be affected with a hot iron. Dr Scott relates a case in which a threat to apply a red-hot iron to the feet of a boy who had been frequently attacked with epilepsy upwards of a year, was perfectly successful in preventing the recurrence of the disease.

A variety of conjectures might be offered to account for many of these phenomena, but none would be perfectly satisfactory to the minute and philosophical inquirer. Too much attention however cannot be paid to that mysterious union which exists between mind and body. The ancients were well convinced of this, though they effected little towards turning their opinion to advantage. Plato says,

> The office of the physician extends equally to the purification of mind and body; to neglect the one is to expose the other to evident peril. It is not only the body that by its sound constitution strengthens the soul, but the well-regulated soul by its authoritative power maintains the body in perfect health.

The mind without the body, nor the body without the mind cannot be well. '*Non sine animo corpus, nec sine corpore animus bene valere potest.*'

Sir Alexander Crichton, in his admirable work on *Mental Derangement*, in which he has no less powerfully than philosophically delineated the several passions and their varied operations, observes, that 'the passions are to be considered, in a medical point of view, as a part of our constitution, which is to be examined with the eye of a natural historian, and the spirit and impartiality of a philosopher.' At a meeting (1834) of the British Association for the Advancement of Science, Dr Abercrombie drew the attention of the medical section to the importance of the study of mental philosophy. He urged the propriety of treating it as a branch of physiology, and recommended the cultivation of it on strict philosophical principles as a science of observation, and as likely to yield laws, principles, or universal facts, which might be ascertained with the same precision as the laws of physical science. He, however, abjured all speculations respecting the nature and essence of mind, and contended for the necessity of confining these researches to a simple and careful study of its operations. The purposes to which this study should be applied, in the opinion of this learned physician and most excellent man, were the education of the young and the cultivation of a sound mental discipline at any period of life – the intellectual and moral treatment of insanity – the prevention of this disease in individuals in whom there exists the hereditary predisposition to it – and the study of mental science as the basis of a philosophical logic.

Too little attention is paid by physicians in general to the influence of the mind or the operations of the passions in the production and in the removal of disease. We know, it is true, that some of the passions excite whilst others depress; and we see how quickly and often how permanently changes are produced in the offices of different parts of the body. Whilst anger, on the one hand, accelerates the progress of the blood, hurrying on the circulation with fearful impetuosity, to the destruction of either the brain or the organs contained within the chest; grief, on the other, depresses the action of the heart, and causes serious accumulations in the larger vessels and in the lungs. Grief has not inaptly been styled 'an heavy executioner; nothing more crucifies the soul, nor overthrows the health of the body than sorrow.' The Psalmist beautifully expresses it: 'My soul melteth away for very heaviness.' Shakespeare's picture is not more true morally than physically, when he makes Macbeth to ask the physician:

> Canst thou minister to a mind diseas'd,
> Pluck from the memory a rooted sorrow,
> Raze out the written troubles of the brain,
> And with some sweet oblivious antidote
> Cleanse the stuff'd bosom of that perilous stuff
> Which weighs upon the heart?*

Violent grief may be speedy and fatal in its effects, but that which is slow and continued is most inimical to health. It undermines the strongest and best of constitutions, and is the cause of a long catalogue of diseases. The energy of the nervous system is weakened, the functions are carried on in a slow and an unequal manner, so that in these cases the body and soul may literally be said 'reciprocally to prey on each other.'

> ' 'Tis painful thinking that corrodes our clay.'
>
> (ARMSTRONG.)

From the operation of anger or of grief, either in excess or under a modified condition, various disorders may arise; and to the influence of the passions generally, therefore, in health as well as in disease, should the attention of the medical practitioner be directed. It has been well said by Dr Reid that he who in the study or the treatment of the human machinery, overlooks the intellectual part of it, cannot but entertain very incorrect notions of its nature, and fall into gross and sometimes fatal blunders in the means which he adopts for its regulation or repair. Intellect is not omnipotent; but its actual power over the organized matter to which it is attached is much greater than is usually imagined. The anatomy of the mind, therefore, should be learnt, as well as that of the body; the study of its

* Mr Collier's excellent edition.

constitution in general, and its peculiarities, or what may be technically called its idiosyncrasies, in any individual case, ought to be regarded as one of the most essential branches of a medical education.

The power of the mind exerted over the body has been rendered conspicuous by many remarkable cases on record:

> Men may die of imagination,
> So depe may impression be take.
>   (CHAUCER – *The Milleres Tale*, v. 3612.)

Fienus mentions an instance of a malefactor who was carried out, as he conceived, to execution; and in order thereto his cap was pulled over his eyes, and a cold wet cloth being struck hastily about his neck, he fell down dead, under the conceit of his decapitation. Charron records a similar case: A man having his eyes covered to be put to death, as he imagined – being condemned, – and uncovering them again to receive his pardon, was found really dead on the scaffold. It is commonly told, but I am unacquainted with the authority, that a person was directed to be bled to death; his eyes were blinded and he was made to believe, by water trickling down his arm, that the sentence was being carried into effect. The mimicry is said to have produced his death as effectually as would the real operation. The powers of life were destroyed by the power of his imagination.

Excessive joy has been known to occasion death equally with, nay, more frequently than, fear and terror. Sir Alexander Crichton relates, that

> in the year 1544 the Jewish pirate, Sinamus Taffurus, was lying in a port of the Red Sea, called Arsenoe, and was preparing for war, being then engaged in one with the Portuguese. While he was there he received the unexpected intelligence that his son, who in the siege of Tunis had been made prisoner by Barbarossa and by him doomed to slavery, was suddenly ransomed, and coming to his aid with seven ships well armed. The joyful news was too much for him: he was immediately struck as with an apoplexy, and expired on the spot.

Valerius Maximus relates the case of two women, matrons, who died with joy on seeing their sons return safe from battle at the lake Thrases. One died while embracing her son; the other was suddenly surprised by the sight of her son while she was deeply lamenting his supposed death. Sophocles, at an advanced age and in the full possession of his intellectual power, composed a tragedy, which was crowned with such success that he died through joy. Chilon of Lacedemon died from joy whilst embracing his son, who had borne away the prize at the Olympic Games. Juventius Thalma, to whom a triumph was decreed for subjugating Corsica, fell down dead at the foot of the altar at which he was offering up his thanksgiving. Fouquet, upon receiving the intelligence of Louis XIV having restored him to liberty, fell down dead. There are many cases of a similar nature on record.

The cases of sudden death from powerful emotions and unexpected joys or sorrow are numerous in the writings of the ancients. They are doubtless to be attributed to the effects produced by means of the nervous system acting chiefly upon other organs, particularly those which appertain to the sanguiferous system, where either disease or a strong predisposition to it had previously existed. Most of the cases of sudden death which now occur – and they have been lamentably numerous of late – are shown by dissection to arise from disorder of the heart or its large vessels.

Sympathy appears to exert itself more particularly between the mind and certain organs of the body than with others. Any excitement of mind quickens the circulation, and occasions the heart to palpitate, that is, to beat quickly and tremulously. Senac quotes a case from Blancard of a person, who, being witness to a dreadful shipwreck, was so operated upon by distress and terror, that palpitation of the heart, succeeded by oppressed breathing, syncope, and death ensued. Upon examination, the heart was found enlarged. The same author mentions other fatal cases occasioned by mental emotions and passions in those in whom, upon examination, the heart was found unnatural and unhealthy. Next to the heart, the organs of digestion seem most susceptible of the effects from mental emotions; and an ingenious writer, Mr Fletcher, of Gloucester, has ventured to designate the effect of the passions upon the stomach as a 'Mental Indigestion', in contradistinction to that dyspepsia which arises from physical causes. The reciprocity of action between certain passions and certain organs is a subject highly deserving of investigation. Fear, as already stated, produces its most decided effects upon the heart, and it is the especial condition of all who have disease of this organ to be under continual apprehension and dread. . . .

Disease is well known to depress the powers of the understanding as well as the vigour of the muscular system, and will also deprave the judgment as well as the digestion. A sick person is, in particular, extremely credulous about the object of his hopes and fears. Whoever promises him health may easily obtain his confidence, and he soon becomes the dupe of quacks and ignorant pretenders.

Medical faith is a matter of very great importance in the cure of diseases, and Dr Haygarth was quite justified in expressing his wish never to have a patient who did not possess a sufficient portion of it. A doctor being asked the question, why he could not cure his mother-in-law as well as his father? wittily replied, that his mother-in-law had not the same confidence, or rather fancy for him, as his father had, otherwise the cure would have been effected. The administration of new medicines, without possessing anything particularly novel or powerful, will frequently induce an amendment in the disease: this may probably arise, in some instances, from the presence of a new stimulus to which the frame has therefore not been accustomed; but in the majority of cases it will be found to be the result of an effect of the imagination. Hippocrates admitted that that physician performed most cures in whom the patients placed the greatest reliance. Medicines when prescribed by a physician of celebrity have been known to succeed better in his hands than that of other persons. Where faith is wanting little success is to be expected. The influence of hope is necessary to procure relief, and the alleviation or removal of diseases is in a great number of cases dependent upon the condition of the mind. An agreement between the mind and the body is constant; and Sterne truly though singularly expressed this opinion, when he said, 'The body and mind are like a jerkin and a jerkin's lining, rumple the one and you rumple the other.'

From On Superstitions connected with the History and Practice of Medicine and Surgery *(1844) pages 28–29, 32–35, 90–97, 110–111.*

CHAPTER THIRTEEN

Mesmerine

John Jones

The powers of hypnosis are so prevalent in *Dracula* that they appear almost to provide a plot within a plot. It is part of the Count's armoury that he can induce submission into his victims simply by applying the hypnotic, animalistic stare. Perhaps Stoker was giving a new slant to the term 'animal magnetism'. Dracula's first victim upon arriving in Britain is Lucy, a young girl prone to somnambulism. Somnambulism is itself a form of trance. Dracula tunes into this susceptibility in order to entice Lucy from her room for the purpose of a cliff-top rendezvous.

Lucy's sleep-walking, in fact, provides Stoker with the opportunity to engage in a little innovation of his own. Although she must meet the brutal fate of all vampires, Stoker wants to exonerate her from full complicity arising from her pact with the devil. Her somnambulism provides him the means to do so. She meets Dracula in trance. She also dies, before she can become a vampire, in trance. Let Van Helsing explain, as he examines her dead body:

> Here, there is one thing which is different from all recorded; here is some dual life that is not as the common. She was bitten by the vampire when she was in a trance, sleep-walking – oh, you start; you do not know that, friend John, but you shall know it all later – and in trance could he best come to take more blood. In trance she dies, and in trance she is Un-Dead, too. So it is that she differ from all other. Usually when the Un-Dead sleep at home – as he spoke he made a comprehensive sweep of his arm to designate what to a vampire was 'home' – their face show what they are, but this so sweet that was when she not Un-dead [sic] she go back to the nothings of the common dead. There is no malign there . . .'
> (*Dracula* Chapter 15)

With the demise of Lucy, attention turns to the fate of her friend, Mina. Here Stoker describes more conventional hypnotic procedures. He had already declared his familiarity with this subject by having Van Helsing mourn the death of the celebrated French neurologist and hypnotist Charcot, who died in August 1893 – midway through the novel's timetable. After Mina has been 'introduced' to Dracula, Van Helsing resorts to hypnotising her as a means of discovering the Count's whereabouts. This he does by commencing 'to make passes in front of her, from over the top of her head downward, with each hand in turn'. (*Dracula* Chapter 23) Hey presto, Mina is hypnotised.

Stoker's reference to Charcot raises questions about the attitudes of *Dracula*'s author towards his heroines. Charcot was indeed an eminent advocate of hypnosis, except that he firmly believed that only certain persons of morbid personality, namely hysterics, were susceptible to it. Lucy's capacity for somnambulism and Mina's easy succumbing to Van Helsing's hand-passes marks them both in Stoker's eyes, as of hysterical temperament.

This brief simplistic account of the induction process might suggest that Stoker was not greatly acquainted with the mechanics of hypnosis. In fact, his sources indicate that he read a great deal on that subject. It is difficult from today's vantage point to appreciate just how excited and agitated Victorian society was by the mysterious 'science' of mesmerism. Along with its associated phenomena, clairvoyance and spiritualism, it constituted a mounting challenge to perceived ways of thought, drawing both passionate support and vehement criticism from among the ranks of the Church. Pick up at random any Victorian book on contemporary medicine, science or Christianity and there is a fair chance that it will have something to say about mesmerism. At least half a dozen of Stoker's sources, while making no mention of hypnosis in the title, turn out to contain disquisitions on the subject.

A case in point is John Jones' *The Natural and the Supernatural: or, Man – Physical, Apparitional, and Spiritual* (1861). This is an extraordinary book. Like others of similar mind, Jones sets about examining the entire field of other-worldly beliefs, as a glance at some of his chapter-headings indicates: Mental currents and Storms; Phrenology; Instinct; Clairvoyance; Spiritualism; Fortune-Telling and Divination; Second Sight; Risings – Anti-Gravitation; Touching by Angels; Dream Visions; etc. Initial wonder at such a quest, however, soon gives way to irritation, then dismay. Of all Stoker's sources for *Dracula* none reads so strangely as Jones', which instantly makes one aware of the chasm which exists between nineteenth and twentieth century thought. The chapter on the mysterious substance known as mesmerine, and which Jones takes to be at the core of mesmerism, perfectly illustrates this chasm.

*

Mesmerine

The power of 'Mesmerine' may be observed in the sick chamber; let the patient be afflicted with small-pox, putrid fever, or other contagious disease; and when a stranger comes into the room, if ventilation has been neglected, the effluvia or 'mesmerine' which has streamed from the afflicted is offensive; and if the visitor be in a negative or sickly condition, he imbibes a portion of that effluvia. Sometimes the *point* or sting of the vapour or disease, with lightning speed, darts upon the stranger, leaves the patient, who recovers; and enters the receptive body of the visitor; and if we could *see* the operation in action, we should be witness to a phenomenon similar to that we call the thunder-bolt, when the point of the fluid darts out and penetrates the atmosphere through the weakest of its negative parts, and enters and kills its receiver; we should witness the disease in the form of a thunder-cloud, surrounding the invalid, and discharging itself by a point of light on the new influence placed within its power. Well is it for man that his organs of sight are so opaque as to prevent him from seeing the more inner or subtler operations of nature. If he were witness to them, life would be a task, fearful and severe; those emanations, and lights, and tempests, would so occupy his energies, and so cloud his vision of the solid, on which he has to depend for support; that life under such a phase would be a misery, and death happiness. It is these death-clouds which hang over the patient, and which are seen, and felt by sensitive animals (such as the dog) and cause the frequent occurrence of 'death-tokens' by howling under the windows of the afflicted; the dog passing *perceives* that which we do not, and his fear finds vent in howlings. Dogs are excessively sensitive to smell, and carry it to such a degree, that where the effluvia or mesmerine proceeding from any human being is agreeable to them, they will follow and endeavour to make friends with those they never saw before: even roughness has little effect, they will run off, only to draw near when opportunity offers.

The law of positive and negative runs through nature. The giver and receiver must be in different conditions, and throw off different effluvia; and if we could *see* the operation, we should find that each effluvia had a substantive existence, as real as the physical human body; all in nature are both receivers and givers, are positive to some powers, and negative to others; all have what is scientifically called Polarity. The very magnet which draws the needle is a receiver and giver; it receives an influence or atmosphere which penetrates its solid, and passes off imbued with the nature of the metal it passes through, and that power is so strong, as I have in past pages stated, that it jets out the emanation, *lays hold* of the iron, if sufficiently powerful, and draws it to itself. In one sense, all seen substances are negatives, as it is only the ethereal influence which enters at one end, and passes off at the other; in another sense, they are positives, as the influence while so passing through becomes a negative, and *receives* of the special quality of the substances passed through; which, borne on the atmosphere, are carried hither and thither, and absorbed by their affinities. Having thus generalized, to show the universal prevalence of 'influence' from all substances; it follows that man has also an influence, which has a powerful effect on his fellow-man, and which we distinguish by the word 'mesmerine'; from Mesmer, the re-discoverer of the power man has, by the exercise of his spirit or will, in directing the route of the *chemical heat* which passes off from his body. Mesmer found out a power, but did not understand the principles on which the effects stood. He had a tub filled with various articles, glass, stone, minerals, &c; the feet of his patients were put into the tub, and while he stood by, most surprising results were produced; faintings, convulsions, trances, elevations of mental power in patients, and cures of many of the diseases the parties were afflicted with. He found also that *he* had power to produce phenomena, it was all a mystery to him; and as these results were noised about, the usual opposition to new things arose, and the schools of medicine, or rather the professors or teachers, ignored the facts, and branded him as an impostor; as in later days, George Stephenson was in a committee of the House of Commons branded with the name of 'lunatic', because he declared that locomotive engines would be able to travel along railways at the rate of twelve miles an hour. Since Mesmer's days the practitioners with 'Mesmerine' have been thousands, and its phenomena have been marvellous; so much so, that the materialist has simply denied the facts, and the religionists, when they could not gainsay them, attributed them to 'Satanic agency'; a slough for all the works of Deity which were not explained at school when they were boys.

Having made the declaration, that a 'chemical aura' proceeds from *every* living substance; let us individualize the subject by creating in the mind's eye; two men, one with black hair, and healthy; the other light hair, and unwell; and a phenomenon will be produced which any man or woman can verify by his own observation, within his own domestic or social circle, and thus *test* the existence of mesmerine and its astonishing results on human nature. Let Light hair extend the palm of his hand towards Black, let Black gently move his fingers a few times, from the wrist down the centre of the palm, to the end of the middle finger, at about half an inch to an inch from the flesh; then pass the hand up again to the wrist and repeat the movement, say, five to seven times, avoiding every time he returns to the wrist, the passing of the operative hand *over* the palm; and the person operated upon will perceive, as it were, a cool or hot breeze, gentle and soft, passing along the palm as the operator moves his hand, and in most cases the operator can tell the *exact spot* the operated upon, felt the current most powerfully. That current is mesmerine, and is the agent or substance which enters the body, and, like the essence of seidlitz powders, effervesces in the body and neutralizes the excess of acidity in the system. So with all medicines, it is not the solid, but the essence or *soul power* contained *in* the visible medicine, which acts on the human system.

Mesmerine is a chemical combination scientifically mixed by nature, and found in *every healthy* human body, male and female; and when applied with an earnest will by passing the warm hand over, but not touching a diseased part, or as near that part as possible, it acts at once; and by stimulating the physical powers, enables them to overcome an obstruction, and perform their functions naturally. Mesmerine has a living energy and power – a subtilty of action in its sphere, which the mere mineral or vegetable cannot have; it is not possible that minerals, collected, ground to powder, and boxed up in a laboratory; or that the root, bark, or leaves of the vegetable dry and withered, can have the same active chemical power that the essence has when streaming from the healthy vital body; and as the surface of the body is crowded with innumerable pores, it presents a natural and incomparable passage for the mesmerine to be thrown by the operator into that part of the body which is diseased; say the chest, the lungs, the head, the foot, the spine, the arm, &c; whereas ordinary medicines have to be swallowed, digested, extracted, and absorbed, and in many cases almost uniformly unsuccessfully.

Disease, in ninety-five cases out of a hundred, is simply an obstruction of the blood vessels, created by the languid action of the blood, for want of the due admixture of chemical substances producing inflammation, ulceration, death. It is evident, therefore, that if the stoppage could be removed, inflammation would cease; disease would be removed, and the healthy tone of the body be in full power. The Essence streaming from man when directed by the will, and poured, shall I say, upon the diseased part; be it rheumatism in the arm or wrist, where the action can be watched; causes a powerful heat to be felt by the patient, frequently accompanied by a 'tingling' sensation; the veins *visibly* swell, the chemical action of the essence acts upon, and appears to dissolve the obstruction; the enlarged veins, like an enlarged drain, give passage for carrying off the inflammatory matter; and the ever onward course of the life blood, forces the way, and the restored action and cessation of pain, attests the cure.

The mesmeric passes are generally made by pointing the fingers at a distance of a quarter of an inch to two inches from, and over the diseased part; by contracting the fingers, and holding them over it with the same kind of *feeling*, and in the same *position* as if a pen were in the hand, and in the act of writing: and after holding the hand in that position for a short time, say a minute, gradually move the fingers from the diseased part, and at the same distance, and draw off the hand at a more rapid pace to the nearest extremity; thus, for the head, over the ears, and off at the shoulders; for the arm, off at the fingers; for the legs, the feet; repeat the process, do it heartily, kindly, and you will, in from five to fifteen minutes, be gratified with the result.

On the essence being absorbed by the disease, it is more than likely the operator will feel as if something were coming off at his finger ends; and it is also frequently accompanied by a throbbing, accelerated pulsation in one or more of his fingers; a sensation which reminds one of water pouring out of a narrow-necked phial. Nature is then carrying out the well-known law of demand and supply. Fire attracts air, and combustion is the result; heat attracts electricity, and the flash of the lightning, and the roll of the thunder, proclaim that atmospheric health is restored. Animal inflammation attracts animal essence, and health is the result. Thus nature is everywhere in its several divisions, carrying out the great law of *equilibrium*; and as the atom, minute of itself, has within its acknowledged littleness all the qualities, character, and laws of a mountain; so a human body, minute of itself, has within itself all the qualities, character, and laws which govern the mass of animal matter existing on the surface of the globe.

Returning to the action of the mesmerine on a diseased part, if at the close of the sitting, say from fifteen to thirty minutes, there should be any stiffness in the limb operated on; blow over the part, and the stiffness will be removed. Let the plan indicated be carried out once or twice a-day till the cure is effected. If it should happen that the patient be inclined to sleep, which is likely, when operating on the chest or lungs; encourage it, as it shows that the essence is laying hold of the system, the same as laudanum or morphine does in the usual routine of medicine. . . .

Sleep can be produced by artificial means. Morphine, opium, and other narcotics or modifications of narcotics, produce slumber, they wrap the mental energies in quiet; the nerves get rest; the organs of the head, and the sinews of the body, get rest; the involuntary nerves, and other self-operative powers, are allowed to do their work without let or hindrance from their companions, – the voluntary powers; and physical nature is refreshed. Mesmerine acts on some patients as a narcotic, it soothes – a quiet steals over the body, as the chemical heat of the hand slowly passes over the brain, the face, and the chest, and gets absorbed by the pores of the flesh. I have frequently caused the same result by simply holding the ends of the fingers of one hand, under the palm of the hand, not touching it; the heat ascends, and as a positive, is absorbed by the patient, who in his state of disease has become a negative; it ascends the arm, and steadily passes onwards *in* the body, till it arrives at the greatest negative or most diseased part in the system; it there acts, allays irritation, and soothes: with a few, it so steeps them in forgetfulness, that as with opiates, you may talk, shout, and shake them, without producing any effect: in such cases, its medicinal energies are acting, and the patient ought to be undisturbed till he *awakes himself*: no harm can arise, the longer the slumbers the more powerful the mesmerine, and more effectual the cure. I have seen this power in action, over and over again.

From The Natural and the Supernatural *(1861) pages 119–124, 127.*

CHAPTER FOURTEEN

Trance-sleep, Somnambulism, and Trance-Waking

Herbert Mayo

There are to be found in *Dracula* three different types of trance state. Dracula can produce it by eye-power alone. Renfield says of him that his 'eyes burned into me, and my strength became like water'. Mina, on the other hand, offers herself to straightforward clinical hypnosis, which she achieves as a result of Van Helsing's attentions. This is a quite separate phenomenon from the hypnotic power at Dracula's disposal, who has no need to make rhythmic movements with his hands to achieve his desired effects. As for Lucy, her situation bears little comparison with either case. Her sleep-walking and the consequent nature of her vampire death-trance illustrates a quite distinct psychological relationship with her master, unique in vampire literature.

The reason for Stoker's concern with trance-like features in *Dracula* is not surprising, given the almost morbid fascination for that subject among learned circles of his time. But why so many varieties of trance, and where did he learn of them? Herbert Mayo's investigation *On the Truths contained in Popular Superstitions – with an Account of Mesmerism* goes some way to answering these questions.

Mayo has already featured in this study, in Chapter 3, with his account of vampyrism. He seemed almost to wish to be rid of such a distraction before settling down into the subject of mesmerism. Stoker might have taken note of Mayo's distinction between sleeping trance and waking trance. Each possesses several sub-types, leading Mayo to put forward what he sees as five overlapping varieties: death-trance, trance-coma, simple (or initiatory) trance, half-waking trance (or somnambulism), and full-waking trance (or catalepsy).

What links together, in Mayo's mind, all these different kinds of trance is the mysterious 'Od-Force'; as espoused by the Viennese natural philosopher Von Reichenbach. Persons of strong constitution are apparently immune from this force – an exemption which, he insists, necessarily excludes most young ladies. To those who are susceptible it is suggested that magnets moved parallel with the body produce weird sensations, tingling, numbness, or a faint draft as if produced by moving air. In some cases flames are reported around the poles of the magnet. The 'force' supposedly responsible was given the name of 'Od' or 'Odyle'.

This odylic force was proposed as an advancement in the search for the hidden physical fluid proposed by Anton Mesmer – similar to what John Jones had described as 'mesmerine'. This search continued long after the demonstration in 1841 by the Scotsman James Braid that the same patient's sensations could be produced as a result of simple suggestion. There was no force at work other than the power of the human imagination. Braid coined the term 'hypnosis' to account for this power of suggestion, and in Mayo's later editions he managed to squeeze in a concluding chapter on these developments – though he sidesteps the problem by proposing that hypnosis is really nothing more than self-mesmerism and, in any case, Braid could only have achieved his successes through his own Od-influence! Indeed, Mayo likens the effects of so-called hypnosis to conscious clairvoyance, and he conveniently conjures up a sixth heading to accommodate it within his original schema – 'trance-umbra'.

Mayo's arguments, naturally enough, cannot be applied to Dracula's peculiar animal-magnetic powers, though it is possible that he provided Stoker with valuable insights regarding the novel's other two cases of mesmerism – relating to the contrasting susceptibilities of Lucy and Mina. Mayo's book was, of course, nearly half a century out of date by the time *Dracula* was published. By the 1890s it was widely accepted that there was no 'substance' passing between master and subject, be it mesmerine, Od, or anything else. It is therefore curious that although Mina Harker requests that Van Helsing 'hypnotise' her, he does not ask her to fix her gaze on anything, offers no verbal suggestions of any kind, but simply goes through the routine of rapid hand passes in the largely outmoded mesmeric tradition.

*

Trance-Sleep, Somnambulism, and Trance-Waking
Trance, then, it appears, is a peculiar mental seizure liable to supervene in persons of an irritable nervous system, either after

mental excitement or in deranged bodily health. The seizure may last for a few hours, or a few days, or for weeks, or years; and is liable to recur at regular or irregular intervals.

Trance again, it has been observed, has phases corresponding with the sleeping and waking of our natural state. And as natural sleep presents three varieties – the profound and heavy sleep of extreme exhaustion, ordinary deep sleep, and the light slumber of the wakeful and the anxious, so trance-sleep is threefold likewise. But as in trance everything is magnified, the differences between the three states are greater, and the phenomena of each more bold and striking.

Two conditions are common, however, to every phase of trance-sleep; these are, the occurrence of complete insensibility, and that of vivid and coherent dreams.

The insensibility is so absolute that the most powerful stimulants are insufficient to rouse the patient. An electric shock, a surgical operation, the amputation even of a limb, are seemingly unfelt.

The dreams of trance-sleep have a character of their own. It is to be remarked, that in the dreams of ordinary sleep the ideas are commonly an incoherent jumble; and that, if they happen to refer to passing events, they commonly reverse their features. The attention seems to be slumbering. Thus Sir George Back told me, that in the privations which he encountered in Sir John Franklin's first expedition, when in fact he was starving, he uniformly dreamed of plentiful repasts. But in the dreams of trance-sleep, on the contrary, the impressions of the waking thoughts, the exciting ideas themselves, which have caused the supervention of trance, are realised and carried out in a consecutive train of imaginary action. They are, accordingly, upon the patient's awaking, accurately remembered by him; and that with such force and distinctness, that if he be a fanatic or superstitiously inclined, he very likely falls into the belief that the occurrences he dreamed of actually took place in his presence. A temperate fanatic goes no further, under such circumstances, than to assert that he has had a vision. The term is so good a one, that it appears to me worth retaining, in a philosophical sense, for the present exigency. I propose to restrict the term vision to the dreams of persons in trance-sleep.

Then of the three different forms of trance-sleep.

I. *Death-trance* – Death-trance is the image of death. The heart does not act; the breathing is suspended; the body is motionless; not the slightest outward sign of sensibility or consciousness can be detected. The temperature of the body falls. The entranced person has the appearance of a corpse from which life has recently departed. The joints are commonly relaxed, and the whole frame pliable; but it is likely that spasmodic rigidity forms an occasional adjunct of this strange condition. So the only means of knowing whether life be still present is to wait the event. The body is to be kept in a warm room, for the double purpose of promoting decomposition if it be dead, and of preserving in it the vital spark if it still linger; and it should be constantly watched. But should every recently dead body be made the subject of similar care? it is natural to ask. There are, of course, many cases where such care is positively unnecessary – such, for instance, as death following great lesions of vital organs; and in the great majority of cases of seeming death, the bare possibility of the persistence of life hardly remains. Still it is better to err on the safe side. And although in England, from the higher tone of moral feeling, and from the respect shown to the remains of the dead, the danger of being interred alive is inconsiderable, still the danger certainly exists to a very considerable degree of being opened alive by order of a zealous coroner. But for the illustration of this danger, and examples of the circumstances under which death-trance has been known to occur, and of its usual features, I refer the reader back to the second Letter of this series. Let me, however, add, that it is not improbable that, by means of persons susceptible of the influence of Od, or of persons in induced waking-trance, the question could be at once decided whether a seeming corpse were really dead.

In England, during the last epidemic visitation of cholera, several cases of death-trance occurred, in which the patient, who was on the point of being buried, fortunately awoke in time to be saved. Death-trance, it is probable, is much more frequently produced by spasmodic and nervous illness than by mental causes: it has followed fever; it has frequently attended parturition. In this respect it differs from other forms of trance-sleep, which mostly, when spontaneous, supervene upon mental impressions.

The only feature of death-trance which it remains for me to exemplify is the occurrence in it of visions. Perhaps the following may be taken as an instance:

Henry Engelbrecht, as we learn in a pamphlet published by him in 1639, after an ascetic life, during which he had experienced sensorial illusions, fell into the deepest form of trance, which he thus describes:

In the year 1623, exhausted by intense mental excitement of a religious kind, and by abstinence from food, after hearing a sermon which strongly affected him, he felt as if he could combat no longer; so he gave in and took to his bed. There he lay a week, without tasting anything but the bread and wine of the sacrament. On the eighth day, he thought he fell into the death-struggle. Death seemed to invade him from below upwards. His body became to his feelings rigid; his hands and feet insensible; his tongue and lips incapable of motion; gradually his sight failed him. But he still heard the laments and consultations of those around him.

This gradual demise lasted from mid-day till eleven at night, when he heard the watchmen. Then he wholly lost sensibility to outward impressions. But an elaborate vision of immense detail began; the theme of which was, that he was first carried down to hell, and looked into the place of torment; from whence, after a time, quicker than an arrow he was borne to Paradise. In these abodes of suffering and happiness, he saw and heard and smelt things unspeakable. These scenes, though long in apprehension, were short in time; for he came enough to himself, by twelve o'clock, again to hear the watchmen. It took him another twelve hours to come round entirely. His hearing was first restored; then his sight; feeling and power of motion followed; as soon as he could move his limbs, he rose. He felt himself stronger than before the trance.

II. *Trance-coma.* The appearance of a person in trance-coma is that of one in profound sleep. The breathing is regular, but extremely gentle; the action of the heart the same; the frame lies completely relaxed and flexible, and, when raised, falls in any posture, like the body of one just dead, as its weight determines. The bodily temperature is natural. The condition is distinguishable from common sleep by the total insensibility of the entranced person to all ordinary stimulants: besides, the pupil of the eye, instead of being contracted to a minute aperture, as it is in common sleep, is usually dilated; at all events it is not contracted, and it is fixed.

Perhaps the commonest cause of trance-coma is hysteria; or by hysteria is meant a highly irritable state of the nervous system, most commonly met with in young unmarried women. There seems to be present, as its proximate cause, an excessive nervous vitality: and that excess, in its simplest manifestation, breaks out in fits of sobbing and crying, alternating often with laughter—a physical excitement of the system which yet fatigues and distresses the patient's mind, who cannot resist the unaccountable impulses. It is at the close of such a paroxysm of hysteria that trance-coma of a few hours' duration not unfrequently supervenes. It is almost a natural repose after the preceding stage of excitement. Hysteria, besides giving origin to a peculiar class of local ailments, is further the fruitful mother of most varieties of trance.

Trance-coma sometimes supervenes on fever, and the patient lies for hours or days on the seeming verge of death. I have known it ensue after mesmeric practice carried to an imprudent excess. Religious mental excitement will bring it on. In the following instance, which I quote from the Rev. George Sandby's sensible and useful work on Mesmerism, the state of trance so supervening was probably trance-coma:

> George Fox, the celebrated father of Quakerism, at one period lay in a trance for fourteen days, and people came to stare and wonder at him. He had the appearance of a dead man; but his sleep was full of divine visions of beauty and glory.

Here is another instance, wherein the prevailing state must have been trance-coma. I quote it from the letter of an intelligent friend. It will help the reader to realise the general conception I wish to raise in his mind:

> I heard [says my correspondent] through the newspapers, of a case of trance ten miles from this place, and immediately rode to the village to verify it, and gain information about it. With some difficulty I persuaded the mother to allow me to see the entranced girl. Her name is Ann Cromer; she is daughter of a mason at Faringdon Gournay, ten miles from Bristol. She was lying in a state of general but not total suspension of the symptoms of life. Her breathing was perceptible by the heaving of the chest, and at times she had uttered low groans. Her jaws are locked, and she is incapable of the slightest movement, so as to create no other wrinkle in her bed-clothes but such as a dead weight would produce. When I saw her, she had not been moved for a week. Upon one occasion, when asked to show, by the pressure of the hand, if she felt any pain, a slight squeeze was perceptible. A very small portion of fluid is administered as food from time to time, but I neglected to discover how. Her hands are warm, and her mother thinks that she is conscious. Three days before I saw her, she spoke (incoherently) for the first time since her trance commenced. She repeated the Lord's Prayer, and asked for an aunt; but she rapidly relapsed, and her locked-jaw returned. Her mother considered this revival a sign of approaching death. The most

remarkable feature in the case is the length of time that the girl has remained entranced. She was twelve years old when the fit supervened, and the locked-jaw followed in sixteen weeks afterwards. She is now twenty-five years of age, and will thus, in a month, if alive, have been in this condition for thirteen years. In the mean while she has grown from a child to a woman, though her countenance retains all the appearance of her former age. She is little else than skin and bone, except her cheeks which are puffy. She is as pale as a corpse, and her eyes are sunk deep in the sockets.

III. *Simple or Initiatory Trance.* – In the lightest form of trance-sleep, the patient, though perfectly insensible to ordinary impressions, is not necessarily recumbent. If he is sitting when taken, he continues sitting; if previously lying, he will sometimes raise himself up when entranced. His joints are neither relaxed nor rigid: if you raise his arm, or bend the elbow, you experience a little resistance; and immediately after, probably, the limb is restored to its former posture. Such is the ordinary degree of muscular tone present; but either cataleptic immobility, or catochus, may accidentally coexist with initiatory trance. The patient may even remain standing rapt in his trance. I quote the following classic instance from the *Edinburgh Review*:

> There is a wonderful story told of Socrates. Being in military service in the expedition to Potidea, he is reported to have stood twenty-four hours before the camp, rooted to the same spot and absorbed in deep thought, his arms folded and his eyes fixed upon one object, as if his soul were absent from his body.

It is not my intention to dwell more on this form of trance at present. Various cases, exemplifying its varieties, will be found in the letter on Religious Delusions. It is the commonest product of fanatical excitement. I have called this form initiatory trance, because, in day-somnambulism, it always precedes the half-waking which constitutes that state; and because it is the state into which mesmeric manipulators ordinarily first plunge the patient. Out of this initiatory state I have seen the patient thrown into trance-coma; but the ordinary progress of the experiment is to conduct him in the other direction – that is, towards trance-waking. . . .

A curious fate somnambulism has had. While other forms of trance have been either rejected as fictions, or converted to the use of superstition, somnambulism with all its wonders, being at once undeniable and familiar, has been simply taken for granted. While her sisters have been exalted into mystical phenomena, and play parts in history, somnambulism has had no temple raised to her, has had no fear-worship, at the highest has been promoted to figure in an opera. Of a quiet and homely nature, she has moved about the house, not like a visiting demon, but as a maid of all work. To the public the phenomenon has presented no more interest than a soap-bubble, or the fall of an apple.

Somnambulism, as the term is used in England, exactly comprehends all the phenomena of half-waking trance.* The seizure mostly comes on during common sleep. But it may supervene in the daytime; in which case the patient first falls into the lightest form of trance-sleep. After a little, still lost to things around him, he manifests one or more of three impulses: one, to speak, but coherently and to a purpose; a second, to dress, rise, and leave his room with an evident intention of going somewhither; a third, to practise some habitual mechanical employment. In each case he appears to be pursuing the thread of a dream. If he speaks, it is a connected discourse to some end. If he goes out to walk, it is to a spot he contemplates visiting; his general turn is to climb ascents, hills, or the roofs of houses: in the latter case he sometimes examines if the tiles are secure before he steps on them. If he pursues a customary occupation, whether it be cleaning harness or writing music, he finishes his work before he leaves it. He is acting a dream, which is connected and sustained. The attention is keenly awake in this dream, and favours its accomplishment to the utmost. In the mean time the somnambulist appears to be insensible to ordinary impressions, and to take no cognisance of what is going on around him – a light may be held so close to his eyes as to singe his eyebrows without his noticing it – he seems neither to hear nor to taste – the eyelids are generally closed, otherwise the eyes are fixed and vacant. Nevertheless he possesses some means of recognising the objects which are implicated in his dream; he perceives their place, and walks among them with perfect precision. Let me narrate some instances. The first, one of day-somnambulism, exemplifies, at the same time, the transitions to full waking, which manifest themselves

---

* Many writers employ the term somnambulism to denote indiscriminately several forms of trance, or trance in general. I prefer restricting it to the peculiar class of cases commonly known as sleep-walking.

occasionally in the talking form of the trance. The case is from the *Acta Vratisv.* ann. 1722.

A girl, seventeen years of age, was used to fall into a kind of sleep in the afternoon, in which it was supposed, from her expression of countenance and her gestures, that she was engaged in dreams that interested her. (She was then in light trance-sleep, initiatory trance.) After some days she began to speak when in this state. Then if those present addressed remarks to her, she replied very sensibly, but then fell back into her dream discourse, which turned principally upon religious and moral topics, and was directed to warn her friends how a female should live – Christianly, well governed, and so as to incur no reproach. When she sang, which often happened, she heard herself accompanied by an imaginary violin or piano, and would take up and continue the accompaniment upon an instrument herself. She sewed, did knitting, and the like. She imagined, on one occasion, that she wrote a letter upon a napkin, which she folded for the post. Upon waking, she had not the slightest recollection of anything that had passed. After a few months she recovered. . . .

The following case of somnambulism, allied with St Veitz's dance, is given by Lord Monboddo:–

The patient, about sixteen years of age, used to be commonly taken in the morning a few hours after rising. The approach of the seizure was announced by a sense of weight in the head and drowsiness, which quickly terminated in sleep, (trance-sleep,) in which her eyes were fast shut. She described a feeling beginning in the feet, creeping like a gradual chill higher and higher, till it reached the heart,when consciousness left her. Being in this state, she sprang from her seat about the room, over tables and chairs, with astonishing agility. Then, if she succeeded in getting out of the house, she ran, at a pace with which her elder brother could hardly keep up, to a particular spot in the neighbourhood, taking the directest but the roughest path. If she could not manage otherwise, she got over the garden wall, with astonishing rapidity and precision of movement. Her eyelids were all the time fast closed. The impulse to visit this spot she was often conscious of during the approach of the paroxysm, and afterwards she sometimes thought that she had dreamed of going thither. Towards the termination of her indisposition, she dreamed that the water of a neighbouring spring would do her good, and she drank much of it. One time they tried to cheat her by giving her water from another spring, but she immediately detected the difference. Near the end, she foretold that she would have three paroxysms more, and then be well; and so it proved. . . .

Under the heading of trance-waking are contained the most marvellous phenomena which ever came as a group of facts in natural philosophy before the world; and they are reaching that stage towards general reception when their effect is most vivid and striking. Five-and-twenty years ago no one in England dreamed of believing them, although the same positive evidence of their genuineness then existed as now. Five-and-twenty years hence the same facts will be matters of familiar knowledge. It is just at the present moment (or am I anticipating the march of opinion by half a century?) that their difference, and distinctness, and abhorrence even, from our previous conceptions are most intensely felt; and that the powers which they promise eventually to place within human control excite our irrepressible wonder.

I shall narrate the facts, which loom so large in the dawning light, very simply and briefly, as they are manifested in catalepsy.

An uninformed person being in the room with a cataleptic patient, would at first suppose her, putting aside the spasmodic affection of the body, to be simply awake in the ordinary way. By-and-by her new powers might or might not catch his observation. But a third point would certainly escape his notice. I refer to her mental state of waking trance, which gives, as it were, the local colouring to the whole performance.

To elucidate this element, I may avail myself of a sketch ready prepared by nature, tinted with the local colour alone – the case of simple trance-waking, unattended by fits or by any marvellous powers, as far as it has been yet observed, which is known to physicians under the name of double consciousness.

A single fit of the disorder presents the following features: The young person (for the patient is most frequently a girl) seems to lose herself for a moment or longer, then she recovers, and seems to be herself again. The intervening short period, longer at first, and by use rendered briefer and briefer, is a period of common initiatory trance. When, having lost, the patient thus finds herself again, there is nothing in her behaviour which would lead a stranger to suppose her other than naturally awake. But her friends observe that she now does everything with more spirit and better than before – sings better, plays better, has more readiness, moves even more gracefully, than in her usual state. She manifests an innocent boldness and disregard of little conventionalism, which impart a peculiar charm to her behaviour. Her mode of speaking is perhaps something altered; a supernumerary consonant making its undue appearance, but upon a regular law, in certain syllables. But the most striking thing is, that she has totally forgotten all that has passed during the morning. Inquire what her last recollections are, they leave off with the termination of her last fit of this kind; the intervening period is for the present lost to her. She was in her natural state of waking when I introduced her to your notice; she lost herself for a few seconds, found herself again; but found herself not in her natural train of recollections, but in those of the last fit.

These fits occur sometimes at irregular intervals, sometimes periodically and daily. In her ordinary waking state, she has her chain of waking recollections. In her trance-waking state, she has her chain of trance-waking recollections. The two are kept strictly apart. Hence the ill-chosen term, double-consciousness. So at the occurrence of her first fit, her mental existence may be said to have bifurcated into two separate routes, in either of which her being is alternately passed. It is curious to study, at the commencement of such a case, with how much knowledge derived from her past life the patient embarks on her trance-existence. The number of previously realised ideas retained by different patients at the first fit is very various. It has happened that the memory of facts and persons has been so defective, that the patient has had to learn even to know and to love her parents. To most of her acquaintances she is observed to give new names, which she uses to them in the trance-state alone. But her habits remain; her usual propriety of conduct: the mind is singularly pure in trance. And she very quickly picks up former ideas, and restores former intimacies, but on a supposed new footing. To complete this curious history, if the fits of trance recur frequently, and through some accidental circumstance are more and more prolonged in duration, so that most of her waking existence is passed in trance, it will follow that the trance-development of her intellect and character may get ahead of their development in her natural waking. Being told this, she may become anxious to continue always in her entranced state, and to drop the other: and I knew a case in which circumstances favoured this final arrangement, and the patient at last retained her trance-recollections alone, from long continuances in that state having made it, as it were, her natural one. Her only fear was – for she had gradually learned her own mental history, as she expressed it to me – that some day she should of a sudden find herself a child again, thrown back to the point at which she ceased her first order of recollections. This is, indeed, a very extreme and monstrous case. Ordinarily, the recurrence of fits of simple trance-waking does not extend over a longer period than three or four months or half-a-year, after which they never reappear; and her trance-acquirements and feelings are lost to the patient's recollection for good. I will cite a case, as it was communicated to me by Dr G. Barlow, exemplifying some of the points of the preceding statement.

> This young lady has two states of existence. During the time that the fit is on her, which varies from a few hours to three days, she is occasionally merry and in spirits; occasionally she appears in pain, and rolls about in uneasiness; but in general she seems so much herself, that a stranger entering the room would not remark anything extraordinary: she amuses herself with reading or working, sometimes plays on the piano – and better than at other times – knows everybody, and converses rationally, and makes very accurate observations on what she has seen and read. The fit leaves her suddenly, and she then forgets everything that has passed during it, and imagines that she has been asleep, and sometimes that she has dreamed of any circumstance that has made a vivid impression upon her. During one of these fits she was reading Miss Edgeworth's *Tales*, and had in the morning been reading a part of one of them to her mother, when she went for a few minutes to the window, and suddenly exclaimed, 'Mamma, I am quite well, my headach is gone.' Returning to the table, she took up the open volume, which she had been reading five minutes before, and said, 'What book is this?' she turned over the leaves, looked at the frontispiece, and replaced it on the table. Seven or eight hours afterwards, when the fit returned, she asked for the book, went on at the very paragraph where she had left off, and remembered every circumstance of the narrative. And so it always is; she reads one set of books during one state, and another during the other. She seems to be conscious of her state; for she said one day, 'Mamma, this is a novel, but I may safely read it; it will not hurt my morals, for, when I am well, I shall not remember a word of it.'

Abridged from On the Truths contained in Popular Superstitions *(1851) pages 89–111.*

CHAPTER FIFTEEN

Spiritual Powers of the Church . . . and Exorcism

Frederick Lee

One of the central conflicts in *Dracula* is that between the Roman Catholic and Protestant faiths. Stoker's dilemma was that, although a staunch Protestant himself, the battle against an agent of the devil rooted in the Hungarian Empire would need to be waged with Catholic weapons. It is a feature of the competing faiths that vampires do not normally rear their heads in Protestant lands; only Catholic or Orthodox ones. This is principally a doctrinal matter relating to the fate of the dead. The Roman Church linked vampirism with excommunication and with purgatory. Vampires were, so to speak, serving their time. Denying the existence of purgatory, Protestantism needed an alternative explanation for supposedly reanimated beings. They could not be the spirits of the departed temporarily returned to earth. The explanation was laid at the door of witchcraft, leading to the different colour of demonology to be found in different parts of Christendom.

All this caused Stoker to plot his characters with care. The upright, professional Englishmen – Harker and Seward – are necessarily Protestant, sceptical of the idolatrous use of crucifixes and communion wafer. But in order to believe in the vampire they have to believe in the weapons of its destruction. These are taught by the Catholic Dutchman, Van Helsing, himself almost as much of an outside intrusion into Britain as Dracula.

Britain could not provide Stoker with much in the way of indiginous vampire lore, but in the pages of Frederick Lee's two volume *Glimpses of the Supernatural – Being Facts, Records and Traditions relating to Dreams, Omens, Miraculous Occurrences, Apparitions, Wraiths, Warnings, Second-Sight, Witchcraft, Necromancy Etc.* (1875), (elsewhere titled *The Other World*), he discovered a compendium of battles successfully waged against the devil. More importantly, all these battles take place in England and are told from a Catholic standpoint. Lee is not one for understatement. He explores the same other-worldly phenomena as did many others in his time, and he writes with the same uncritical eye. He takes on trust the most outlandish apocryphal tales, constantly reassuring the reader of the veracity of his sources – even if some of them date back centuries. The consequences of dreams are to be taken as authentic simply on account of the natural honesty of the dreamer.

Lee's value for Stoker lies not merely in providing an English record of the devil vanquished by Catholic means. It lies in the abundance of little anecdotes recorded by Lee and which remind the reader of similar scenes in *Dracula*. Of course, Stoker had been reading books on other-worldly topics all his life. Even so, he would have found it difficult to ignore some of the dramas described in *Glimpses of the Supernatural*.

There is the episode of the bridegroom setting eyes on a woman 'dressed in white, with flowing hair and a wild look, holding up in both hands her little infant' (Vol 1, p. 120). Lucy Westenra is similarly described wandering in a deserted churchyard. Lee even relates a tale of teeth: a vault is opened, a coffin unscrewed, blood spots are found spattered on the shroud, and upon pulling it back the corpse is exposed with every one of its teeth drawn (Vol 1, pp. 234–35).

In *Dracula* Mina Harker describes her first dream-like vision of the Count as like mist or smoke, with the energy of boiling water, becoming thicker and thicker till it congealed into a pillar of cloud. (*Dracula* Chapter 19) Where did Stoker find this image? Possibly from Lee's account of an Oxford student:

> All of a sudden I saw what seemed to be an elongated perpendicular cloud of foggy-looking grey smoke, collected in the right-hand corner of the room. I could not comprehend what it was. While looking steadily at it, and rubbing my eyes (doubting for a moment whether I was awake or asleep), it seemed to form itself, by a kind of circular rolling motion of the smoke or luminous mist, into a human shape (Vol 2, p. 71).

There is also the business of exorcism. In effect, Van Helsing exorcises the vampire in Lucy as he restores her to natural death. But Van Helsing is not ordained. He also claims to have an indulgence for the desecration he commits. Lee might have given Stoker guidance on this, and also on the spiritual powers of the magic circle, within which Van Helsing protects Mina in the novel's climax. In addition, when the Professor places a holy wafer on Mina's forehead, she is branded in a manner reminiscent of another of Lee's reports.

*

Spiritual Powers of the Church . . . and Exorcism

For generations, up to the very earliest age of Christianity, there have been officers of the Church duly set apart and ordained for the particular work of exorcism. Amongst the minor orders of Western Christendom the exorcist has always found a place; and although, in later years, this special work, when undertaken, has been more frequently done by persons in the higher or sacred orders, yet the very office itself, and its title, as well as the existing forms for casting out evil spirits, abundantly attest the Church's divine and spiritual powers.

In countries which are specially and eminently Christian, where churches, sanctuaries, and religious houses are numerous; where, by the road-side and on the hill-top, stand the signs and symbols of the Faith of Christendom; where the Sacrament of Baptism is shed upon so many; where post-baptismal sin is remitted by those who have authority and jurisdiction to bind and loose in the Name of their Master; and where the Blessed Sacrament of the Altar, God manifest in the Flesh, reposing in the tabernacle, or borne in triumph through aisle and street and garden, hallows and feeds the faithful – there the power and influence of the Evil One is circumscribed and weakened. Sacred oil for unction, and holy water and the life-giving power of the Cross, and the relics of the beatified as well as of the favoured and crowned servants of the Crucified, make the devils flee away, and efficiently curb their power. Hence it is found that in countries where the Catholic Faith has been halved or rejected, Superstition has taken the place of the first theological virtue, Faith; and the Prince of the Powers of the air comes back again, with his evil and malignant spirits to vex mankind anew, and mar and stay the final triumph of Him to Whom all power is given in heaven and in earth. . . .

The following extract from Mr Ruddle's MS. Diary, was taken by the Rev. R.S. Hawker, M.A., vicar of Morwenstow, the accomplished and well-known Christian poet, and appears in his interesting 'Footprints of Former Men in Far Cornwall' (London, 1870). . . .

January 12th, 1665. Rode into the gateway of Botathen, armed at all points, but not with Saul's armour, and ready. There is danger from the demons, but so there is in the surrounding air every day. At early morning then and alone, for so the usage ordains, I betook me towards the field. It was void, and I had thereby due time to prepare. First I paced and measured out my circle on the grass. Then did I mark my pentacle in the very midst, and at the intersection of the five angles I did set up and fix my crutch of raun [rowan]. Lastly I took my station south, at the true line of the meridian, and stood facing due north. I waited and watched for a long time. At last there was a kind of trouble in the air, a soft and rippling sound, and all at once the shape appeared, and came on towards me gradually. I opened my parchment scroll, and read aloud the command. She paused and seemed to waver and doubt; stood still: and then I rehearsed the sentence again, sounding out every syllable like a chant. She drew near my ring, but halted at first outside, on the brink. I sounded again, and now at the third time I gave the signal in Syriac – the speech which is used, they say, where such ones dwell and converse in thoughts that glide.

She was at last obedient and swam into the midst of the circle: and there stood still suddenly. I saw, moreover, that she drew back her pointing hand. All this while I do confess that my knees shook under me, and the drops of sweat ran down my flesh like rain. But now, although face to face with the spirit, my heart grew calm and my mind composed, to know that the pentacle would govern her, and the ring must bind until I gave the word. Then I called to mind the rule laid down of old that no angel or fiend, no spirit, good or evil, will ever speak until they be spoken to. N.B. – This is the great law of prayer. God Himself will not yield reply until man hath made vocal entreaty once and again. So I went on to demand, as the books advise; and the phantom made answer willingly. Questioned, wherefore not at rest? Unquiet because of a certain sin. Asked what and by whom? Revealed it; but it is *sub sigillo*, and therefore *nefas dictu**; more anon. Inquired, what sign she could give me that she was a true spirit and not a false fiend? Stated [that] before next Yule-tide a fearful pestilence would lay waste the land, and myriads of souls would be loosened from their flesh, until, as she piteously said, 'Our valleys will be full.' Asked again, why she so terrified the lad? Replies, 'It is the law; we must seek a youth or a maiden of clean life, and under age, to receive messages and admonitions.' We conversed with many more words; but it is not lawful for me to set them down. Pen and ink would degrade and defile the thoughts she uttered, and which my mind received that day. I broke the ring and she passed, but to return once more next day. At evensong a long discourse with that ancient transgressor, Mr B——. Great horror and remorse; entire atonement and penance; whatsoever I enjoin; full acknowledgment before pardon.

January 13, 1665. At sunrise I was again in the field. She came in at once, and, as it seemed, with freedom. Inquired if she knew my thoughts,

---

* 'The seal of the confessional, and therefore it cannot be said.' – C.L.

and what I was going to relate? Answered, 'Nay, we only know what we perceive and hear: we cannot see the heart.' Then I rehearsed the penitent words of the man she had come up to denounce, and the satisfaction he would perform. Then said she, 'Peace in our midst.' I went through the proper forms of dismissal, and fulfilled all, as it was set down and written in my memoranda; and then with certain fixed rites, I did dismiss that troubled ghost, until she peacefully withdrew, gliding towards the west. Neither did she ever afterwards appear; but was allayed, until she shall come in her second flesh, to the Valley of Armageddon on the Last Day.

Another example, giving with singular power and effect a very striking Glimpse of the Supernatural, from the experiences of a venerated and exemplary Roman Catholic clergyman, the late Rev Edward Peach, of S Chad's, Birmingham, is here given at length. The events narrated occurred in the year 1815, and Mr Peach deliberately affirmed of the following account that it '*may be relied on in every particular as being strictly true.*' 'I,' he continues, in a formal record of the successful exorcism, 'was the minister of God employed on the occasion; and truth is more to me than all the boastings of pride and vain glory.'
The authentic record stands as follows:

Somme time after Easter, in the year 1815, I was informed that a young married woman of the name of White, in the parish of King's Norton, Worcestershire, a Protestant, was afflicted with an extraordinary kind of illness, and that her relations, who occupied a small farm, were convinced that her illness arose solely from the malice of a rejected admirer, who, they said, had employed the assistance of a reputed wizard at Dudley to do her a mischief. These were their terms. I paid but little attention to this story. Afterwards I was informed by a sister who frequents our markets, and supplies with butter a respectable family of my congregation, Mr Powell, Suffolk Street, that the young woman was married in the beginning of the preceding Lent; that her former admirer repeatedly declared that, if she did marry any other, she should never have another happy day; that the day after her marriage she was seized with an extraordinary kind of mental complaint; that she became suddenly delirious; that she raved, and declared that a multitude of infernal spirits surrounded her; that they threatened to carry her away; that she must go with them. The poor sister informed my friend, with tears streaming down her cheeks, that she continued in that state, day and night, for nearly two months, and that the whole family were almost exhausted with the fatigue of constantly attending her, for, she said, they could not leave her alone, lest she should put her threats of destroying herself into execution.

At the end of about two months, according to the relation of the same sister, the poor creature was so spent that her medical attendant (who, during the whole time of his attendance, declared that her illness arose more from a mental than corporeal cause,) declared that, in all probability, she could not survive four-and-twenty hours. The clergyman of the parish was called in to assist her in her last moments; but he found her in a state not to be benefited by his assistance, and he departed.

Amongst the neighbours who came to make a tender of their good offices for the relief of the afflicted family was a Catholic woman. Her offers were accepted, and she was frequently with her. Finding her reduced almost to a state of inanition, and hearing her speak of these infernal spirits every time she opened her lips, the thought came into her mind of applying to her some holy water. She accordingly procured some, dipped her finger into it, and made the sign of the cross upon her forehead. Instantly the poor sufferer started, and, in a faint voice, exclaimed, 'You have scalded me.' However, she leaned upon the bosom of her attendant, and, what she had not done for a considerable time before, she fell into a gentle sleep. On awaking, she continued to hold the same language as before. The Catholic put a little holy water into her mouth. But the very instant it entered her mouth she seemed to be in a state of suffocation. She and the others who were with her were alarmed, and expected that every instant would be her last. In a short time, however, she swallowed it, and after many convulsive struggles she regained her breath, and exclaimed with violence, 'You have scalded my throat, you have scalded my throat.' In a few minutes she fell again into a comfortable sleep, and continued so for some hours. The next morning she appeared refreshed, and spoke reasonably for a short time. Being informed of what had been applied to her, she seemed to wish for more. The swallowing was attended with the same sensation of scalding, and the same convulsive struggles as before; but it seemed to give her ease. From that time the danger of death seemed to decrease by degrees. She enjoyed lucid intervals from time to time; and invariably after the application of holy water, although attended with the same sensations as before, she fell into a slumber.

One remarkable circumstance deserves notice. In one of her paroxysms, she insisted on getting up, and going out of doors. She said that there was a large snake in front of the house, that she would go and kill it, and then one of her enemies would be removed. Nothing would satisfy her, till this same sister, who gave the account, assured her that she would go down and kill it. She went down, and, to her great astonishment, found a large snake, and succeeded in destroying it.

This in substance is the account which the sister gave of Mrs White's extraordinary illness. At the same time it was asked whether I could be of any assistance to her, or whether it was probable that I could be prevailed on to go and see her? My friend who related to me the whole of the above account, asked me to go. I replied that I knew nothing of them, nor they of me; but that if she would walk over, and examine into the state of the poor woman, I would go, if there appeared to her to be any probability of my being of service. She went, and, on her return, she informed me that all she had heard seemed to be true, and assured me that all the family were desirous of seeing me, and particularly the young woman herself.

However, I still delayed, till at length, on Tuesday in Rogation Week, May 2nd, 1815, a special messenger came over to inform me that Mrs White was in a worse state than ever, and to request me to go and see her without delay.

I obeyed the call, and I may say with truth that it was the most awful visit I ever made during the whole course of my ministry. The distance was about six miles. No sooner had I cleared the skirts of the town than I heard the distant thunder before me. Before I had proceeded two miles, the storm was nearly over my head; and I may say the remainder of my walk, and during the time I was with her, there was hardly cessation of one minute between the claps of thunder. I do not say that in this there was anything supernatural, but, knowing the business I was upon, it was truly awful.

When I arrived at the house, I was informed that she was in a dreadful state, and that the strength of two persons was necessary to keep her in bed. I went up-stairs, and on entering into the room, before she saw me, the curtains being drawn on the side where I entered, she turned to the other side of the bed, and struggled so violently to get away that it was with difficulty that her husband and two women overpowered her. In a few minutes, before she had lifted up her eyes to see me (for she had turned her face downwards) she stretched out her hand to me, in a convulsive manner, and fell speechless and spent upon her back.

After a time she opened her eyes, and in a faint whisper, answered a question that was put to her, and said she knew who I was. She revived by degrees, and in a short time could speak in an audible voice. Her friends having requested me to try if I could discover what it was that weighed most upon her mind, for they said they had tried to no purpose, I requested them to withdraw. Being alone, she related to me, as far as she could recollect, the circumstances of her illness, and I found that they corresponded exactly with the accounts given by her sister. I questioned her as to the cause, but I could not discover that it was owing to anything weighing heavy on her mind. She was positive, she said, that it was the young man who had done her a mischief.

I then proceeded to explain to her some of the articles of the Catholic Faith. She listened with every attention; and when I assured her that she must believe the Holy Catholic Church before she could obtain relief, she, without hesitation, declared that she did believe, and that she believed from the moment she knew what holy water was, and experienced its effects. From the time it was first applied, she said that the devils seemed to keep at a greater distance from her, and that the number seemed to be diminished.

Such were the ideas on her mind at the time. She was convinced, she said, that it was not the effect of imagination – that she was not delirious – that she knew everything that was said to her, and that she could recollect everything that had passed. I asked her to tell me where the holy water was. Her voice immediately faltered; and with every endeavour, I perceived that she could not point out with her finger, nor tell me by words where it was. She was like an infant attempting to point out an object.

I looked about and found it. I dipped my finger into it, and made the sign of the cross on her forehead. She started as soon as I touched her, and was a little convulsed. I asked her what was the matter. For a few moments she could not articulate; but as soon as she could speak, she said that it scalded her.

After a little more conversation, I desired her to join with me in repeating the Lord's Prayer. She consented, and without difficulty repeated the first words. But when we came to the petitions, her voice faltered; she was labouring for breath, and appeared to be almost suffocated: her countenance and limbs were convulsed. The greatest stammerer could not find greater difficulty in pronouncing words than she did in pronouncing every word of the petitions. At one time I was inclined to desist, thinking that it was impossible for her to finish it; but we laboured on, and at length came to the end.

After a short pause, she again began to converse with a free voice, without the least faltering. I explained to her the nature of exorcisms, and proposed to read them over her. She consented, and said that she would endeavour to offer up her prayers to God during the time in the best manner she could. As soon as I began the exorcisms, she fell into a state of convulsive agitation, not indeed endeavouring to get away; but every limb, every joint seemed to be agitated and convulsed, even her countenance was distorted, – it required constant attention to keep her covered.

Now it was that I felt in a particular manner the awful situation in which I was. All alone with a person in a distressed condition, – the lightning flashing, the thunder rolling, and I with an imperative voice commanding the evil spirit to reply to my interrogatories, and to go forth from her. I acknowledge that my flesh began to creep and my hair to stand on end. However, I proceeded on till I came to the conclusion, and nothing happened except the violent agitation of the poor sufferer, which continued uninterrupted during the whole time.

After I had finished, she became calm, and in a few minutes began to converse with me with the same ease as before. Among other things, I asked her whether she had felt any particular sensations during the time that I was coming to see her? She said that during the whole afternoon she had felt the most determined resolution to destroy herself; that she employed every means to induce her friends to leave the room, or to make her escape from them; and that if she had succeeded, she would have laid violent hands on herself the moment she was at liberty. I explained to her the nature of baptism, the necessity of receiving it, and the effects produced by it.

During the course of our conversation, discovering that there were strong reasons to doubt whether she had been baptized at all, or whether the essential rites had been observed in her baptism, I conceived that it would be advisable to re-baptize her conditionally. I proposed it, and she readily consented. I gave her what instructions were necessary, and repeated several acts of contrition. Finding her in dispositions the most satisfactory, I made use of the holy water, and baptized her, subject to the condition, *if she was not baptized.* During the time she trembled like a leaf, and the features of her countenance were distorted, like those of a person in acute pain. Upon my putting the question to her, she replied as she did before, that it gave her as much pain as if boiling water had been poured over her.

Immediately after the ceremony was concluded, she began to speak to me with all the cheerfulness of a person in perfect health and spirits. We conversed together for a few minutes, and I took my leave, promising to see her again the next day. Her sister went to her, and her first request was that she might have a cup of tea and something to eat; and before I left the house, she eat and drank as she had done before her affliction. I went to see her the next day, and found her down-stairs in perfect health; at least, no effects of her illness were perceptible, except a weakness of body. From that time to this, she has enjoyed good health, and not the least symptom of her former complaint has been felt. It is more than a twelvemonth since.

P.S. In the act of exorcism, of course it is not necessary that the exorcist be a clergyman, in other words, in holy orders. An 'exorcist' technically so called, when formally ordained, is only in 'minor' and not in 'holy' or 'sacred orders.' Any Christian layman, with faith and a hearty desire and readiness to abide by the rules of the Church, can perform the act of exorcism, if no duly-ordained exorcist can be had.

From The Other World: Or, Glimpses of the Supernatural *(1875)* *pages 57–58, 64, 66–79.*

CHAPTER SIXTEEN

The Devil

Rev Albert Réville

Count Dracula is something more than one of Victorian fiction's unsavoury characters. He is evil incarnate. Given the religious dimension of the novel Stoker clearly wanted Dracula to be identified with the devil. This is made clear in several passages. Firstly, the Count's appearance – a tall thin man dressed in black – is the standard fictional representation of the devil here on earth. Secondly, when Dracula arrives in London he operates under a fitting pseudonym – Count *de Vil*le. Third, when Van Helsing is informed of Dracula's earlier, human, existence back in the fifteenth century he also learns of his studies at the Scholomance, otherwise known as the Devil's Academy. One student in ten – Dracula, naturally – came to serve as the devil's accomplice.

Count Dracula, in other words, is no mindless ghoul operating in a zombie-like vacuum. He has a powerful sponsor. But, as Stoker knew, attitudes towards the devil have changed over the centuries. What sort of devil did he have in mind as the co-conspiritor with Dracula?

In this connection we should observe the words 'Réville's History of the Devil' on Stoker's list of sources. Stoker was referring to the astute little book by the Rev Albert Réville *The Devil: His Origin, Greatness and Decadence*, translated from the French in 1871, which traces the evolution of the devil in Jewish and Christian thought.

The Old Testament depiction of Satan as an abstract adversary, or accuser of man, slowly gave way to an image of a malign *agent provocateur*. The devil adds hatred of God to his hatred of man, and, banished from heaven, establishes a separate kingdom in a subterranean Hell. This early Christian interpretation viewed the devil as the harbinger of death and the source of certain types of inexplicable torment, such as madness and epilepsy.

But it is the view of the devil prevailing in the Middle Ages that Stoker unveils in *Dracula*. The mediæval fear of the incubus and succubus were symptomatic of the ascetic war being waged upon the body and its appetites. This sexual orientation implied that the devil had somehow become humanised, and a 'human' devil would naturally require human servants to do his bidding. Dracula recruits Lucy and Renfield for this purpose.

In recent centuries perceptions of the devil have continued to adapt, a consequence of the fresh perspectives introduced by the Renaissance, the Protestant reformation, and the rise of modern science. Declining belief in supernatural agencies meant that the oppressive mediæval fears of the devil would, in time, also recede. By the nineteenth century Satan had, for many, returned to what he was at the time of Christ: as Réville puts it, 'a tempting, invisible, impalpable spirit'.

There are indications that Stoker, personally, might have clung to belief in a more virulent, and active, devil. Either way he was unable to implant the watered-down contemporary view of diabolism into a novel like *Dracula*. For one thing, he faces the problem of Lucy's (and Mina's) culpability for their liaisons with the Count. Stoker needs to pronounce them guilty of submission to, even acquiescence in, Dracula's advances. To a tolerant eye they were both innocent of intentional complicity: after all, they only sinned in the face of an infinitely stronger power controlling their minds. But Stoker cannot allow that defence. Their flirtations with the devil must invoke the full weight of an Inquisitorial response. Witches were burned: Lucy is staked – and a similar fate awaits Mina but for the Count's destruction.

It will be noted that Stoker's return to the diabolism of the Middle Ages and Van Helsing's role as chief Inquisitor ties in neatly with the era of Vlad the Impaler. This has the curious effect of placing the novel in two different timescales simultaneously – the fifteenth and the nineteenth centuries. Vlad had not been dead twenty years when the *Malleus Maleficarum* unleashed its horrors on Europe. The background to this notorious publication, which was given the blessing of Pope Innocent VIII, is provided by Réville. Its chilling pages detailed the torture procedures to be adopted for unearthing and punishing instances of alleged devil-worship.

But they also suggest another parallel with the nineteenth century. The medical sources consulted by Stoker, and especially those concerned with trance-states and disorders of the mind, were at pains to present a picture of female fragility and susceptibility to the effects of hysteria. Put simply, women were viewed as weaker than men. According to the *Malleus Maleficarum*, four centuries earlier, women are also more evil and eager to have commerce with the devil. Both strands of misogyny merge into the complex portrait of women represented in *Dracula*.

*

The Devil

The Jewish Messiah became to Christians the Saviour of guilty humanity. This is why we see the radical antagonism between Satan and the Messiah reflected in the primitive doctrine of redemption. From the close of the second century, this doctrine is summed up in a grand drama in which Christ and the devil are the principal actors. The multitude were contented to believe that Christ, descending into hell, had, in virtue of his right as the stronger of the two, taken from Satan the souls he had carried captive. But this rude idea underwent a refinement. Irenæus taught that man, after the fall, having become Satan's rightful property, it would have been unjust on the part of God to deprive him by violence of his own; and that Christ, as a perfect man, and therefore independent of the devil, offered himself a ransom for the human family, which bargain the devil accepted. Soon, however, it became clear that the devil had made a very foolish reckoning, as Christ did not remain, after all, in his power. Origen, whose ecclesiastical teachings must not always be taken as literally exact representations of his real opinions, became the organ of views which freely admitted that both Christ and Satan had played their parts very cleverly, seeing that the devil believed he should keep in his power a prey which was worth more to him than the whole human race, while Christ knew very well that he should not remain in Satan's hands.

This view, which made Jesus the deceiver at the cost of Satan, scandalous as it appears to us, was, nevertheless a success, and long predominated in the Church. Ecclesiastical poetry, popular preaching, and even pontifical assertion, extended it in all directions, dramatised it, consecrated it. One can readily understand that this way of regarding redemption did not go towards diminishing the devil's sway over men's minds. Nothing did more to increase fear of the enemy, than vague descriptions of the immensity of his power, and of the risk run by exposure to his attacks; especially as, by a singular contradiction from which the ancient theology never succeeded in extricating itself, the devil, although declared vanquished, overthrown, and rendered powerless by his victor Christ, did not the less maintain his infernal sway over a large majority of mankind. The saints alone could count themselves safe from his ambushes; and, according to the legends which now began to spread, great was the prudence and energy they required to escape him! Everything turned upon this constant state of watchfulness. Baptism dwindled into an exorcism. To become a Christian, was to renounce the devil with his pomps and works. Expulsion from the fold of the Church, whether for immoral behaviour, or for heterodoxy, was the being 'delivered over to Satan'.

It was thus that during this period the doctrine of the fall of the evil angels was developed. Now, we find it taught that devils were referred to in that mythic passage of Genesis where the 'sons of God saw the daughters of men that they were fair, and took them wives of all that they chose,' licentiousness being considered as the original sin and never-ending concern of evil spirits; and again, as this hypothesis did not explain the anterior presence of a wicked angel in the earthly paradise, the fall of the rebel fiends was dated from the moment of the Creation. Augustine thought that in consequence of this fall, their bodies, which were formerly subtle and invisible, became dense. And here we have the beginning of a belief in the visible apparitions of the devil. Then came another notion, that devils, in order to gratify their lust, took advantage of the night to surprise young persons while asleep; and hence the *succubæ* and *incubi* which played such a prominent part in the middle ages. Saint Victor, according to the legend, was overcome by a demon who had artfully assumed the form of a young seductress who had lost her way at night time in the woods. The councils, from the fourth century, enjoined bishops to keep a close watch over those in their dioceses who practised magic arts, the inventions of the devil, and wicked women are spoken of who are supposed to run the fields by night in the train of Diana and other heathen goddesses. But as yet these imaginary *sabbaths* are regarded as but dreams suggested by Satan to those whose vicious inclinations gave him a hold over them.

Ere long, however, all became real and material. There was not a saint to whom the devil did not at least appear once under a human form. Saint Martin even met him so disguised as to represent Christ. For the most part, however, in his quality of angel of darkness, he appeared as a man, and quite black, under which colour he was wont to escape from the heathen temples and idols that had been thrown down by the zeal of converts to the new religion. And then came the idea that one could make an agreement with the devil, by which the soul might be exchanged for the object of one's greatest desire. This notion dates from the legend of Theophilus, a sixth century saint. He, in a moment of wounded pride, made himself over formally to Satan; but, being devoured by remorse, he got the Virgin Mary to recover the fatal document from the evil one.

This legendary episode, written with the express object of extending the worship of Mary, necessarily had important results. The devil, moreover, saw his prestige increase still further, when the conversion of the invaders of the Empire, and the missions sent into countries that had never formed part of the Roman dominions, introduced into the bosom of the Church a mass of grossly ignorant people, who were still impregnated with polytheism. The Church and State, which had been united since Constantine's time, and were still more closely cemented under Charlemagne, did what they could to refine the coarse minds of those whose teachers they had become; but, to do this effectually, the temporal and spiritual powers had need to be themselves less under the sway of the very superstitions they desired to repel. If some among the more clever of the Popes succeeded in combining with their political plans a certain amount of toleration for customs and errors that seemed ineradicable, the great majority of bishops and missionaries firmly believed that by insisting upon the extirpation of polytheism they were fighting against the devil and his host. They inoculated their converts with the same belief; and thereby considerably prolonged the existence of the heathen divinities.

The good old rural spirits died hard. The sacred legend contains many of them, and comparative mythology recognises not a few ancient Keltic and Teutonic gods among the patron saints of our ancestors. Saint Nicolas, Saint Victor, Saint Denis with the 'head-carrying' saints in general, Saint Ursula (Horsela), Saint Venetia, and many others of less fame, enter into this category. For a long time, and without its being looked upon as a renunciation of the catholic faith, it was usual in England, France, and Germany, to offer presents, now out of gratitude, now through fear, to the spirits of the fields and forests; women, especially, adhering to such old customs. But as the Church still regarded as demons and devils all superhuman beings who were not saints or angels, seeing that the character of the old gods had nothing angelical in it, an interchange, or, rather a transformation, was effected. The good side of these deities served, under new names, to enrich the kingdom of the saints, the kingdom of the demons had what was left. Belief in the devil, which in the earlier ages had something elevated in it, became simply gross and stupid. At the beginning of the middle ages certain animals, as cats, toads, rats, mice, black dogs, wolves, were regarded as specially selected by the devil and his servants for symbols, auxiliaries, and even as temporary disguises. In our own times even, we generally find these animals were consecrated or sacrificed to the divinities whom demons have replaced. Traditions of human sacrifices offered up in honour of the ancient gods, account doubtless for the notion that Satan and his slaves have a relish for human flesh. The werewolf who eats children has been by turns a god, a devil, and a sorcerer who went to the *sabbath* under the guise of a wolf that he might not be recognised. We all know that there is no witch without her cat. Vermin, that sore which then as now was but too common a scourge among populations devoid of all sense of cleanliness, was also to be laid at the door of the devil and his servants. A time came when the idea that the devil had a distinct bodily shape became settled; and this form was that of the ancient fauns and satyrs, with horns, protruding legs, hairy skin, tail, cloven foot or horse's hoof.

It would be easy to accumulate here semi-burlesque, semi-tragic details. But we prefer marking the salient points of the development of the belief. We have reached a period at which we must look at it under a new light. Among the Jews of the times immediately preceding the Christian era, Satan had become the *adversary* of the Messiah; with the early Christians he was the direct antagonist of the Saviour of mankind: but to the middle ages Christ was up in heaven, far away, and the immediate, living organism in which his kingdom on earth was to be realized was the Church, between which and the devil the war was thenceforward to be waged. The faith of the peasant consists simply in believing what the Church believes. Ask him what the Church believes, and he will answer boldly, 'What I believe.' And if in the times of which we are speaking the question had been put, 'What does the devil do?' the answer would have been, 'What the Church does not do'; while to the question, 'And what is it that the Church does not do?' the response would have amounted to this, 'What the devil does.' The *sabbaths* which the ancient councils, when referred to thereupon, treated as appertaining to imaginary regions, had now been something very real. . . .

At Carcassonne, from 1320 to 1350, more than four hundred executions for witchcraft are on record. Up to the end of the fourteenth century, however, these horrible displays were localized; but in 1484 a decree of Pope Innocent VIII extended trial for witchcraft over the whole of Christendom. Then began in Europe that hideous witch-hunt which marks the climax of the belief in the devil, which concentrated and condensed it during more than three centuries; and which at last, succumbing to the moral force of modern times, was to carry away with it the dark belief from which it arose.

In the fifteenth century a momentary lull of orthodox fanaticism rendered the inquisitor's task somewhat difficult in the treatment of heresy proper. On the banks of the Rhine as well as in France, it seems people began to be weary of the insatiable ghoul that threatened everybody, while it healed none of the ills of the Church to which it had been applied as a sovereign remedy. Faith in the Church itself as a perfect and infallible institution was tottering, and the inquisitors carried to the Holy See their murmurs at the increasing obstacles placed in their way by local powers and parish clergy. Still, even those whose faith in the Church was shaken, and who inclined towards religious toleration, did not propose to leave a free course to the devices of the devil and his agents. It was at this time that the famous bull *Summis desiderantes* appeared, by which Innocent VIII added to the power of the officers of the Inquisition that of prosecuting those guilty of witchcraft, and of applying to them the rules which hitherto had only been aimed at *depravatio heretica*. Long is the list of machinations enumerated in the pontifical bull, from tempests and the destruction of crops to the spells cast upon men and women to prevent the increase of the human family. Armed with this bull, which thundered the severest pains and penalties against the refractory, and which was confirmed by other decrees of the same sense and origin, the inquisitors, Henry Institoris and Jacob Sprenger wielded that *Witch Hammer, Malleus Malificarum,* – which was long throughout Europe the standard code of action against those suspected of sorcery. It received the sanction of the Pope, and the approval of the Emperor Maximilian and of the theological faculty of Cologne. The perusal of this heavy and wearisome treatise can hardly fail to provoke a shudder; a careful study of the false put in the stead of the true, of the repeated sophisms with which the book abounds, of the pedantic folly with which its authors heap together whatever can give a shadow of likelihood to their nightmares, together with the cold-blooded cruelty which dictates their prosecutions and summonses, – this could not but disgust the modern student, were it not his duty to bring to the bar of history one of the most lamentable aberrations that have warped the conscience of humanity.

Everything is explained in this conjuring-book. We learn why the devil enables his servants to change themselves *reali transformatione et essentialiter* into wolves and other dangerous animals; why it is heresy to disbelieve in the power of magic; how the *incubi* and *succubæ* work their ends; why the number of witches is greater than ever; why David in olden time drove away the spirit that troubled Saul by showing him a harp in the form of the cross, &c. We are told, again, that the reason why there are more witches than wizards lies in the fact that women are more ready than men to be beguiled by the devil's promises; and this, because the *fluidity* of their temperament makes them more easily acted upon by his inspiration; in a word, because being weaker than men they readily seek supernatural aid in order to satisfy their vengeance or their sensuality. All manner of recipes are recommended to persons who have the good sense to guard themselves against the charms that may be practised upon them. The sign of the cross, holy water, the judicious use of salt, and of the name of the Holy Trinity, are among the principal exorcisms. The sound of bells is accounted a very energetic preservative; and therefore it is well to ring them during storms, as the evil spirits, who cannot support the sacred sound, are thereby driven away, and checked in their work of perturbation. This superstitious custom, which has lasted to our own day, denotes clearly the confusion of demons, ecclesiastic with the old divinities of storm and tempest.

But what is above all worthy of attention, is the mode of criminal action developed in this book, and which became law everywhere. It is exactly based upon the prosecutions instituted by the Inquisition against heretics. As witchcraft was the outcome of a league with the devil it presupposed the abjuration of the baptismal vow, and was, consequently, a kind of apostasy, a heresy of the gravest order. Denunciations without proof were admitted. Even public hearsay sufficed to bring the charge under the judge's scrutiny. The depositions of all comers were received, no matter how infamous, no matter whether or not they were the enemies of the accused parties. The trial was to be as summary as possible, and useless formalities cut short. The witch was to be cross-questioned until something peculiar was detected in her life that served to strengthen the suspicions which hung over her. The judge was not obliged to name her accusers. She was allowed a defender, who knew no more of the matter than she did, and who had to limit what he said to the defence of the person accused, but not of her criminal acts, as this would turn suspicion upon himself. Confession was to be obtained by torture, together with all the circumstances connected with the offence.

In order to obtain full and prompt confession, her life might be promised her; but – and this is expressed in so many words – such promise was not binding. Torture was to be repeated every three days: and the judge was to use all needful caution lest its effects should be neutralised by charms hidden about the person of the accused. He was even to abstain from looking her in the face, seeing that witches had been known to be gifted by the devil with an influence which made judges who thus gazed on them unable to pronounce their condemnation. When at last she had been well and rightly convicted, she was to be delivered over to the secular arm, to be put to death without further parley.

This rapid glance is enough to show that the unhappy creatures who fell into the clutches of this terrible tribunal, might well leave all hope at their prison door. There is nothing more shocking than an attentive examination of witch trials. Women were always, as we have seen it learnedly explained, in the majority. Hatred, jealousy, vengeance, and, more than all, suspicions caused by wretchedness and ignorance, found in these trials a vent of which they did not fail to avail themselves. Not unfrequently, poor creatures were the victims of their own imagination, stimulated by an hysterical temperament, or by the fear of hell fire. Those who in our own day have had an opportunity of examining cases of religious mania know how readily women believe themselves fallen from grace and given over to the power of the evil one. All such sad cases, which are now treated with the greatest tenderness, in institutions devoted to their care, were then looked upon as 'possessions' of the devil, or as witches, and horrible to think of, not a few of them believed it themselves! Many related that they had been to the *sabbath* and had given themselves up to the most shameful excesses. Greatly must such confessions have aggravated the danger of those who denied with the firmness of innocence that they had committed the abominations of which they were accused! Torture was at hand to tear from them what they refused to say, and thus the belief took deep root in the minds of the judges, even when they were comparatively humane and just, that over and above crimes committed by natural means, there was a long list of offences the supernatural origin of which made them doubly heinous. And how was it possible to deal too sharply with such offences?

In the single year 1485, and in the district of Worms alone, eighty-five witches were delivered to the flames. At Geneva, at Basle, at Hamburg, at Ratisbon, at Vienna, and in a multitude of other towns, there were executions of the same kind. At Hamburg, among other victims, a physician was burnt alive because he saved the life of a woman who had been given up by the midwife. In Italy, during the year 1523, there were burnt in the diocese of Como alone, more than two hundred witches. This was after the new bull hurled at witchcraft by Pope Adrian VI. In Spain it was still worse; there, in 1527, two little girls of from nine to eleven years of age denounced a host of witches, whom they pretended to detect by a mark in their left eye. In England and Scotland, political influence was brought to bear upon sorcery; Mary Stuart was animated by a lively zeal against witches.

From The Devil: His Origin, Greatness and Decadence *(1871) pages 27–35, 44–51.*

CHAPTER SEVENTEEN

The Inquisitorial Process

Henry C. Lea

Bram Stoker was a man of the law. His early years as a civil servant in Dublin involved him in legal work. His first book, *The Duties of Clerks of Petty Sessions in Ireland*, necessitated painstaking research into that country's lawcourts. Later, as manager of Irving's Lyceum, Stoker was entrusted with its legal and contractual responsibilities. He also found time to study for the Bar, being called to the Inner Temple in 1890.

This legal background spills over into much of his fiction, not least *Dracula*. Stoker's alter ego, Jonathan Harker, is a young, recently-qualified, provincial solicitor. It is he who takes care of any legal obstacles supervening between the Count and his pursuers, save those concerned with avoiding inquests into Dracula's victims, which fall to Seward and Van Helsing – himself another lawyer.

The presence of two legal minds in the novel does not always signify a respect for the law that one might expect. The Dracula-hunters breach the law regularly and with impunity, breaking and entering into the Count's London house, and resorting to bribery at every turn. There is no attempt to bring Dracula before the courts and try him fairly and in public – the right of everyone, no matter how debased. Nor is there any intention of hearing his version of events. Dracula's guilt is assumed unquestioningly, and although he has not performed any capital offence (of the kind to satisfy a jury), the death sentence awaits him upon capture. That death sentence, it should be noted, is performed outside the law: Dracula – and his female vampires – are in effect the victims of a lynch mob.

As noted in the previous chapter, there is something reminiscent of the Holy Inquisition in Van Helsing's religious zeal. He likens himself and his fellow pursuers to the old knights of the Cross (*Dracula* Chapter 24), and their quest to a nineteenth-century Inquisition (*Dracula* Chapter 17). However, the circumstances of the

Church's tribulations in fifteenth and sixteenth-century Europe were as much legal as theological. And if Stoker's knowledge of the legal background to the Inquisition was wanting, help was at hand among his source books.

From its title, Henry C. Lea's *Superstition and Force*, (1878), sounds like another of the popular supernatural texts of which Stoker availed himself. From its sub-title *Essays on The Wager of Law, the Wager of Battle, the Ordeal, and Torture* it is apparent that Lea's is a juridical work. Indeed, it turns out to be a voluminous tome on jurisprudence, or, as Lea puts it: 'a brief investigation into the group of laws and customs through which our forefathers sought to discover hidden truth when disputed between man and man'. In sum, how does God manifest his will when arbitrating in the disputes of his children?

Impeccably scholarly, Lea's pages nevertheless make grim reading. He spares us no details when relating techniques used in history to determine an accused's guilt. The foundations of all justice depend on what constitutes admissible 'evidence'. In Roman law, for example, the taking of an oath was assumed to produce reliable testimony, for it formed the basis of the Roman legal system. In *Dracula* the 'Inquisitors' pledge an oath of mutual support on three separate occasions. Their honour is therefore at stake, no less than that of an petty thief pleading his innocence before a Roman court.

Implicit in most legal systems is the belief that God is on the side of justice, and works in mysterious ways to bring it about. This principle can be seen at work in the judicial duel – the assumption that God's desire for justice makes itself known through the accuracy of the sword or the pistol shot. Soldiers in battle, on both sides, likewise presume theirs to be the just cause, with the outcome divinely ordained – in their favour, naturally.

It was but a short step to conceive of more direct appeals for God to declare his hand. The so-called 'Ordeal' provided a straightforward test of the accused's guilt or innocence. Boiling water, red-hot irons, fire, poison, or some other test would be administered in the expectation that God's miraculous intervention could inhibit pain or disfigurement, thereby indicating aquittal or condemnation. The automatic request for Divine providence in matters of law meant that 'miracles' came to be considered natural, commonplace, inviting neither wonderment nor surprise. There is something of the 'Ordeal of the Eucharist' in Van Helsing's placing of the holy wafer on Mina's forehead: her guilt being plainly registered by the searing of her skin.

There is, however, another means of determining guilt – by torture. And it was to this end that the techniques of the Inquisition were directed.

*

The Inquisitional Process

About this time we also find, in the increasing rigor and gradual systematizing of the Inquisition, an evidence of the growing disposition to resort to torture, and a powerful element in extending and facilitating its introduction. The church had been actively engaged in discountenancing and extirpating the ordeal, and it now threw the immense weight of its authority in favor of the new process of extorting confessions. When Frederic II, in 1221, published at Padua his three constitutions directed against heresy, cruel and unsparing as they were, they contained no indication that torture was even contemplated as a mode of investigation. In conformity with the provisions of the Lateran Council of 1215, parties suspected on insufficient evidence were directed to prove their innocence by some fitting mode of purgation, and the same instructions were given by Gregory IX in 1235. In 1252, however, when Innocent IV issued his elaborate directions for the guidance of the Inquisition in Tuscany and Lombardy, he ordered the civil magistrates to extort from all heretics by torture not merely a confession of their own guilt, but an accusation of all who might be their accomplices; and this derives additional significance from his reference to similar proceedings as customary in trials of thieves and robbers. It shows the progress made during the quarter of the century, and the high appreciation entertained by the church for the convenience of the new system.

As yet, however, this did not extend beyond Italy. There is extant a tract, written not long after this time, containing very minute instructions as to the established mode of dealing with the Waldensian sectaries known as the 'Poor Men of Lyons'. It gives directions to break down their strength and overcome their fortitude by solitary confinement, starvation, and terror, but it abstains from recommending the infliction of absolute and direct torture, while its details are so full that the omission is fair negative evidence that such measures were not then customary.

The whole system of the Inquisition, however, was such as to render the resort to torture inevitable. Its proceedings were secret; the prisoner was carefully kept in ignorance of the exact charges against him, and of the evidence upon which they were based. He was presumed to be guilty, and his judges bent all their energies to force him to confess. To accomplish this, no means were too base or too cruel. According to the tract just quoted, pretended sympathizers were to be let into his dungeon, whose affected friendship might entrap him into an unwary admission; officials armed with fictitious evidence were directed to frighten him with assertions of the testimony obtained against him from supposititious witnesses; and no resources of fraud or guile were to be spared in overcoming the caution and resolution of the poor wretch whose mind, as we have seen, had been carefully weakened by solitude, suffering, hunger, and terror. From this to the rack and estrapade the step was easily taken, and was not long delayed. In 1301, we find even Philippe-le-Bel protesting against the cruelty of Fulk, the Dominican Inquisitor, and interfering to protect his subjects from the refinements of torture to which, on simple suspicion of heresy, unfortunate victims were habitually exposed. Yet when, a few years later, the same monarch resolved upon the destruction of the Templars, he made the Inquisition the facile instrument to which he resorted, as a matter of course, to extort from De Molay and his knights, with endless repetition of torments, the confessions which were to recruit his exhausted treasury with their broad lands and accumulated riches. . . .

During [the sixteenth and seventeenth centuries], while Central and Western Europe had advanced with such rapid strides of enlightenment, the inquisitorial process, based upon torture, had become the groundwork of all criminal procedure, and every detail was gradually elaborated with the most painstaking perverseness.

Allusion has already been made to the influence of the Inquisition in introducing the use of torture. Its influence did not cease there, for with torture there gradually arose the denial to the accused of all fair opportunity of defending himself, accompanied by the system of secret procedure which formed so important a portion of the inquisitorial practice. In the old feudal courts, the prosecutor and the defendant appeared in person. Each produced his witnesses; the case was argued on both sides, and unless the wager of battle or the ordeal intervened, a verdict was given in accordance with the law after duly weighing the evidence, while both parties were at liberty to employ counsel and to appeal to the suzerain. When St Louis endeavored to abolish the duel and to substitute a system of inquests, which were necessarily to some extent *ex parte*, he did not desire to withdraw from the accused the legitimate means of defence, and in the Ordonnance of 1254 he expressly instructs his officers not to imprison the defendant without absolute necessity, while all the proceedings of the inquest are to be communicated freely to him. All this changed with time and the authoritative adoption of torture. The theory of the Inquisition, that the suspected man was to be hunted down and entrapped like a wild beast, that his guilt was to be assumed, and that the efforts of his judges were to be directed solely to obtaining against him sufficient evidence to warrant the extortion of a confession without allowing him the means of defence – this theory became the admitted basis of criminal jurisprudence. The secrecy of these inquisitorial proceedings, moreover, deprived the accused of one of the great safeguards accorded to him under the Roman law of torture. That law, as we have seen, required the formality of inscription, by which the accuser who failed to prove his charge was liable to the *lex talionis**, and in crimes which involved torture in the investigation, he was duly tortured. This was imitated by the Wisigoths, and its principle was admitted and enforced by the Church before the introduction of the Inquisition had changed its policy; but modern Europe, in borrowing from Rome the use of torture, combined it with the inquisitorial process, and thus in civilized Christendom it speedily came to be used more recklessly and cruelly than ever it had been in pagan antiquity.

In 1498, an assembly of notables at Blois drew up an elaborate ordonnance for the reformation of justice in France. In this, the secrecy of the inquisitorial process is dwelt upon with peculiar insistence as of the first importance in all criminal cases. The whole investigation was in the hands of the government official, who examined every witness by himself, and secretly, the prisoner having no knowledge of what was done, and no opportunity of arranging a defence. After all the testimony procurable in this one-sided manner had been obtained, it was discussed by the judges, in council with other persons named for the purpose, who decided whether the accused should be tortured. He could be tortured but once, unless fresh evidence meanwhile was collected against him, and his

---

* 'An eye for an eye.' – C.L.

confession was read over to him the next day, in order that he might affirm or deny it. A secret deliberation was then held by the same council, who decided as to his fate.

This cruel system was still further perfected by Francis I, who, in an ordonnance of 1539, expressly abolished the inconvenient privilege assured to the accused by St Louis, which was apparently still occasionally claimed, and directed that in no case should he be informed of the accusation against him, or of the facts on which it was based, nor be heard in his defence. Upon examination of the *ex parte* testimony, without listening to the prisoner, the judges ordered torture proportioned to the gravity of the accusation, and it was applied at once, unless the prisoner appealed, in which case his appeal was forthwith to be decided by the superior court of the locality. The whole process was apparently based upon the conviction that it was better that a hundred innocent persons should suffer than that one culprit should escape, and it would not be easy to devise a course of procedure better fitted to render the use of torture universal. There was some protection indeed, theoretically at least, in the provision which held the judge responsible when an innocent prisoner was tortured without sufficient preliminary proof to justify it; but this salutary regulation, from the very nature of things, could not often be enforced, and it was so contrary to the general spirit of the age, that it soon became obsolete. Thus, in Brittany, perhaps the most independent of the French provinces, the Coutumier, as revised in 1539, retains such a provision, but it disappears in the revision of 1580.

But even this was not all. Torture, as thus employed to convict the accused, became known as the *question préparatoire*; and, in defiance of the old rule that it could be applied but once, a second application, known as the *question définitive* or *préalable*, became customary, by which, after condemnation, the prisoner was again subjected to the extremity of torment in order to discover whether he had any accomplices, and, if so, to identify them. In this detestable practice we find another instance of the unfortunate influence of the Inquisition in modifying the Roman law. The latter expressly and wisely provided that no one who had confessed should be examined as to the guilt of another; and in the ninth century the authors of the False Decretals had emphatically adopted the principle, which thus became embodied in ecclesiastical law, until the ardor of the Inquisition in hunting down heretics caused it to regard the conviction of the accused as a barren triumph unless he could be forced to incriminate his possible associates.

Torture was also generically divided into the *question ordinaire* and *extraordinaire* – a rough classification to proportion the severity of the infliction to the gravity of the crime or the urgency of the case. Thus, in the most usual kind of torment, the strappado, popularly known as the *Moine de Caen*, the ordinary form was to tie the prisoner's hands behind his back with a piece of iron between them; a cord was then fastened to his wrists by which, with the aid of a pulley, he was hoisted from the ground with a weight of one hundred and twenty-five pounds attached to his feet. In the extraordinary torture, the weight was increased to two hundred and fifty pounds, and when the victim was raised to a sufficient height, he was dropped with a jerk that dislocated his joints, the operation being thrice repeated.

Thus, in 1549, we see the system in full operation in the case of Jacques de Coucy, who, in 1544, had surrendered Boulogne to the English. This was deemed an act of treachery, but he was pardoned in 1547; yet, notwithstanding his pardon, he was subsequently tried, convicted, condemned to decapitation and quartering, and also to the *question extraordinaire* to obtain a denunciation of his accomplices.

When Louis XIV, under the inspiration of Colbert, remoulded the jurisprudence of France, various reforms were introduced into the criminal law, and changes both for better and worse were made in the administration of torture. The Ordonnance of 1670 was drawn up by a committee of the ablest and most enlightened jurists of the day, and it is a melancholy exhibition of human wisdom when regarded as the production of such men as Lamoignon, Talon, and Pussort. The cruel mockery of the *question préalable* was retained; and in the principal proceedings all the chances were thrown against the prisoner. All preliminary testimony was still *ex parte*. The accused was heard, but he was still examined in secret. Lamoignon vainly endeavored to obtain for him the advantage of counsel, but Colbert obstinately refused this concession, and the utmost privilege allowed the defence was the permission accorded to the judge, at his discretion, to confront the accused with the adverse witnesses. In the *question préliminaire*, torture was reserved for capital cases, when the proof was strong and yet not enough for conviction. During its application it could be stopped and resumed at the pleasure of the judge, but if the accused were once unbound and removed from the rack, it could not be repeated, even though additional evidence were subsequently obtained.

It was well to prescribe limitations, slender as these were, but in practice it was found impossible to enforce them, and they afforded little real protection to the accused, when judges, bent upon procuring conviction, chose to evade them. A contemporary whose judicial position gave him every opportunity of knowing the truth, remarks: 'They have discovered a jugglery of words, and pretend that though it may not be permissible to *repeat* the torture, still they have a right to *continue* it, though there may have been an interval of three whole days. Then, if the sufferer, through good luck or by a miracle, survives this reduplication of agony, they have discovered the notable resource of *nouveaux indices survenus*, to subject him to it again without end. In this way they elude the intention of the law, which sets some bounds to these cruelties and requires the discharge of the accused who has endured the question without confession, or without confirming his confession after torture.' Nor were these the only modes by which the scanty privileges allowed the prisoner were curtailed in practice. In 1681, a royal Declaration sets forth that, in the jurisdiction of Grenoble, judges were in the habit of refusing to listen to the accused, and of condemning him unheard, an abuse which was prohibited for the future. Yet other courts subsequently assumed that this prohibition was only applicable to the Parlement of Grenoble, and in 1703 another Declaration was necessary to enforce the rule throughout the kingdom.

The Ordonnance of 1670, moreover, gave formal expression to another abuse which was equally brutal and illogical – the employment of torture *avec réserve des preuves*. When the judge resolved on this, the silence of the accused under torment did not acquit him, though the whole theory of the question lay in the necessity of confession. He simply escaped the death penalty, and could be condemned to any other punishment which the discretion of the judge might impose, thus presenting the anomaly of a man neither guilty nor innocent, relieved from the punishment assigned by the law to the crime for which he had been arraigned, and condemned to some other penalty without having been convicted of any offence.

This punishing for suspicion was no new thing. Before torture came fully into vogue, in the early part of the fourteenth century, a certain Estevenes li Barbiers of Abbeville was banished under pain of death for suspicion of breach of the peace, and was subsequently tried, acquitted, and allowed to return. About the same period a barber of Anet and his sons were arrested by the monks of St

Martin-des-Champs on suspicion of killing a guard who was keeping watch over some hay. The evidence against them was insufficient, and they were taken to the gallows as a kind of moral torture not infrequently used in those days. Still refusing to confess, they were banished forever under pain of hanging, because, as the record ingenuously states, the crime was not fully proved against them. So in the records of the Parlement of Paris there is a sentence rendered in 1402, against Jehan Dubos, a procureur of the Parlement, and Ysabelet his wife, for suspicion of the poisoning of another procureur, Jehan le Charron, the first husband of Ysabelet, and Dubos was accordingly hanged, while his wife was burnt. Jean Bodin, one of the clearest intellects of the sixteenth century, lays it down as a rule that the penalty should be proportioned to the proof; he ridicules as obsolete the principle that when the evidence is not sufficient for conviction the accused should be discharged, and mentions stripes, fines, imprisonment, the galleys, and degradation as proper substitutes for death when there is no evidence and only violent presumption. He gives in illustration of this a case personally known to him of a noble of Le Mans, who was condemned to nine years of the galleys for violent suspicion of murder. The application to the torture-process of this determination not to allow a man to escape unless his innocence was proved led to the illogical system of the *réserve des preuves*.

The theory on which the doctors of the law proceeded was that if there were evidence sufficient for conviction and the judge yet tortured the criminal in surplusage without obtaining a confession, the accused could not be condemned to the full punishment of his offence, because the use of torture in itself weakened the external proofs, and therefore the culprit must be sentenced to some lighter punishment – a refinement worthy of the inconsequential dialectics of the schools. The cruel absurdities which the system produced in practice are well illustrated by a case occurring in Naples in the sixteenth century. Marc Antonio Maresca of Sorrento was tried by the Admiralty Court for the murder of a peasant of Miani, in the market place. The evidence was strong against him, but there were no eye-witnesses, and he endured the torture without confession. The court asserted that it had reserved the evidence, and condemned him to the galleys for seven years. He appealed to the High Court of the royal council, and the case was referred to a distinguished jurisconsult, Thomaso Grammatico, a member of the council. The latter reported that he must be considered as innocent, after having passed through torture without confession, and denied the right of the court to reserve the evidence. Then, with an exhibition of the peculiar logic characteristic of the criminal jurisprudence of the time, he concluded that Maresca might be relegated to the islands for five years, although it was a recognized principle of Neapolitan law that torture could be inflicted only in accusations of crimes of which the penalty was greater than relegation. The only thing necessary to complete this tissue of legal wisdom was afforded by the council, which set aside the judgment of the Admiralty Court, rejected the report of their colleague, and condemned the prisoner to the galleys for three years. Somewhat less complicated in its folly, but more inexcusable from its date, was the sentence of the court of Orléans in 1740, by which a man named Barberousse, from whom no confession had been extorted, was condemned to the galleys for life, because, as the sentence declared, he was *strongly suspected* of premeditated murder. A more pardonable, but not more reasonable example occurred at Halle in 1729, where a woman accused of infanticide refused to confess, and as she labored under a physical defect which rendered the application of torture dangerous to life, the authorities after due consideration and consultation of physicians, spared her the torture and banished her without conviction.

The same tendency to elude all restrictions on the use of torture was manifested in the Netherlands, where the procedure was scarcely known until the 16th century, and where it was only administered systematically by the ordonnance on criminal justice of Philip II in 1570. When once employed it rapidly extended until it became almost universal, both in the provinces which threw off the yoke of Spain, and in those which remained faithful. The limits which Philip had imposed on it were soon transcended. He had forbidden its employment in all cases '*où il n'y a plaine, demye preuve, ou bien où la preuve est certaine et indubitable*,' thus restricting it to those where there was very strong presumption without absolute certainty. In transcription and translation, however, the wording of the ordonnance became changed to 'plaine ou demye preuve, ou bien où ia preuve est incertaine ou douteuse,' thus allowing it in all cases where the judge might not have a doubt not of the guilt but of the innocence of the accused; and by the time these errors were discovered by a zealous legal antiquarian, the customs of the tribunals had become so fixed that the attempt to reform them was vain.

In Germany, torture had been reduced to a system, in 1532, by the Emperor Charles V, whose 'Caroline Constitutions' contain a more complete code on the subject than had previously existed, except in the records of the Inquisition. Inconsistent and illogical, it quotes Ulpian to prove the deceptive nature of the evidence thence derivable; it pronounces torture to be *'res dira, corporibus hominum admodum noxia et quandoque lethalis, cui et mors ipsa prope proponenda**'; in some of its provisions it manifests extreme care and tenderness to guard against abuses, and yet practically it is merciless to the last degree. Confession made during torture was not to be believed, nor could a conviction be based upon it; yet what the accused might confess after being removed from torture was to be received as the deposition of a dying man, and was full evidence. In practice, however, this only held good when adverse to the accused, for he was brought before his judge after an interval of a day or two, when, if he confirmed the confession, he was condemned, while if he retracted it he was at once thrust again upon the rack. In confession under torture, moreover, he was to be closely cross-questioned, and if any inconsistency was observable in his self-condemnation, the torture was at once to be redoubled in severity. The legislator thus makes the victim expiate the sins of his own vicious system; the victim's sufferings increase with the deficiency of the evidence against him, and the legislator consoles himself with the remark that the victim has only himself to thank for it, 'de se tantum non de alio quæratur'. To complete the inconsistency of the code, it provided that confession was not requisite for conviction; irrefragable external evidence was sufficient; and yet even when such evidence was had, the judge was empowered to torture in mere surplusage.

Yet there was a great show of tender consideration for the accused. When the weight of conflicting evidence inclined to the side of the prisoner, torture was not to be applied. Two adverse witnesses, or one unexceptionable one, were a condition precedent, and the legislator shows that he was in advance of his age by ruling out all evidence resting on the assertions of magicians and sorcerers. To

---

* 'a terrible thing for the bodies of men, generally painful and sometimes deadly, next to which death itself is to be placed.' – C.L.

guard against abuse, the impossible effort was made to define strictly the exact quality and amount of evidence requisite to justify torture, and the most elaborate and minute directions were given with respect to all the various classes of crime, such as homicide, child-murder, robbery, theft, receiving stolen goods, poisoning, arson, treason, sorcery, and the like, while the judge administering torture to an innocent man on insufficient grounds was liable to make good all damage or suffering thereby inflicted. The amount of torment, moreover, was to be proportioned to the age, sex, and strength of the patient; women during pregnancy were never to be subjected to it; and in no case was it to be carried to such a point as to cause permanent injury or death.

From Superstition and Force *(1878) pages 425–427, 451–463*

Complete List of Bram Stoker's Sources for *Dracula*

Rev Sabine BARING-GOULD MA
The Book of Were-Wolves: Being an Account of a Terrible Superstition Smith, Elder & Co – London 1865
Curious Myths of the Middle Ages Rivingtons – London 1877
Germany, Present and Past (2 vols) Kegan Paul, Trench – London 1879
Curiosities of Olden Times John Grant – Edinburgh 1895

Fletcher S. BASSETT Lieutenant US Navy
Legends and Superstitions of the Sea and of Sailors – In all Lands and at all Times Sampson Low, Marston, Searle & Rivington – London 1885

Isabella L. BIRD
The Golden Chersonese John Murray – London 1883

Charles BONER
Transylvania: Its Products and its People Longmans, Green, Reader and Dyer – London 1865

Sir Thomas BROWNE
Religio Medici

Andrew F. CROSSE
Round About the Carpathians Blackwood – London 1878

Rushton M. DORMAN
The Origin of Primitive Superstitions: And Their Development into the Worship of Spirits and the Doctrine of Spiritual Agency Among the Aborigines of America Lippincott & Co – London 1881

A Fellow of the Carpathian Society
'Magyarland': Being the Narrative of our Travels Through the Highlands and Lowlands of Hungary (2 vols) Sampson Low, Marston, Searle and Rivington – London 1881

Emily GERARD
'Transylvanian Superstitions' in The Nineteenth Century July 1885

Major E.C. JOHNSON MAI, FRHistS
On the Track of the Crescent: Erratic Notes from the Piræus to Pesth Hurst and Blackett – London 1885

John JONES
  The Natural and the Supernatural: Or, Man – Physical, Apparitional and Spiritual   H. Bailliere – London 1861

William JONES FSA
  Credulities Past and Present   Chatto and Windus – London 1880
  History and Mystery of Precious Stones   Richard Bentley & Son – London 1880

Rev W. Henry JONES and Lewis L. KROPF
  The Folk-Tales of the Magyars   Elliot Stock – London 1889

Henry Charles LEA
  Superstition and Force – Essays on: The Wager of Law, The Wager of Battle, The Ordeal and Torture   H.C. Lea – Philadelphia 1878

Rev Frederick George LEE DCL Vicar of All Saints', Lambeth
  The Other World: Or, Glimpses of the Supernatural – Being Facts, Records and Traditions (2 vols)   Henry S. King and Co – London 1875

Henry LEE FLS, FGS, FZS Sometime Naturalist of the Brighton Aquarium
  Sea Fables Explained   William Clowes and Sons – London 1883
  Sea Monsters Unmasked   William Clowes and Sons – London 1883

Sarah LEE (sometimes classified under her former name, Mrs Bowdich)
  Anecdotes of Habits and Instincts of Birds, Reptiles and Fishes   Lindsay Blalmston – Philadelphia 1853
  (see also *Anecdotes of Habits and Instincts of Animals*)   Lindsay Blalmston – Philadelphia 1853

L.F. Alfred MAURY (no titles given, but probably include the following)
  Essai sur les Légendes Pieuses du Moyen-Age   Chez Ladrange – Paris 1843
  La Magie et L'Astrologie dans L'Antiquité et au Moyen Age: ou, Étude sur les Superstitions Païennes qui sont Perpétuées jusqu'a jours   Didier et Cie – Paris 1860
  Le Sommeil et Les Rêves: Études Psychologiques sur ces Phénomènes et les divers États qui s'y Rattachent   Didier et Cie – Paris 1865

Herbert MAYO MD
  On the Truths contained in Popular Superstitions – with an Account of Mesmerism   William Blackwood and Sons – London 1851

Thomas Joseph PETTIGREW FRS, FSA
  On Superstitions connected with the History and Practice of Medicine and Surgery   John Churchill – London 1844

Rev Albert RÉVILLE DD
  The Devil: His Origin, Greatness and Decadence   Williams and Norgate – London 1871

F.C. and J. RIVINGTON
  The Theory of Dreams (2 vols)   62 St Paul's Churchard – London 1808

F.K. ROBINSON
A Whitby Glossary 1876

Robert H SCOTT MA, FRS Secretary of the Meteorological Office
Fishery Barometer Manual H.M.S.O. – London 1887

William WILKINSON Late British Consul Resident at Bukorest
An Account of the Principalities of Wallachia and Moldavia: with various Political Observations Relating to Them Longman, Hurst, Rees, Orme and Brown – London 1820